The Underground World
of Secret Jews and Africans

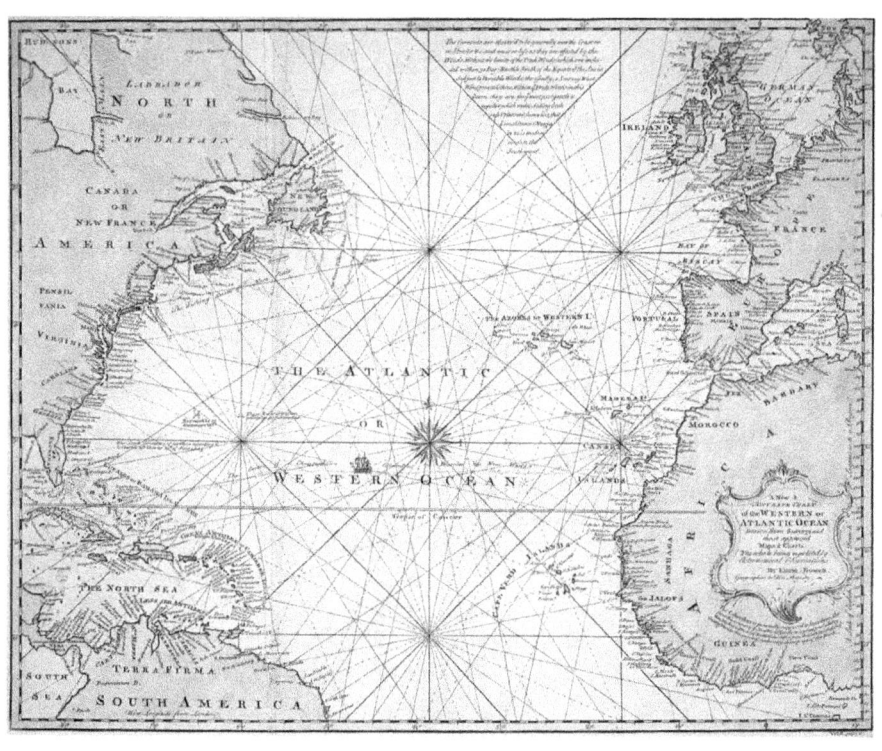

Atlantic world map, 17th Century.
A new and accurate chart of the Western or Atlantic Ocean drawn from surveys and most approved maps and charts, the whole being regulated by astronomical observations
Bowen, Emmanuel (1693?-1767). Map, 1744, English, Toronto Public Library

THE UNDERGROUND WORLD OF SECRET JEWS AND AFRICANS

Two Tales of Sex,
Magic, and Survival in
Colonial Cartagena and Mexico City

BY JONATHAN SCHORSCH

Markus Wiener Publishers
Princeton

Two women on the cover in front of the image of 17th-century Mexico City:

(Left) Queen Esther, Savior of the Jewish people in Persia, which Jews celebrate as Purim. The Festival of Santa Esterica is a holiday that was created as a substitute for Purim by the "conversos" (Sephardic Jews forced to convert to Catholicism) after their expulsion from Spain in the late 15th century. The festival featured a fictional saint called "Esterica," who was heavily based on Queen Esther. During the festival the New Christian women fasted for 3 days, as did Esther herself in the Book of Esther prior to her meeting with the Persian King Achashverosh.

(Right) Yemoja is the water goddess from West Africa in the Afro-Caribbean and Brazilian diaspora. She is often blended with Virgin Mary figures of the Catholic Church, a practice that emerged during the era of the Trans-Atlantic slave trade. Yemoja is also the Queen of the Ocean, the patron spirit of fishermen and survivors of shipwrecks, the feminine principle of creation, and the spirit of moonlight. Yemoja is often depicted as associated with the moon (in some diaspora communities), water, and feminine mysteries. She is the protector of women.

Copyright © 2021 by Markus Wiener Publishers

All rights reserved. No part of this book may be reproduced or transmitted in any form or by any means, whether electronic or mechanical—including photocopying or recording —or through any information storage or retrieval system, without permission of the copyright owners.

For information write to:
Markus Wiener Publishers, 231 Nassau Street, Princeton, NJ 08542
www.markuswiener.com

Book Design by Cheryl Mirkin, CM Design

Library of Congress Cataloging-in-Publication Data

Names: Schorsch, Jonathan, 1963- author.
Title: Underground world of secret Jews and Africans : two tales of sex, magic, and
    survival in 17th century Cartagena and Mexico city / by Jonathan Schorsch.
Description: Princeton, N.J. : Markus Wiener Publishers, 2020. |
    Includes bibliographical references and index.
Identifiers: LCCN 2020022455 |
    ISBN 9781558769526 (hardcover) |
    ISBN 9781558769533 (paperback)
Subjects: LCSH: Church history—17th century. | Inquisition—Colombia—
    Cartagena—History—17th century. | Inquisition—Mexico—Mexico city—
    History—17th century. | Blacks—Relations with Jews—History—17th century. |
    Race relations—Religious aspects—History—17th century. | Jews—Colombia—
    Cartagena—History—17th century. | Jews—Mexico—Mexico city—History—
    17th century. | Blacks—Colombia—Cartagena—History—17th century. |
    Blacks—Mexico—Mexico city—History—17th century.
Classification: LCC BR440 .S458 2020 | DDC 277.2/5306—dc23
LC record available at https://lccn.loc.gov/2020022455

Markus Wiener Publishers books are printed in the United States of America
on acid-free paper and meet the guidelines for permanence and durability
of the Committee on Production Guidelines for Book Longevity
of the Council on Library Resources.

— Table of Contents —

Acknowledgements vii
Preface ix

Introduction 1
    Jews and Judeoconversos 3
    Africans and Afroiberians 6
    Caste and Christianity 11
    Inquisition 13

The Clash of Two Surgeons and a Slave 17
    A Portuguese-Born New Christian is Accused and Tortured 22
    An Ex-Slave Surgeon and his Witchcraft-Practicing Lover 30
    Knowledge is Power, Especially Through the Gaze of the Invisible 41
    The Meaning-Making of Afroiberian Magic 45
    Denouncing Injustice? 48
    Spilling One's Guts 55
    Trials and Errors 60

Esperanza Rodríguez: A Life In-between 69
    An Extended Family of Fervent Crypto-Jews? 73
    Becoming a Crypto-Jew 77
    Within the Bosom of the Clan: From Slave to Elder 89
    The Attraction of the Other 99
    The Tragic Sense of Humor of the Cosmos 108

Conclusion 113
    Tying up Toxic Loose Ends 124
    Final Thoughts 128

Notes 131
Bibliography 171
Index 185
About the Author 188

— Acknowledgements —

This volume contains material adapted from my book, *Swimming the Christian Atlantic: Judeoconversos, Afroiberians and Amerindians in the Seventeenth Century* (Leiden: Brill, 2008). The adaptation was carried out by Craig Leisher, for whose skillful editorial hand I am very grateful.

Additional research for the story of Esperanza Rodríguez in the Inquisition holdings of the Archivo Histórico Nacional (Madrid) was conducted by Isabel Boyano. I am thankful for her assistance.

I owe a real debt of gratitude to the publisher, Markus Wiener, for his belief in the quality and relevance of the tales I tell within the pages that follow and his persistence in urging me to allow him to present them anew to a wider audience.

May knowledge of the past help lead to a more human and more godly future.

New York City
January 2020

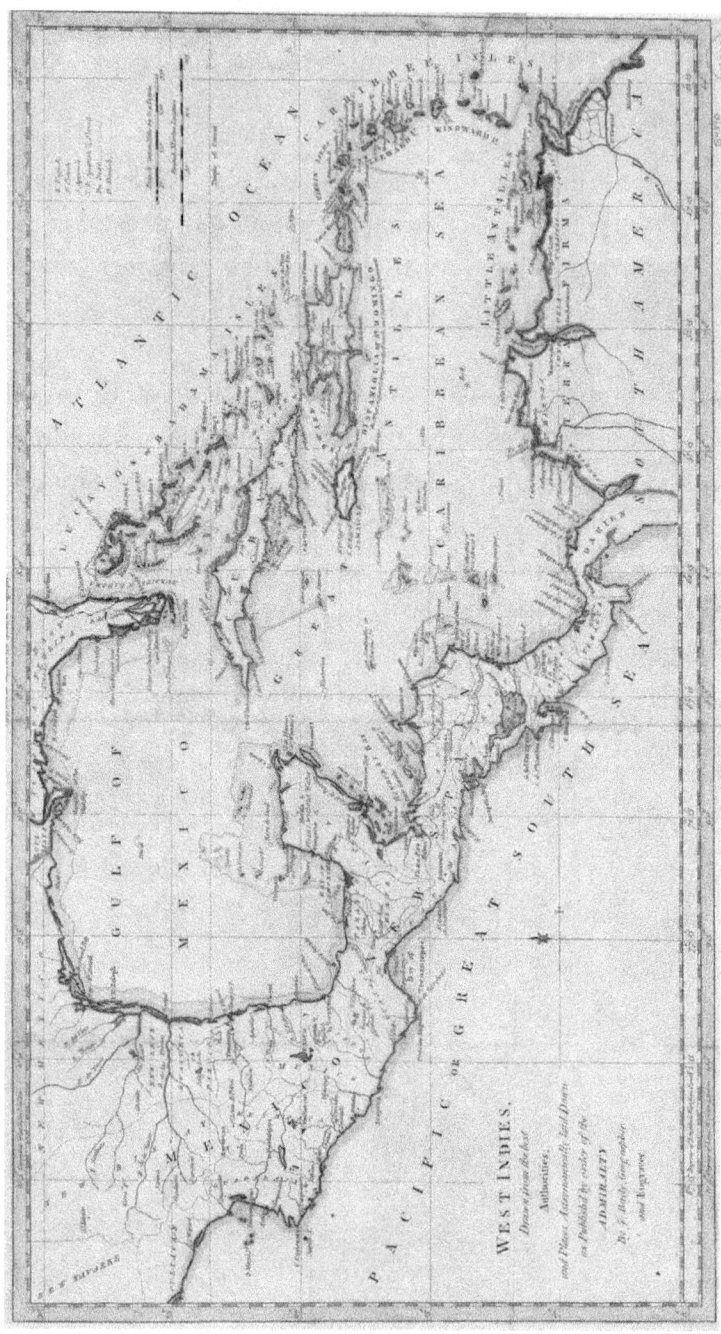

Historical Map of the Caribbean
An accurate map of the West Indies with the adjacent coast by John Gibson, active 1750-1792.
[London : Printed for R. Baldwin, 1762.] Library of Congress Geography and Map Division, Washington, D.C.

— Preface —

In this book, I try to understand the way in which two dominated groups within the Spanish and Portuguese empires — Judeoconversos and Afroiberians — perceived one another and interacted with each other. Though I investigate the political, religious, and social contexts in which individuals from these subaltern groups circulated in the Atlantic world of the seventeenth century, I am more concerned with the less-studied horizontal relations *between* Judeoconversos and Afroiberians. This book presents not a sweeping overview but a series of textual moments and physical sites of interaction between members of these groups. The material presents an immanent view, exploring the statements and sentiments of members of these groups. Two episodes of tragically intertwined lives from the seventeenth century make up the scene of action, one in Cartagena de las Indias, the other in Mexico City, two of the major urban centers of the Spanish Empire in the Americas.

The topics in this book conjure a mood, a dark mood, informed by cruelties, brutalities, the stuff of nightmares so horrific as to make the averting of the eyes in Maimonidean negative theology seem by comparison a game of coquetry. Torture on racks with screams duly recorded by the scribes. People burned while still alive as punishment for upholding the wrong form of religion. Survivors and sociologists have taught us about the upside-down world of the Nazi concentration or death camps. Was the early modern Atlantic world a long-term equivalent for many of its inhabitants?

A woman from a synagogue my wife and I used to attend was at our house one day. In the course of conversation about Jews and Blacks and my research she asked to see a copy of my first book, *Jews and Blacks in the Early Modern World*. I was opening to the first page of the Introduction to show her how I state there that extreme Black charges against Jews regarding slavery should be treated with skepticism when she said, in an offhanded way, "Oh, I was told by someone at *shul* [synagogue] that your work is anti-Semitic." (I am not sure whether I had already told her that one of my essays was put online by a rabidly anti-Jewish Black nationalist website.[1]) All this confirmed my wife's worries that the book would make me public enemy number one in the Jewish world. But the deeper meaning is more frightening. After all, what is "anti-Semitic" about a book treating, in a scholarly methodology of moderate tone and fact-based argumentation, Jewish relations with Blacks? Likely for some Jews *any* conclusion that deems Jews to have been less than angelic in some way, that dares raise a critical voice suggesting that Jews behaved like others — that airs dirty laundry in public — verges on anti-Semitism.

Characterizing "Black-Jewish" relations in the seventeenth century almost inevitably retrojects today's socioeconomic and political tensions. The very question itself divulges this fact. Yet, despite some significant and vast differences between the two eras and situations, it is hard not to recognize some similarities. As two groups of intermediaries or go-betweens that served vastly different purposes for the empires, Judeoconversos and Afroiberians stood very much in conflict, often quite direct, with one another. Added to this was a very real religious and theopolitical divergence. Nonetheless, it is difficult to detect much, if any, *particular* animus between members of the two groups in documentation from the time.

Some words about terminology. In this book, I am careful to distinguish Jews from Judeoconversos. When I use the former term it never refers to Judeoconversos who are living, regardless of their inner feelings, outwardly as Catholics. When I use the term Judeoconverso, it is as a synonym for New Christian, meaning there is no implication regarding religious loyalty; it is a purely sociological category. When discussing an individual Converso or group of Conversos still loyal to Judaism, I use the term Crypto-Jew. *Marranos* is the insulting term used for Judeoconversos and is said to derive from a word for pig, but the more likely etymology is that given in anti-Jewish literature: that *marranos* feign (*marran*) Christianity. I avoid the term in this book.

I capitalize ethnic, caste and/or racial markers, such as Judeoconverso, Black, Mulato, and Mestizo. However distasteful or ridiculous the terms may seem to us now (though perhaps not to enough of "us"), these were the categories constructing reality in the seventeenth century. My capitalizing them aims to remind us of their status as proper nouns, where not capitalizing them — mulato, mestizo, black — strikes me as not granting them the same kind of legitimacy as terms such as French, Catholic, or Jewish.

Unless otherwise noted, all translations from languages other than English are my own. When I quote primary material that has been directly quoted in secondary sources, I note as much. Inquisition sources contain all the orthographic inconsistencies of writing in an age before standardization. Within quotes, generally I have kept this non-standardized spelling, even of proper and place names, as it appears in the original Spanish or Portuguese. Frequently, then, I have chosen to leave all spellings and capitalization, or lack thereof, as they appear in the original. Unless otherwise noted, comments or clarifications that appear amid quoted material within square brackets are mine. When relating what is said to have occurred within such documents, I use the present tense, the mode of conveying that which must remain eternally textual. I have maintained the flavor (or lack thereof) of the original "legalese" to be found in Inquisition documents and have not "improved" the language or style. Since such was the stylistic choice of the Inquisition functionaries, I thought it worth retaining.

Las castas. Casta painting showing 16 racial groupings.
Anonymous, 18th century, oil on canvas, 148×104 cm, Museo Nacional del Virreinato, Tepotzotlán, Mexico/Bridgeman Image

Introduction

The tragic end of medieval Spanish and Portuguese Jewry, a history filled with long moments of coexistence and rich accomplishment, is well known. A 1492 royal edict ordered the expulsion from Castilian territories of all Jews who did not convert to Catholicism. Many thousands fled to Portugal, who, together with the Jews already residing there, faced another royal edict in 1497 commanding the forced conversion of every Jew in Portugal, this time without the option of leaving. According to many sources, both contemporary and modern, the manner of the sudden, collective conversion in Portugal generated a community far more knowledgeable in and committed to Judaism, as least for the next few generations.[2] The problem of so-called *cristianos nuevos* or *cristãos novos* (New Christians) — Jews who had been forced to or chose to become Christians — began in earnest with anti-Jewish persecutions and massacres in Spain toward the end of the fourteenth century (mainly 1391) and led to the re-establishment of the medieval Inquisition there in 1478.[3]

King Ferdinando and Queen Isabella of Castile re-established the Inquisition at the behest of the leadership of the Dominican order, in particular the queen's confessor, friar Tomás de Torquemada. The initial worry was that Jews who converted (Judeoconversos) may not have been living up to their professed Christianity. The inquisitors quickly expanded their targets to include Muslims who had likewise been for the most part forcibly converted to Catholicism during and after the Reconquista, the growing number of Protestants, and other religious deviancies such as witchcraft, self-proclaimed mystics, transgressive priests, blasphemers, those who engaged in sex deemed sinful by the church, as well as those who made heretical statements.

Spanish and Portuguese Jews who had fled Iberian territories not only found an increasingly tolerant welcome but also gained previously unheard-of privileges and rights. This trend seems to have reached its zenith in the Dutch colonies, where Jews constituted roughly a third of the European population. These New Jews, Judeoconversos who came out as open Jews or turned to Judaism for the first time, played an important role, even a dominant one, in various aspects of Atlantic and general international commerce. In family-based networks that spanned European motherlands and their colonies, Crypto-Jews and New Jews of Iberian background at various times were active in trading and/or processing pepper and spices, sugar, indigo, chocolate, slaves, coral and diamonds, not to mention more mundane goods such as wool and wine. They participated as well, insofar as they were able, in the more exploitative aspects of colonialism, though they are underrepresented, often significantly, in the more directly dominating, martial or violent activities.[4]

Mikvé Israel-Emanuel Synagogue (The Hope of Israel-Emanuel Synagogue), in Willemstad, Curaçao, is the oldest surviving synagogue in the Americas. The congregation Mikvé Israel dates from the 1650s, and consisted of Spanish and Portuguese Jews from the Netherlands and Brazil.

Jews and Judeoconversos

One crucial aspect of Judeoconverso identity is the peculiar position of Jews in European society, where they often found themselves between the colonizers and the colonized.[5] Just as in England after the Norman invasion, where Jews were used by the conquerors as tax collectors, Jews made up the majority of tax farmers in many of the kingdoms in Moslem and Christian Spain, serving the interests of the monarchy and nobility "against" the internally colonized peasants. It was convenient and for the most part effective for medieval Christian Europe, a cluster of societies that for the most part despised, shunned and even demonized physical and cultural mobility, to have Jews and later Judeoconversos serve as commercial intermediaries.[6] All this helped create the position of Judeoconversos and Spanish and Portuguese Jews in the Atlantic world. Jonathan Israel hints at the economic uses to which Jews were often put by European countries (his examples are all from the mid-seventeenth century):

> At Hamburg, the rules imposed by the Senate excluded the Jews from practically every form of activity other than overseas trade [...] Even at Amsterdam, guild restrictions excluded Jews from most crafts and forms of shop-keeping and those crafts they were allowed to practice, such as diamond-processing, tobacco-spinning, and chocolate-making, were, generally speaking, closely connected with colonial trade.[7]

In light of the difficulties of attracting Europeans to settle in the new-found overseas colonies, Jews were offered rights and privileges if they would settle, for example, in early Dutch Surinam, rights and privileges which were reaffirmed by later conquerors who wanted to keep the Jews there. Conversos fulfilled similar commercial functions in the Iberian empires. From the beginning, Spain and Portugal forbade Jews and Conversos to emigrate to the New World.[8] Yet the economic benefits of tolerating not only New Christians but even Jews swayed some to seek to rein in theological zealotry for "reasons of state." The Portuguese mercantilist Duarte Gomes Solís, himself a New Christian, "urged Philip III not just to restrain persecution of New Christians but to allow professing Jews to settle in the Portuguese colonies in Asia and have ghettos there 'as they do in Rome and other parts of Italy' as a means of defeating Dutch and English commercial rivalry in the east."[9]

This is not to imply that Jews and Conversos were unwilling converts to colonialism. Where possible, they were seeking their own survival and gain like everybody else. (It needs to be kept in mind that most Jews in *every* early modern city in both the old and new worlds were poor.) Like so many Europeans, Conversos flocked to the Americas in the hope of obtaining the privileges that in Europe remained the prerogative of the nobility. Many Conversos also fled to the Americas in order to escape the tyranny of the motherlands' Inquisitions which hovered over them regardless of their religious orientation. Conversos were officially not allowed to emigrate to the Americas and so often took a circuitous route via Guinea or Angola.[10]

It was precisely the confluence of Jewish self-interest and European colonial desires that put Jews and Conversos into often problematic situations vis-à-vis other colonized peoples. Conversos or Jews were but a minority of the actual colonialists but carried out much of the trading. Just as lower-class Europeans found an elevated status in the Americas — as Whites living above Amerindians and Blacks — so did Judeoconversos.[11] Nonetheless, the New World was not necessarily a paradise for Judeoconversos, particularly as their commercial success only attracted greater inquisitional interest. The Inquisition followed these refugee colonialists there, and "Jews" and "heretics" were hunted out beginning in 1570 in Peru, 1571 in Mexico, and 1579 in Brazil. The few Judeoconversos who made their way to Portuguese Angola were likewise followed by an inquisitorial visitation in 1626.

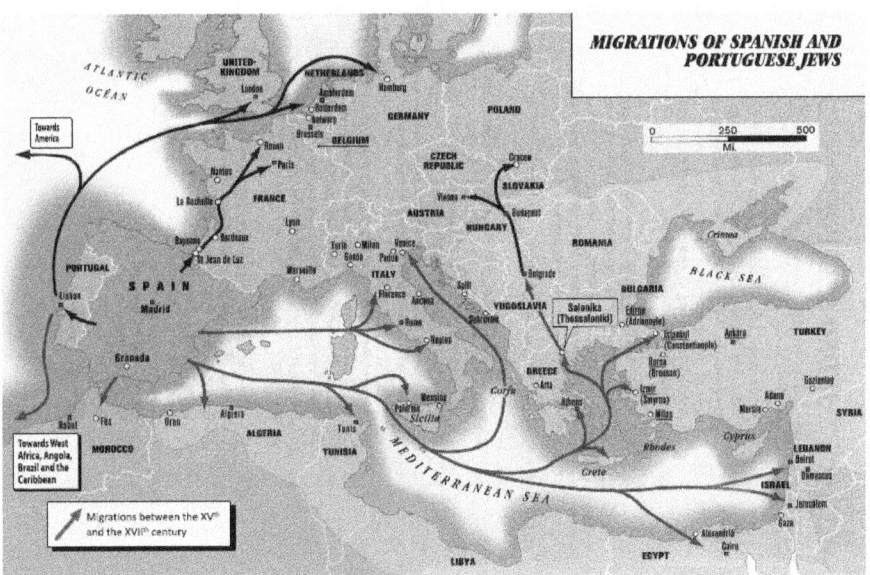

Sepharadic migrations map

Africans and Afroiberians

Beginning in 1595, Spain outsourced the supply of its enslaved men and women to Portuguese slave traders in a mutually beneficial arrangement that lasted, despite official interruptions, for well over a hundred years.[12] Many of the slavers were New Christians.[13] The Africans bought or stolen into slavery and sent to Europe and the Americas found themselves in an often severe predicament. In these locales, Africans usually became slaves put to lowly, arduous and dangerous tasks. Despite their frequent use as brute labor in mines and plantations, African slaves were also needed for the skills they brought with them and for the skilled work they contributed to the building of the Spanish and Portuguese colonial societies. Gwendolyn Midlo Hall reminds us that:

> Enslaved Africans were blacksmiths, metallurgists, toolmakers, sculptors and engravers, silversmiths and goldsmiths, tanners, shoemakers, and saddle-makers. They were designers and builders of warehouses and docks, barracks and homes, public buildings, churches, canals, and dams. They were coopers, draymen, and coach drivers; breeders, groomers and trainers of horses; and cowboys skilled in cattle rearing and herding. They were hunters and fishermen, as well as pearl divers. They were ship builders, navigators, sounders, caulkers, sailmakers, ship carpenters, sailors, and rowers. They were indigo-makers, weavers and dyers of cloth, tailors and seamstresses. They were basket weavers, potters, and salt-makers. They were cooks, bakers, pastry chefs, candy-makers, street vendors, innkeepers, personal servants, housekeepers, laundresses,

King of Kongo giving audience to Portuguese guests and his subjects. The Portuguese initially fostered a good relationship with the Kingdom of Kongo. Civil war within Kongo would lead to many of its subjects ending up as enslaved people in Portuguese and other European vessels. Created before 1850 AD; Library of Congress Prints and Photographs Division, Washington, D.C. 20540.

domestics, doctors or surgeons, and nurses. They cultivated corn, rice, garden crops, tobacco, poultry, pigs, sheep, and goats.[14]

By the middle of the seventeenth century, perhaps some 15 percent had escaped their slave status by one means or another to become free. Enslaved females, who often served their masters romantically or sexually, whether voluntarily or not, were manumitted more readily than enslaved males. Whatever ethnic or national identities these men and women may have had back home — Fon, Mandinka, Ewe, Bantu, among others — in their new settings they became simply Africans, but more ubiquitously, *negros*, Blacks to their overlords. Their generally darker skin color may or may not have served as an excuse or cover for the already traditional European denigrations of their culture, seen as primitive and barbaric, but in any case, skin color quickly came to serve as a metonym for their status as natural born slaves for the "higher" and lighter skinned Iberians. In the early seventeenth century, the Portuguese Jesuit Antonio Vieira preached to the enslaved in Brazil that they should "thank God for having removed them 'from the country where [they] and [their] ancestors lived like savages,' " who would "burn in Hell," while they, now living among Christians "would go to heaven instead."[15] Enslaved or free, Africans and their descendants were subject to persistent and widespread dehumanization, denigration, marginalization and cruelty.

Beyond "pure" Blacks, many of the Iberian terms denoted, as Douglas Cope reminds us, "new kinds of people for whom new names had to be invented: *mestizos* (children of a Spaniard and an Amerindian), *castizos* (children of a Spaniard and a Mestizo), *zambos* (children of an African and an Amerindian), and many others."[16] Mulatos can be added to the list (children of an African and a

Spaniard), along with Conversos and New Christians.[17] Though this contemporary identification must be taken seriously as the governmental and, to some degree, social perspective that constructed ethno-racial identity, it also comprised something that was questioned and modified, where possible, by the individuals living "under" the designated categories. Approaching this multicultural, polyglot yet strictly hierarchical Iberian Atlantic world, Stuart Hall's discussion of hegemony is useful. He argues that the "cohesion and stability of [the] social order" is achieved "in and through (not despite) its 'differences,' " and that "what matters is not simply the plurality of their internal structures, but the articulated relation between their differences."[18]

Afroiberians were unaware of the details of Catholic doctrine, yet they adapted selected parts of it for their own needs. Their misappropriation of this doctrine, coupled with their continued involvement in the religious ways of their homeland, they often found themselves the target of inquisitorial jurisprudence. Blasphemy, especially in response to mistreatment by their mistresses or masters, constituted one of the most prevalent offenses by enslaved individuals punished by the Inquisitions, though, ironically, many of those charged might well have blasphemed in order to beseech the Inquisition to intervene in their cases against their owner.[19]

Most Afroiberians were not able to produce and leave the kind of paper trail that the educated and socially ascendant Latinos did. Hence the attraction of Inquisition trials and records for scholars of Afroiberian history, culture and religion, which afford an invaluable window. Yet, unlike the extremely familiar and well-documented *"judaísmo"* as known by the Inquisition machinery (accurately or not), the nature and even names of the "pagan" religions of the Africans remained unknown to the overwhelming majority of government and church functionaries. Occasional efforts at such understanding did spring forth, such as *Naturaleza, historia sagrada y profana, costumbres y ritos, disciplina y catecismo evangélico de todos etíopes* (Seville, 1627), a thick description produced by P. Alonso de Sandoval, rector of the Jesuit college at Cartagena de Indias and experienced preacher to the area's enslaved Africans. In terms of the most basic level of self-location, one that was particularly important to Iberians, most Afroiberians who had been born in Africa could not trace their genealogy beyond their parents. Inquisition officials thus often simply assumed that Blacks were bereft of any proper lineage.[20]

While Afroiberians were not technically New Christians, a term invented for Judeoconversos and then applied to Amerindians and Moriscos (Muslims forcibly converted to Christianity during and after the Spanish Reconquista), they were similarly "newly transplanted to the faith," as wrote the biographer of Father Pedro Claver, missionizer to Blacks around Cartagena de Indias.[21] Frederick Bowser claims that in the Americas "the African, unlike the Indian, was not granted the status of neophyte in the Faith," though Jonathan Israel writes that in the Jesuit view Blacks, Mulatos as well as Mestizos were considered "neophytes of the Church."[22] It is unclear whether these authors use the term "neophytes" technically or figuratively. While in the Americas Blacks were forbidden to receive holy orders (along with Amerindians), Africans had not been forbidden to do so in Africa or in Portugal. Some jurists, such as Juan de Solórzano Pereira, author of the most important collection of laws covering American Spanish territories, distinguished the less problematic background and coming-to-Christianity of Africans and Amerindians from the more problematic "race" of Judeoconversos.

Caste and Christianity

The seventeenth century, on which this book focuses, witnessed the continued playing out of the seismic confrontations and couplings of the sixteenth century. The medieval world that was ever so gradually dissipating was one that prized homogeneity, feared and even hated outsiders, foreigners, others. Assumptions of caste and race (and class) were ubiquitous. They led to the fact that from 1580 to 1820 the vast majority of immigrants to the Americas arrived involuntarily. From 1580 to 1640, according to David Eltis, 67 percent of the immigrants were enslaved, 6 percent servants (indentured servants or contract migrants) and 1 percent convicts, while between 1640 and 1700, 65 percent were enslaved, 18 percent servants, and 2 percent convicts.[23] The original Amerindian inhabitants of nearly every American colony first served for the most part as a source for enslaved or forced labor for the extraction of the natural resources of what had been their homelands.

The caste system that created race and races was one invented in the late Middle Ages by an expansionist Christendom in order to construct the community's boundaries. These boundaries were increasingly measured by the conflation of sanctity, purity and worth; blood became "the site and marker of theological [...] investments."[24] It was, to paraphrase Bruno Latour, a network, constructed by communities of political authorities, theologians, clerics, writers, law enforcement experts who claim to have "discovered" it in nature — though they had in fact constructed it. María Elena Martínez shows how anti-Jewish attitudes and strategies of control and exclusion morphed into the racial caste system of the Iberian colonial worlds.[25] The racial caste system was a confused fusing "of 'nation' with religion, of religion with ancestry, and of ancestry with political loyalty."[26] Race was/is both real and constructed, "much more than an illusion and much less than an essence."[27] Consciousness of racial difference permeated daily life and discourse high and low, print and oral. Countervailing rhetoric notwithstanding, all of the three monotheisms (Judaism, Christianity and Islam) were essentially communal demarcations and to some degree even ethnic demarcations.

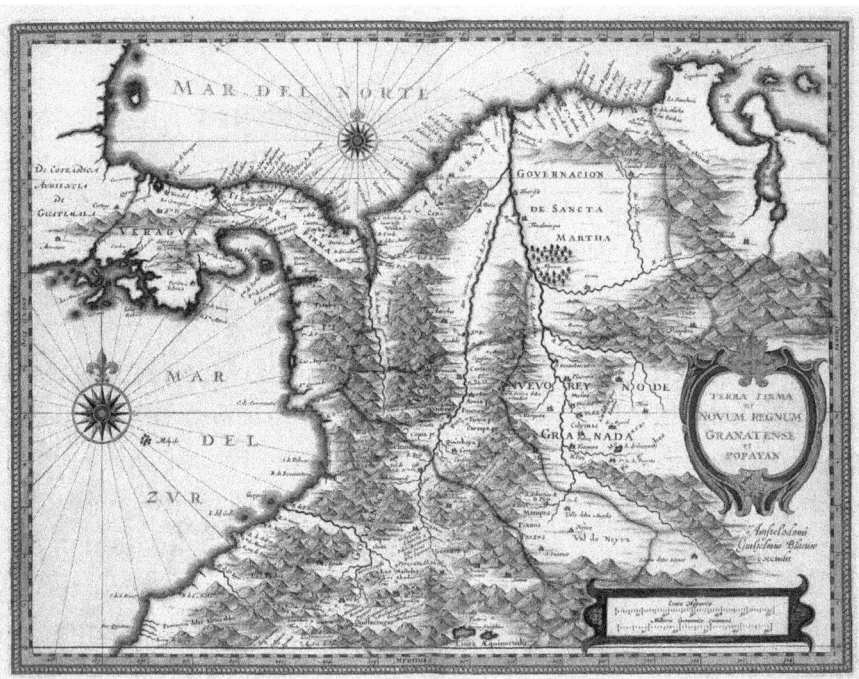

Map of Terra Firma, made up of the New Kingdom of New Granada, the Royal Audiencies of Panamá and Santa Fe de Bogotá, and Provinces of Santa Marta, Popayan, Venezuela, and Guyana. Library of Congress, Geography and Map Division, Washington, D.C.

Inquisition

Partly responsible for the homogeneity of caste and religion as factors in social interaction was the global surveillance apparatus of the Inquisitions of Spain and Portugal, encouraged by the leadership of the Catholic Church, serving the political aims of a monarchy and a culture seeking uniformity. What is more important is the very nature of the Inquisitions as an institution for the policing of political theology. In a theistic society, heresy, because it violates divine law, also violates civil law. Religious dissent is therefore both a sin and a crime.

Inquisition trial records yield a plethora of information about how Judaism and Christianity intersected with caste to shape the interactions and mutual understandings, or misunderstandings, of Judeoconversos and Afroiberians within the orbit of the Iberian empires. From the perspective of Judeoconversos (if not Jews as well) and those of African descent, the seventeenth century Atlantic remained all too monolithically Christian. As Jorge Cañizares-Esguerra has argued, Catholic and Protestant colonizers shared the view that the New World and its inhabitants posed a satanic challenge requiring a crusade of forcible chivalric cleansing, if not extirpation.[28] As is well known, though worth repeating, the Atlantic world was to a great extent discovered, constructed, and defended as a Christian space.

The Inquisitions' intimate concern with the ideational and behavioral components of its subject populations' lives, combined with their early modern bureaucratic mode of operation, led to the creation of enormous archives of documents which record the processes and results of the Inquisitions' essentially ethnographic surveillance. There were far more than the 44,000 or so cases now extant which

Inquisition in Lisbon, 1536. An auto-da-fé in Lisbon's Terreiro do Paço.
Engraving by Picart from the book *The Spanish Inquisition* by Cecil Roth, published 1937.

had been prosecuted to some degree by the Portuguese Inquisition. The larger Spanish Inquisition generated over 150,000 cases.

The very possibility of studying Crypto-Jews, Blacks or Mulatos through documents from the sixteenth through eighteenth centuries depends on the ethnic, religious and caste categories that both caused and resulted from the machinery — social, institutional and textual — that produced the documents. Often no way would exist to identify "Blacks," "Mulatos," "judaizers," or "descendants of Jews" in these materials other than the fact that the individuals are throughout identified as such by lettered official functionaries themselves.[29] Officials wanted to know how to categorize individuals and the groups to which they belonged because the caste system and the laws concerning blood purity determined to a great extent how Spanish and Portuguese society functioned, who was permitted to do or be certain things and who was not. Both Judeoconversos and Afroiberians functioned as cultural and political intermediaries, taking advantage of their status for their own benefit but also suffering accordingly.

In the first section, I offer a case study exploring the parallels and explosive contacts that unfolded between a pair of Mulatos, a Judeoconverso, and the local Inquisition of Cartagena de las Indias in the 1620s and 1630s. The two Mulatos, the free Diego Lopez and the enslaved Rufina, discussed and spied on those they suspected of being Crypto-Jews. They were also both involved in circles of magical practitioners. Arrested by the Cartagena tribunal of the Inquisition, Lopez offered denunciations of numerous Judeoconversos, particularly Blas de Paz Pinto, a fellow surgeon. The colorful events that link Rufina, Lopez and Pinto offer evidence of how members of these different subaltern groups sought to survive and thrive despite the theo-political web that attempted to keep them in their societally assigned places and that also often brought them into direct confrontation with one another.

In the second section, I focus on the life of Esperanza Rodriguez, born in Seville toward the end of the sixteenth century, the daughter of a Judeoconverso father and an enslaved African mother. In the Judeoconverso household where she herself served as a slave, the young Rodriguez learned about crypto-Jewish beliefs and practices. She later moved to the Americas, eventually settling down in Mexico City. There, she circulated among the city's Crypto-Jews, many of them her relatives. When the inquisitional authorities cracked down on alleged Crypto-Jews in the early 1640s, Rodriguez found herself arrested, along with her three daughters. Based on the Inquisition record of her trial, among other documents, I explore

Rodriguez's experiences within the Mexico City Crypto-Jewish community and the significance of her newfound religion and kin network. The riveting, troubled life of this vibrant and ambitious woman of color is set amid the context of colonial Iberian theo-politics, in order to evoke the manifold meanings "Jewishness" held for many Afroiberians oppressed by the Atlantic slave system. Research in the archives in Madrid done since the last publication of this material turned up some new information, which is incorporated into the text.

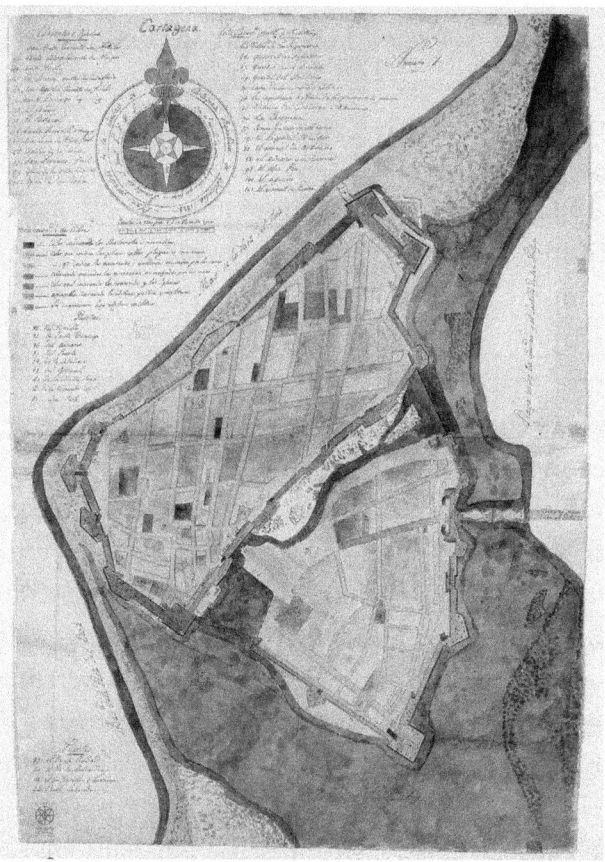

Historical Map of Cartagena.
Archivo General de la Nación, Colombia, Sección: Mapas y Planos. Mapoteca 4 Ref:83A.

The Clash of Two Surgeons and a Slave

In early seventeenth-century Cartagena de las Indias two men, both surgeons, came to know one another, though one was a Judeoconverso and the other a Mulato ex-slave. This inter-racial acquaintanceship, probably fairly typical for urban milieus of the time, evolved into a rather complicated relationship. Both men embodied cultural miscegenation and mobility, though in different ways, and both suffered as a result. Each was accused by the city's inquisitional tribunal, a tribunal increasingly zealous to arrest the perceived threat the colony faced from multicultural witchcraft and sorcery, as well as from wealthy merchants who were allegedly secret Jews. Within the space of a few years, the tribunal seized and charged the Mulato as a *brujo* or practitioner of improper magic and he, for one reason or another, denounced his colleague as a secret Jew. One of the Mulato's lovers had involved herself in the same circle of magical practitioners and had expended much energy gathering information about the city's alleged Crypto-Jews, sometimes in cooperation with her lover. Three interlocking cases, ordinary yet extraordinary, left behind a documentary record whose richness allows us to limn the fragile coexistence and differing trajectories of minority groups in the Spanish Indies.

The port city of Cartagena served as one of the main gateways to the Spanish Indies, both physically and commercially, because it was the beginning of one of the land routes to the thriving city of Lima and the silver mines of Potosí. The anonymous author of the *Description of the Viceroyalty of Peru*, written around 1615, says that

Cartagena, colored woodcut. Cartagena des Indias in the 17th Century. Vue Generalle de Carthagene, Ville de l'Amerique Meridionalle. Paris, c. 1780. Library of Congress Prints and Photographs Division, Washington, D.C.

Cartagena "is better and bigger than Panama City, has very good houses of stone and very good streets, very rich churches and monasteries, stores or merchandise."[30] A 1629 description declares that the city hosts "more than 1,500 Spanish residents."[31] Because of its commercial importance, Cartagena also attracted many non-Spanish Europeans interested in taking advantage of colonial possibilities. One of the city's booming socioeconomic features consisted of the transshipment of enslaved Africans and a dependence on African domestic slaves, which, together with the Amerindians, produced in the population an entire range of Mestizos, Mulatos and other "racial mixtures."

The city's demographic variety obviously was not entirely the result of voluntary immigration. The above-quoted anonymous *Descripción* nodded to the polyglot nature of the city, containing as it did "many settlements [*rancheríos*] of Blacks," since "here many ships arrive which the merchants of Guinea bring, loaded with Blacks."[32] According to historian Charles R. Boxer, Cartagena "was the principle depot for the Portuguese slave-traders," a precedent established already with their first Spanish slave contract (*asiento*) in 1595, which designated Cartagena as the port of primary entry for the Viceroyalties of New Granada and Peru because it was so well situated for the further distribution of enslaved humans into those territories.[33] With the gradual decimation of the Native American population, African slaves became increasingly important as laborers in the colonies' mines and plantations and as servants tending to the needs of the cities' elites.[34] The anonymous seventeenth-century description continues by relating how "here [in Cartagena] arrive merchants from Peru to buy" slaves.[35] The Cartagena customs house reported 6,884 slaves imported between 1585 and 1590.[36] Official letters detail the arrival of 4,810 enslaved individuals between May 1615 and April 1619, and over 6,000 between May 1619 and

Pedro Claver was a Jesuit priest, sent to the New Kingdom of Granada, where he arrived in the port city of Cartagena in 1610. "Claver saw the slaves as fellow Christians, encouraging others to do so as well. During his 40 years of ministry it is estimated that he personally catechized and baptized 300,000 slaves."—*Dominican Journal*

December 1620.[37] These constitute only the official tallies, numbers probably far exceeded by the actual total of arriving enslaved Africans. According to the biographer of Father Pedro Claver, a man who devoted his life to Christianizing the Blacks in and around Cartagena, "In the course of every year, from ten to twelve thousand [Blacks] are brought. And in [16]33, fourteen ships were seen in the port together, without any merchandise other than blacks, with 800 to 900 on each one."[38]

According to this estimate, the minimum total for 1633 would have surpassed 11,000 incoming slaves. Most of the enslaved were sold or shipped off to other locations, but no small number remained to serve individual or institutional masters in the immediate area. A letter of 1619 from a local Franciscan friar, Sebastián de Chumillas, estimates that "there are in [Cartagena] and its district from twelve to fourteen thousand blacks in domestic service."[39]

While Africans came to Cartagena against their will, others sought out the city. Gaspar Rodrigues Nunes, the Converso father of the Amsterdam rabbi Menasseh ben Israel, described in one of the audiences during his Inquisition trial in Lisbon how his first cousin, Manuel Dias, urged him and others to flee Portugal for Cartagena, "because there everyone lived the way he wanted and one was not observed to find out how one was living."[40] Dias' perception had a basis in reality; in 1630 Portuguese, many of them no doubt New Christians, comprised no fewer than 154 of the city's 184 registered foreigners and made up some 10 percent of its White male citizens. Portuguese New Christian merchants indeed dominated the commerce of the Nueva Granada region.[41]

Contrary to Manuel Dias' notions, however, by the seventeenth century Cartagena had become all too Spanish. In 1610 the Inquisition opened a tribunal in the city, a tribunal that ended up overseeing an enormous physical terrain. In the relatively small city itself, "where almost everybody seems to know each other," it had become all too tempting to gather and use knowledge of other people's lives.[42] This explains the interests of two local Mulatos in observing and uncovering the private behavior of other local, mostly Portuguese, residents, whom they suspected of being secret Jews.

A Portuguese-Born New Christian is Accused and Tortured

The alleged Crypto-Jew on whom we focus is Blas de Paz Pinto, a Portuguese surgeon, born in Évora in or around 1590.[43] Until roughly the age of thirty he lived in Lisbon. He is called a *licenciado* in one letter between some of his commercial associates, meaning that he was university trained and passed a medical exam to become a surgeon.[44] Arriving in Cartagena from Angola in 1622, Pinto treated sick slaves in the process of being sold by Portuguese slavers. His medical practice operated out of the Franciscan convent of San Diego.[45] On his farm or ranch (*estancia*) at the edge of the city, he "dedicated himself to the cultivation of medical plants," while also investing in "inter-regional commerce, turning himself into an indispensable partner" and intermediary of merchants from both Lima and Cartagena, including some of the most prominent such as Sebastian Duarte, António Nunes Gramaxo, João Rodrigues Mesa (or Juan Rodriguez Messa) and Manuel Bautista Peres (or Baptista Pérez), all Portuguese.[46] Pinto also traded in slaves, in this connection even working with the slave traders of Lisbon.[47]

The Colombian scholar Itic Croitoru Rotbaum published a photo of Pinto's house in Cartagena, which, according to his book's Index of Illustrations, the author "recently identified" at Plaza Fernández Madrid, No. 37-14.[48] Pinto considered himself "quiet and pacific," according to the official who compiled and submitted the list of the city's foreigners in 1630, who adds a mention of the surgeon's "useful [*menesteroso*] occupation," his being "without suspicion" and the fact that he dutifully pays what he owes the government. For these reasons, and the fact that he paid 350 pesos, it was ordered that he receive a letter of naturalization.[49] None of the documents relating

Palace of the Inquisition, Cartagena, Plaza de Bolívar (Bolívar´s Square), Cartagena de Indias. Colombia: Photo Detlef Langer GNU free documentation library.

to Pinto make clear whether or not he was married. In 1633 he sought help obtaining the certification of naturalization that had still not arrived, turning to the local prominent Portuguese merchant Antonio Nunes Gramaxo, who tried, unsuccessfully, to purchase it for 300 ducats.[50]

When the inquisitional tribunals of Lima and Cartagena became active in fomenting anti-Portuguese hysteria around 1634, Pinto fell into the latter's hands, through the usual web of denunciations targeting outsiders, in this case Portuguese, suspected Jews, merchants, and the wealthy.[51] Of the 81 alleged judaizers sentenced by the Cartagena tribunal in the seventeenth century, 57 were Portuguese and 38 were merchants.[52] The tribunal arrested Pinto on 22 July 1636, the same day it arrested four other Portuguese New Christians. He served as the majordomo of the confraternities of Saint Antonio and of the Immaculate Conception, yet the inquisitors could only see this as a calculating show: "to have it understood that he was a Catholic Christian, being a descendent of Hebrews."[53]

Pinto was denounced to the Inquisition by a number of people, accused by various witnesses of hosting gatherings of Portuguese Conversos in his house, which one witness calls a synagogue.[54]

This same witness testifies that Pinto acknowledged that he was Jewish and that a sister of his was "penitenced" by the Inquisition in Portugal. It is said that he verbally denigrated the holy images in one of the city's churches and even spat on one. The rest of the accusations against Pinto come from other Portuguese New Christian merchants already imprisoned by the same tribunal as suspected judaizers: Manuel Álvarez Prieto, Juan Rodríguez Mesa and Francisco Piñero. Rodríguez Mesa says that Pinto "was a Jewish judaizer, observer of the law of Moses" and was known as such. He supposedly didn't eat pig (*tocino*, bacon); kept fasts, including "the fast of the month of September," i.e., Yom Kippur, when he would not eat

Denunciation window, Palace of the Inquisition.
Cartagena: Photo Detlef Langer GNU free documentation library.

"until the night emergence of the star;" kept the sabbath as a festival, for which he wore new clothes and used fresh linens and tablecloths; and ate fish with scales (one of the requirements for fish to be considered kosher, the other being the presence of fins).[55] According to Francisco Piñero, Pinto participated with the other Portuguese in various "ceremonies and fasts" and "was held to be a man learned and capable among the Jews."[56] Based on the above information, the Cartagena tribunal imprisoned Pinto and sequestered all of his goods. One accused judaizer, Manuel de Fonseca Enríquez, later claims under torture that it was Pinto who had taught him the Law of Moses, beginning in 1632.[57] Another, Francisco Rodríguez de Solís, states that Pinto "gave some talks [pláticas] regarding the observance of the [...] law."[58]

It is difficult to know what to make of the charges against Pinto. Some of the detailed allegations evince familiarity with Crypto-Jewish practices that go beyond the usual litany given in the *edictos de fé* that were read in the churches and posted on church doors, as had been done in Cartagena in 1610 with the opening of the local tribunal.[59] These details may reflect more on the knowledge of the witnesses than the knowledge of Pinto, of course. Some of the purported crimes seem strange, to say the least. For instance, Rodríguez Mesa alleges that Pinto "put his hands behind him above his belt (*que ponía las manos por detrás sobre la cintura*), as a rite and ceremony of the Law of Moses and as his own observance," a ritual of which I have never heard nor found documentation.[60] On the other hand, keeping in mind the usual inquisitorial context, all of those who denounced Pinto were themselves under suspicion by the local tribunal for one reason or another. Protesting that they knew nothing did not spare them in the least. One Portuguese merchant in Cartagena, Luis Gomes Barreto, tried in 1636 by the local inquisitorial tribunal, includes Pinto among the group of Portuguese merchants who got together to conduct business — they were all involved with one or another aspect of the slave trade — though he denies that any discussions of or observance of things Jewish took place.[61] Barreto relates that the group met at Pinto's farm or ranch (*estancia*) around 1630, on which occasion the Senior Inquisitor and Archdeacon were among those present (making it hard to believe anything unsuitable happened).[62] Another Portuguese merchant, Manuel Álvarez Prieto, arrested in April 1636, names Pinto as "his capital enemy" as the rack on which he was strapped was given an excruciating tightening. Álvarez Prieto also accuses Pinto of accusing him falsely and insists that he knows nothing of any Fraternity of Holland (a nation comprising Spain's capital enemy at the time; the fraternity is discussed below). Through seven turns of the rack's wheel (his screams duly recorded by the scribe) Álvarez Prieto offers nothing more substantive, though the Inquisition surgeons confirm that both arms have been broken (three months later he is dead).[63] According to the tribunal's summary, Álvarez Prieto called Pinto a Jewish judaizer, but later retracted his accusation.[64] Finally, it is odd that Pinto is considered by some of his denouncers to be the group's "rabbi," since it seems from the documentation that others knew and practiced much more than he. Still, enough of the Portuguese Conversos confirm the gatherings at Pinto's house that it seems likely that they indeed occurred, though whether they were social affairs or ritual events remains murky. Historian Tobias Green finds that "one of the formulations of Blas de Paz Pinto in his letter to Tomás Rodriguez Barassa of October 12th 1635 — "*Alavo a Dios /* Praise God" — was a variant of a prayer which had been recited by converted Jews in Spain in the 15th century, and also of a favored prayer of Tomás Treviño de Sobremonte, the famous Crypto-Jew of Mexico who declared his Judaism as he was marched to the stake and burnt alive in the great Auto de Fé of 1649."[65]

At first Pinto claims not to know "what caste he was," i.e., whether any of his parents or grandparents were Conversos, and he denies, through all of eight audiences, being anything other than a good Catholic. Continuing to deny all of the charges, the inquisitors and four consultants voted to apply torture (euphemizing it by calling it "the charitable admonition") in the hope of extracting a confession corroborating the charges they take as truth.[66] After three quarters of an hour on the rack, Pinto "wished to confess the truth entirely," stating that he has been "judaizing" for thirty years, since his time in Lisbon, where he was taught by a woman named Violante Duarte.[67] He says that "he had fasted Wednesdays and Fridays of some weeks," kept Saturday sabbaths as a festival, putting on new clothes, and avoided eating pig whenever possible.[68] He names many of the group of Portuguese merchants with whom he would gather to perform rites and "to confess the fast days that they kept:" Juan Rodríguez Mesa, Francisco Rodríguez de Solís, Manuel de Fonseca, Manuel Álvarez Prieto, Manuel de Acosta, Alvaro de Silvera, Francisco Piñero, Luis Gómez Barreto, Francisco de Heredia, Antonio Rodríguez Ferrerín, and Antonio de Acosta. He also denounces as judaizers Amaro Denis, already imprisoned by the Lima tribunal, and the slave traders and brothers Juan Rodríguez de Silva and Jorge de Silva. He claims that it was Álvarez Prieto, whom he met in Angola, who convinced him to keep the Law of Moses. He implies that Rodríguez Mesa's house served as the main gathering place for this group, that Rodríguez Mesa would often conduct ceremonies in which scriptural passages were read and said that "the promised messiah has not come."[69]

Some of the details of Pinto's confession make it appear convincing that he knew something about Crypto-Jewish beliefs and practices. The confession of the fast days to one another was not an element of the *edictos de fé* and would not likely have been known by non-Conversos. In addition, the charges against the other sentenced Portuguese Conversos show impressive variation.[70] Most of the components of Pinto's admission were standard fare, however, and would have been known by most Iberians. Of course, just because Pinto knew these details does not mean he observed the practices themselves, nor can one jump to conclusions because of the knowledge or activities of others in his sphere. It could well have been the accumulated pressure of his imprisonment and trial, and, finally, his torture, that brought forth this gush of information.

He could well have learned in the Inquisition jail just which Portuguese New Christians had been arrested and, possibly, even who had denounced him.

Torture Instruments.
Museum of the Inquisition, Cartagena.

An Ex-Slave Surgeon and his Witchcraft-Practicing Lover

The only non-Portuguese who denounced Blas de Paz Pinto seems to have been the Mulato surgeon Diego López, who had been arrested by the same tribunal for alleged crimes of his own. Almost all of our information regarding him comes from Inquisition sources. He was born into slavery in Cartagena in 1591 or 1592. As a slave, he served in one of the city's hospitals, either San Sebastián founded in 1613, then known also as San Juan de Dios, or San Lázaro founded in 1598. San Sebastián treated and housed incurables, the chronically ill and convalescent, while San Lázaro received lepers and those suffering from sores/ulcers.[71] López took advantage of this opportunity to enter the medical profession, which he practiced for his income once he obtained his liberty. It was not infrequent that Blacks and Mulatos acquired European medical skills through such servitude.[72]

Surgeons comprised a mixed lot, some considered mere bloodletters, others "full" physicians. Still, all had only to obtain the license of a "simple" *protomédico*, along with druggists and barbers. According to colonial legislation from 1605, their exam consisted of relevant questions concerning human anatomy as well as the variety of sores, head wounds, and serious sicknesses. If the questions were answered satisfactorily, the applicant had in addition to agree to cure the poor *pro bono*.[73] Hence both Diego López and Blas de Paz Pinto ministered to the enslaved and the non-White population, though not always for similar motivations. The primary function of surgeons was to treat the blood and/or humors and to prescribe medications. Given the frequent lack of doctors, they often fulfilled the complete range of physicians' functions.[74]

On 8 January 1633, López was incarcerated by the Holy Office on the testimony of nine witnesses, all women over twenty-five, who provided concrete accusations depicting him as a "heretical apostate witch [brujo]." In his first three meetings with his inquisitors he denied absolutely everything. On 7 April 1634, more than a year after having been imprisoned, López began to confess his crimes and to name accomplices.[75]

A close friend of López's and a married lover of his beginning in 1627, if not earlier, was the Mulata Rufina. An enslaved woman, Rufina not only participated in the magical practices that claimed the involvement of a good number of the city's women and men but stood as the only non-White permitted to participate in a select group of White practitioners of magic (brujas), all of whom had supposedly learned their skills from a Black woman named Paula de Eguiluz. Rufina even served as a kind of aide to this locally famous Eguiluz.[76] As Mulatos in an urban setting, López and Rufina represented and enjoyed a cultural integration, social mobility and economic opportunity that, while limited by factors of race, went far beyond the world of newly arrived slaves (bozales) trapped amid mines or plantations.[77]

López and Rufina had a tempestuous relationship. Imprisoned, he denounces her as one of the "enemies" whose testimony had landed him in trouble.[78] She had attempted to wreak vengeance on a new lover he had taken. And in a fit of anger and jealousy when López's wife delivered a baby, she used her magical powers to threaten him that the baby would die shortly, which it did.[79] (The married López's lovers are listed in one of his audiences: first Juana Hortensio, then a different Rufina (slave of Amador Pérez), later "our" Rufina (slave of Rafael Gómez), and finally Ana María of Jamaica, against whom Rufina sought vengeance.)[80] Still, López and "our" Rufina seemed to be constant companions.

One mutual interest shared by Rufina and López, mostly instigated by Rufina, according to López's narration, was spying on the city's suspected Crypto-Jews. Rufina appears to have delighted in spreading gossip about who might be a Jew (and acting on it), telling López, for instance,

> that an old woman who is Portuguese and who lives in the street with the rest [of the Portuguese (?)], in some low houses of Juana Colón, also Portuguese, mother-in-law of Miguel de Chabes, is a Jew and communicates with the mother-in-law of Rafael Gómez, whom he now remembers is called Beatriz López and similarly that the mother-in-law of doctor Báez was a Jewess and all three communicated in secret.[81]

The self-interest motivating at least part of Rufina's curiosity can be gleaned from the appearance of the mother-in-law of her master, Rafael Gómez, and mother of her mistress, Clara Núñez, in this listing of alleged secret Jews, a miniscule portion of the detailed and colorful gossip about secret Jews (among other things) that Rufina shared. It should be recalled that as Portuguese, these individuals were considered outsiders and suspect, especially as Portuguese hostility to the union of Spain and Portugal (1580-1640) grew into outright secession. Other episodes of spying on her mistress and master and their local relatives suggest that her interests in the religious life of her neighbors had roots in possibilities for improving her situation. But her persistent curiosity, stemming perhaps as much from ethnological interests as from ulterior motives, led her to understand the importance of "knowing other people's lives," an importance encouraged by the Inquisitions, not surprisingly.[82]

Rufina's interest in discovering and uncovering the goings-on of those she thought might be Jews spread outward and enveloped López in ways beyond sharing rumors. The Portuguese-born Blas de Paz Pinto became a focal point of her interest. She told Diego that Blas de Paz Pinto has a synagogue at his house and was "desirous that this one [López] see something of what they read at the gatherings which she knew they secretly had [...] sometimes at night and others at midday, she went up to call the accused [López] [...] and, accompanying the accused, the said mulata went ahead and entered and then came out and said to this one [López]: 'now is a good time, go in and see what they are doing.' "[83]

From the way Rufina went into the house or was said to have gone in it would appear that she had entry, that is, she was familiar to either Pinto himself or, more likely, to a member or members of his household staff. These situations remind us of the relative freedom of mobility possessed by those who lived on the margins of respectable society. As Diana Luz Ceballo Gómez writes, "certain service slaves, for example, visit the world of the blacks, that of their own masters and that of the masters of other blacks; they enter the houses, bearing messages and orders, go to the market to shop and enter into contact with the merchants, go freely about the city."[84] López, finding the door closed, had to go around to the house of Martín Sánchez in front, where he remained until five in the afternoon.[85] The street windows of the Pinto house stayed shut the whole time, however, "and the slaves of the above-mentioned [Pinto] were posted at attention in places, in order not to allow entry to anyone who came to do business with him." Eventually, around five o'clock, López saw "ten men, more or less," exit the house, among them some he knew.[86]

Around 1629, perhaps when the two were still lovers, Rufina told López that he should go visit Pinto, who was ill and that [López] said to her, "what sickness does he have?" and she responded that he was like her, he was menstruating and not understanding what the said mulata had told him, he went to the house of the said Blas de Paz and, asking him about his sickness, he told him the cause and that he was bleeding, and that he [López] should see whether he [Blas] had some hemorrhoids or some inflammation in the rear and this one [López] looked at him and told him that he had no inflammation, with which he ordered this accused [López] to go look at the blood, which was in a silver basin and before he did the above-mentioned, the said mulata Rufina had said to this accused [López] that the said Blas de Paz had covered his toilet with a linen on which was an image of a saint with a diadem and [with] the cloth of the toilet over the said image and that he would sit on it when he went [i.e., defecated].[87]

Given the opportunity, López says he looked at the toilet, finding exactly what Rufina had predicted. Though he claims he could not identify the particular saint, he saw that the figure in the image wore the habit of Saint Francis and was a youth. The inquisitors' report about the *auto de fé* in which the late Pinto appeared speculated that "according to everyone it was understood that it was Saint Antonio, of whose confraternity [Pinto] was superintendent [*majordomo*]."[88] Saint Anthony, patron saint of travelers and seafarers, served logically as the patron saint of diasporic Portuguese communities, which set up many chapels in his honor.[89] In other words, Pinto's existence was taken to be not only schizoid — a Jew pretending to be Christian, the inner life differing from the outer — but to comprise a complete and absolute self-negation, intent on destroying precisely that which it upheld, on upholding exactly that which it despised.

Rufina's description of Blas de Paz Pinto's sickness drew on two related, often conflated traditions in Christian discourse. The first and earlier one held that Jews experienced hemorrhoids, bleeding from the anus, as a result of their denial of Christ, either permanently, or every Easter or Good Friday. The second posited that Jewish men menstruated, a theory going back at least as far as the thirteenth-century anatomist Thomas de Cantimpré and recurring among Christian thinkers into the seventeenth century, if not later.[90] The former tradition was "imputed to the paradigmatic enemies of God" from late antiquity through the middle ages: Judas, Arians/heretics, and Jews."[91] Continues scholar Willis Johnson:

> This idea may well have originated when the heresiarch Arius died by prolapse — the herniated extrusion of the intestines — in a public toilet in Alexandria. This death was interpreted by his contemporaries as a divine condemnation of Arius's teachings regarding the physical body of Christ, and exegetically equated with the mysterious bursting of Judas's belly (Acts 1:18) when he hanged himself. As symbolic betrayers of Christ, Jews were exegetically linked with Judas and Arius in many texts through the middle ages. In the twelfth century, a consolidation of Church power that led to the eventual demonization of the Jews coincided with the arrival in the West of the elaborately theorized humoral medicine of the Arabs. Numerous sources from this period reflect a rationalization and medicalization of the formerly religious symbolism of Jewish bleeding. By the thirteenth century, these traditional associations had evolved into a belief in

the annual bleeding of Jews at Easter. For more than a century these two ways of understanding the Jewish flux coincided and occasionally reinforced each other. Jews were thought to suffer a disabling bloody flux from their anuses in annual commemoration of the killing of Christ.[92]

These theories witnessed a revival in seventeenth-century Spain and Portugal, where Old Christians wielded them against suspected Crypto-Jews, whose increasing invisibility heightened fears of their invidiousness. In early 1632, the Spanish court official Juan Quiñones submitted a memorandum to the Inquisitor General Antonio de Sotomayor, suggesting methods for discovering whether a New Christian was a judaizer:

> [...] every month many of them suffer a flowing of the blood from their posterior parts, as a perpetual sign of infamy and shame... Many authors say therefore that when Pilate said, as Saint Matthew relates, that he was innocent of the Just One's blood, all those Jews who shouted and said let his blood be on them and their children, they and all their descendants remained with the blemish, plague, and perpetual sign so that every month they suffer a flow of blood like women... The sign is nothing more than making a mark (on something) so that it is different from others, so that it is not confused with them... and when recognition is difficult from the look of the face, one should resort to the hidden signs that are on the body.[93]

Quiñones had composed his treatise attempting to prove the myth of Jewish male menstruation as an intervention into a particular

Inquisition trial. Quiñones's allegation accompanied a wave of similar insults against "Jews" and "Jewish" doctors in the course of the movement for strengthening purity of blood statutes.[94] The year before, a translation of a Portuguese anti-Jewish tract announced that some "say that on holy [i.e., Good] Friday all the Jews, male and female, have that day a flux of blood, and for that reason almost all are of a pallid color."[95] Similar charges had been raised already in a 1604 text: "[T]he Jews suffer permanently from hemorrhoids and from an anal flux of blood and they are called circumcised because they clean their anus with their fingers."[96] Gerónimo de la Huarta (or Gómez de Huarta; 1573-1643), personal physician of King Felipe IV (reigned 1621-1665), proposed applying purity of blood statutes in the medical profession, a field often seen as monopolized by Jews, a proposal not unconnected to his scientific opinion about "the putrid odor of the Jewish physician caused by his murder of Christ, his permanent condition of hemorrhoids, and the flux of anal blood on his bare fingers."[97] In Portugal, in particular, Old Christians were said to prefer disease or even death to treatment at the hands of a Converso doctor. In short, we have here a discourse constructing Judaism as "one of the incurable diseases," in the early sixteenth-century words of the exiled Spanish-Jewish author Solomon ibn Verga.[98] Perhaps we should not be surprised, then, by the fact that when the charges against Blas de Paz Pinto are drawn up by the tribunal, both in 1636 and when re-presented in 1651, the one regarding male menstruation heads up the list.[99] It is as if the inquisitors find this "condition" the strongest proof of Pinto's Jewishness.

Rufina, an illiterate enslaved individual, might well have picked up the rumor of Jewish flux somewhere, which would indicate that the pseudo-scientific myth had a life beyond "elite" thinkers in Europe.[100] The notion probably did not come from a book produced in Cartagena, as the city possessed no printing press for most of its history before the nineteenth century.¹⁰¹ In this case, Rufina's magico-medical knowledge would have derived from acquaintances or even her mentor Paula de Eguiluz, who might have learned of these notions about Jews from someone in the medical field. Indeed, Eguiluz, who had been arrested twice by the Cartagena Inquisition, in 1624 and 1632, was sentenced at her first trial to work in the city's hospital, where she would also live, among other penalties.¹⁰²

In fact, given the medical provenance of much of this discourse regarding Jewish male menstruation, it is just as likely that Diego López himself applied the theory to Blas de Paz Pinto on his own and simply blamed Rufina when standing before the inquisitors. López, after all, was trained as a surgeon and had worked in one of the city's hospitals, a site where continental "medical" theories regarding Jewish male menstruation might well have been discussed. Though Cartagena does not seem to have had a facility of medical education, it hosted one of the era's most innovative surgeons, Pedro López de León, of Seville, for 24 years. In 1628 he published the book he wrote while in Cartagena, *Theory and Practice of Abscesses*.¹⁰³ Historian Ceballos Gómez points to our Diego López as an example of an individual who is both a cultural intermediary as well as himself a bearer of several biological/cultural traditions, who even comes to learn his practice "alongside a doctor instructed in the Mediterranean tradition" of medicine.¹⁰⁴ The local mistress of magic, Paula de Eguiluz, could be characterized similarly. Though clearly working with African and Amerindian knowledge and practices, as shown by Luz Adriana Maya Restrepo, according to Ceballos Gómez,

> If at first [Eguiluz] did not know the details and twists and turns of the imaginary of European diabolical witchcraft, by the end of her first trial she will know the basics and, by the conclusion of the third she will be the greatest

expert, "educating" in these matters her acquaintances [...] between [her] trials, but also conducting an exchange of magical recipes and love potions with other people in Cartagena [...] or instructing her alleged accomplices in what they should declare before the inquisitors.[105]

It is very possible that López and Eguiluz had come to know one another while each worked at the hospital, though López blames Rufina for introducing him (earlier?) to Eguiluz's circle of magical practitioners.

Sharing this knowledge between them, or perhaps acting on his own, the interest of the "scientifically" oriented López was piqued enough to spur him to take advantage of a chance to investigate its truth. Without mentioning Rufina's mandate, López examines Pinto and tells him that he has no inflammation. His bleeding comes from another cause, says López, implicitly supporting the notion that he is menstruating due to supernatural reasons.[106] Indeed, López's diagnosis that Pinto lacked any medically observable ailment became the basis for the first of the Inquisition's sixteen charges against the alleged judaizer:

> a certain person urging another to go visit Blas de Paz, who was sick, [...] and examining him with care, the said person found that he had no sort of inflammation, because of which it is to be believed that the said Blas de Paz is a descendant of those who, with shouts, said "crucify [him], let his blood be upon us and upon our children [Matt. 27: 23, 25]," and because of which blood goes over him [probably alluding to Matt. 23:35].[107]

These words of the inquisitors resemble the framing of this whole issue in Quiñones and earlier authorities suspiciously closely, down to the invocation of the verses from Matthew. It seems difficult to believe that the illiterate Rufina or even López would have been aware of such theological contexts and connections. The allusion to the Christological punishment of Jewish men for their alleged deicide comes in Latin, but the framing of the episode would appear to point right to López as the author of this charge against Pinto and its formulation. Yet it is not just the formulation of the quoted or paraphrased learned officials which should arouse curiosity. The structure of the entire investigation conducted by López and Rufina appears to be a concrete application of the hermeneutic suggestion proposed by Quiñones: "when recognition is difficult from the look of the face, one should resort to the hidden signs that are on the body."

Knowledge is Power, Especially Through the Gaze of the Invisible

Rufina's hand should not be dismissed too quickly, however. Like the later well-known Marie Laveaux of New Orleans, Rufina, though still enslaved, reigned over a kind of fiefdom.[108] Rufina held a prominent place in the quasi-African magical gatherings headed up by Paula Eguiluz. Like Marie Laveaux, Rufina was highly attentive to gossip, encouraging it, cultivating it, controlling it. Both women understood that knowledge is power and put this understanding into practice. Discussing other cases in Cartagena, Ceballos Gómez calls attention to the way

> blacks testify in the trials against white women and fabricate rumors against them; contrary to Indians, who have keeping quiet as a virtue, they are talkers, prone to gossip and appear with too much frequency as witnesses in the criminal trials, with their world populated by spirits and curses, intriguing against the rest. The slaves talk, comment and return the *vox populi* that certain whites are *brujas*."[109]

When Rufina tells López that Pinto's house serves as a synagogue, he asks her how she knows this. She "responded that every day she hears many things about this in her house [that is, the house of her Portuguese masters Rafael Gomez and Clara Nuñez] and through this she knows."[110] According to López, Rufina had told him that one older Portuguese woman had "gone out in an *auto de fe*" and that Rufina's master's mother-in-law, also Portuguese, "was a descendent of Hebrews."[111] After detailing one episode of spying with Rufina on her master's mother-in-law, who was supposedly abusing a small Christ on a crucifix, an accusation commonly lodged against New Christians, López informs the inquisitors that "Rufina always said with admiration that were one to touch this material it would certainly bring ruin." Here he alludes to the potential harm such knowledge of others' behavior could wreak, as well as to Rufina's seeming enjoyment of this power.[112]

Diego López seems to have been just as curious to know about other people's lives and just as active in gathering information, if his confessions to the inquisitors have any truth in them. Passing the house of one Portuguese whom Rufina has told him "was a Jew when he came from Spain," López supposedly sees him or his young son urinating on an image of the Virgin. López investigates, "in order to better satisfy myself."[113] It appears that he was even caught several times nosing into the business of others. One time, for instance, he comes across one of the men he suspects to be a judaizer sitting in the house of another suspected judaizer, reading a book. Seeing López enter, the man quickly hides the book under folds of cloth or curtain. Recalling Rufina's allegations that this man was a Jew, López imagines

> that that must be some book of his Law and the said man who reads in the book having been called upstairs, [López] remained in the corridor that goes down to the patio where he had to stay until they advised him that he could come, and as he had the suspicion that he related, he took the book with one hand and opened it with it and saw that the beginning of it said "Compilation of the Bible."[114]

Perhaps because López was an ex-slave, perhaps because he was not White, it seems that the Portuguese whom he was surveilling either did not take the threat seriously or could do nothing about it given the necessity for López to carry out his tasks. In many instances, including this one, those being investigated made efforts to explain away things. The brother of João Rodrigues Mesa, finding López looking at the book,

> took the book with great speed and anger and put it under his arm, smiling with the said youth with the large nose, their voices all nervous/agitated, and J[oã]o Rodriguez Messa came out, saying that people came to other people's houses not to conduct business but to see what was up, and [he said] this with much annoyance [...] and then Blas de Paz came to speak with [López] and made particular effort to ascertain whether he had seen what the said book contained.[115]

Pragmatically, López simply lies to him, pretending that he saw nothing. It seems to have been quite clear to López at least what he had done.[116] A long time after an incident in which López claims to have rebutted some anti-Christian remarks by the father of Rufina's mistress, the man (whose name López cannot recall) asks López if he remembers their exchange; again, López simply lies and says he remembers nothing.[117]

The Inquisition as an institution thus did not merely function as a neutral observer. As in quantum physics, the presence of an observing entity actually determined matters to some degree, fanning personal inquisitiveness, producing new opportunities, within the context of the very structure of the socioeconomic hierarchy to produce a war of all against all. Again Ceballos Gómez excellently captures the way pressures led people to "unburden their emotions/grudges in gossip and slanders, among whites to stand out in order to win the favor of the king or of the officials — in order to improve one's position, to obtain mercy or expediting — and among blacks procuring the appreciation of the masters — in order to get better work and be assigned less arduous labor, [all this] had to have created a conflictual environment."[118]

A case of feared witchcraft that exercised the authorities of Cartagena in 1565 serves as an excellent model for understanding the gathering of information by Rufina and the denunciations made by López. A 25-year-old Black slave woman, Guiomar, taken from Africa at the age of 10 or 12, seems to have suffocated or drowned various children of the household in which she served, as well as committing other acts of magical terrorism, in order that her master sell her. Ceballos Gómez, who studied the case of Guiomar and her accomplice, an older Black slave named Bartolomé, finds that throughout the trial Guiomar manifests "a profound hatred toward whites, justifying her acts and her accusations against other blacks by the harmful actions of the masters: the mistreatment, the excessive work to which they were subject, having to raise the masters' children and look after their sustenance, the fact that they would have slaves or, simply, the fact that someone would not want to liberate a slave." Other Blacks who were interrogated (many by the province's Governor, no less) confirmed the sentiments, hoping, in contrast, that through helpful behavior they would be able to "improve their situation [by] giving to their masters herbs so that they would wish them well, others working sensibly so that their master would liberate a child or in order to win his appreciation."[119] Both Bartolomé and Guiomar, on the other hand, confess their having gone out to kill "all the people of Cartagena."[120] Other slaves recognized Guiomar's uniquely deep hatred, having heard her say things such as that she "would eat all [her master's] blacks."[121] James Sweet discusses an early eighteenth-century Brazilian-Portuguese case in which a slave woman used incantations "to attack rival servants" and reads such attacks as "always more than a personal attack; it was also a strike against the master's economic and social well-being."[122]

The Meaning-Making of Afroiberian Magic

Similar motivations seem to have pushed Rufina and López. Their participation in the local circles of *brujería* — López only from 1628 or so, according to his own testimony[123] — reflect their anti-establishment sentiments and acts of counter-hegemonic disobedience, grounded on their understanding that the law and establishment entailed a fundamentally xenophobic and slave-based system. Irene Silverblatt notes how the perceived "political" threat of multicultural magic in Peru increased as the seventeenth century went on; "it was said that [witches] could stop royal officers from carrying out a sentence, or even inquisitors from pursuing a case."[124] The threat may well have been perceived accurately. Michael Taussig asserts that the "leaders of the *palenques* or runaway slave settlements were as likely as not to be wizards and witches, according to the official texts."[125] At the same time, African knowledge, herbal or pharmacological, for instance, served as a means by which the enslaved and the "colored" could sell their expertise, mostly to White Spaniards, and thereby reaffirm their personhood and escape to some degree the condition of objectification imposed on them.[126]

Both López and Rufina participated in Eguiluz's circle, which met on the beaches and fields of *Ciénaga de los Manzanillos* / Swamp of the Manzanillos (Manzanillo is a South American tree with fruit like a small apple), near the city, as well as at the house of Elena de Viloria, in the city itself. One of the major, and first, charges against this group of non-Whites mentioned in the audiences of López is the "crimes, damages [...] which are notorious [...] which they [i.e., the entire group] have caused to many important persons in this Republic."[127] Even before joining these circles, claims López, Rufina had told him with seeming pride who the local *brujas* and *brujos* were, "some [of whom] were referring to the harmful acts that they had done."[128] Many of the murders and casting of spells attributed by López to this circle relate to romantic interests, which James Sweet interprets as efforts to gain "access to members of the opposite sex" by a population suffering from "the void in human contact and affection that was created by slavery."[129] The group's alleged crimes went far beyond this, however. Eguiluz allegedly had one of her minions kill a merchant named Hernando Godo Mexia for reasons left unstated.[130] Some of the acts supposedly perpetrated by Eguiluz herself and others within her circles include mockeries of or attacks on representations of Catholicism in various local churches. Charges from the 1630s as well as from her first trial in 1624 point to other classic forms of satire or rebellion, that is, acts of symbolic or real subversion.[131] Supposedly finding out that Rufina disinterred a recently buried infant girl for nefarious purposes, López accuses her of carrying out acts of horrifying audacity. She, in turn, lays all the blame on her superior in magic, Paula de Eguiluz: "who inspires us to [do it] all, as with [other] similar cases."[132] In what might be an indication of the sway Eguiluz held over her followers, when in front of the inquisitors López seems afraid or unwilling to "believe the said Paula [is behind] any evil [deed] but rather her zamba" — here probably referring to Eguiluz's assistant of mixed African and Amerindian background, Juana Zamba.[133]

At one of his first gatherings with Eguiluz's *junta*, López is assigned, "as a companion" a "devil named Taravira, who appeared in the figure of a man dressed like an Indian," to whom López pledges allegiance and whom he penetrates in anal sex. Later López confessed to bearing a mark on his left rear thigh, made as a demonstration of his loyalty to this "devil," in the inquisitors' terms.[134] The fact that López's spirit guardian was Amerindian points to the increasingly syncretic nature of the magical practices wielded by these Afroamericans as time went on and as they went from being *bozales* (newly arrived enslaved individuals) to becoming part of the cultural mix of their new setting. Things Amerindian possessed enormous potency for many non-Whites of Nueva Granada as a component of their symbolic marronage, subconscious or otherwise.[135] López tells the inquisitors that "when he coupled with his devil Taravira and knew him from behind he had more pleasure with him than as if he were with a woman."[136] López's statement might allude to the kind of proclivities, repressed in upstanding Catholic society, that were allowed, even encouraged to surface in such counter-cultural fora, but also to the intentionally contrarian nature of the acts embodying efforts to challenge or overturn, in whatever manner, an unjust socio-politico-economic system. It is telling that Rufina's spirit companion is named *Rompe sanctos* / Breaks Saints.[137]

Denouncing Injustice?

The interest of Rufina and López in Blas de Paz Pinto thus may have stemmed from more than the latter's allegedly prominent role in the Cartagena Crypto-Jewish community. Though a surgeon by profession, the *licenciado* Pinto also dealt in slaves. Many Portuguese in the Spanish Indies engaged in trading enslaved people, some as a supplement to their principle occupations.[138] Pinto was part of the commercial network of Manuel Bautista Peres and his partner Sebastião Duarte, of Lima, whose firm was involved in transshipping the enslaved as well as silver mining in the Andean mountains and the trade route between Acapulco and Manila.[139] By no means, though, can Pinto be included among the most prominent slave traders, even within Cartagena. Perhaps he picked up this business while in Angola, where he resided after leaving Lisbon. Tobias Green states that Pinto "was so well known in Guiné that on March 4th 1637, 4 people testified in Cacheu that they recognized his handwriting."[140] According to one witness testifying to an inquisitorial visitor in 1635, a 13-year scheme to bribe officials in Cartagena to ignore their illegal importation of enslaved people was arranged by none other than Pinto.[141]

Scholars suggest that New Christians, who were not allowed in the Americas by law, often took a circuitous route via Guinea or Angola, finding entry in the western hemisphere through Buenos Aires or elsewhere "under the guise of bringing along slaves."[142] Jonathan Israel suggests that Portuguese New Christians served as "agents of Lisbon contractors handling the slave trade" in order "both to emigrate and make money."[143] According to Israel, "most of the leading and middling Portuguese Crypto-Jewish merchants of New Spain seem to have got started in trans-Atlantic commerce in this particular way."[144] A glance through the 1630 list of foreigners in Cartagena reveals that a high number of the Portuguese there came by way of Guinea or Angola, many having served in one capacity or another on slaving ships.[145]

Portuguese New Christians testifying (under one or another form of duress) to various inquisitional authorities in the Americas often cite Angola as a place where they were introduced to judaizing practices by a family member or friend.[146] For instance, take the 1641 confession of Gaspar de Robles to the Inquisition in Mexico City: as an adolescent, two uncles convinced him to sail with them in the slave trade to Angola, persuading him en route to believe in the Law of Moses. In Luanda, where they lived, their proselytization continued.[147] Manuel Álvarez Prieto, a slave trader living in Cartagena, confessed in 1636 to the Inquisition there that some twenty years earlier, "being in Angola," a business associate (now deceased) "taught him the Law of Moses." He also mentioned as judaizing mentors "a scribe of the Angola contract, about whom they told him he left for The Hague" and "some priest..., who is in Guinea."[148] The Portuguese Converso Garci Méndez de Dueñas left Portugal around 1590 on a slaving ship to West Africa, "in the company of a certain Ruy Méndez" — a relative? — who, he later stated, had induced him, "in the sweltering heat of Guinea, to forsake Christianity and embrace Judaism."[149] Such allegations were easy to make, of course; West Africa was far away and often those featured in the accusations were already deceased. One corroborating allegation comes from a Portuguese Jesuit visiting Angola in 1593, Pero Rodrigues, who reports the existence of a Torah in Luanda and the celebration of a Passover.[150] Intriguingly, counter to the Inquisitions' view, one Conversa of Mexico City complains about the disinterest of New Christian slave traders in preserving their tradition. Rafaela Enríquez, part of an extended family of judaizers, is accused of criticizing "certain

Portuguese masters/skippers of blacks who are carrying on romances with Old Christian women, not marrying with girls of the Law [of Moses]. [Rafaela,] Inveighing [against them] that they were in a bad state and that they rendered the children that they had with their girlfriends lost, without teaching them the law, which is the goal for which observers [of the law] are married to each other."[151]

Though never making explicit reference to race or slavery as a motivation for surveilling or denouncing Blas de Paz Pinto, López and Rufina seem to have been well aware of the centrality of race in their own lives as well as of the racial and thus "political" context of Pinto's activities. At one point in 1629, Rufina's masters beat or whipped another of their enslaved staff, a Black named Pablos, to extract a confession that Rufina on occasion left the house at night to go sleep with López. As a consequence, Rufina fled the house, not returning for five or six days and the two lovers rendezvoused at night less frequently after this incident.[152] In the wake of this, claims López, Rufina came up with a magical means of "taming" her masters.[153] Along more mundane lines, López also claims to have given Rufina four hundred pesos to buy her own liberty.[154] Afterwards, she tried another magical means of "being able to leave her house more freely," through an accord with the spirit Huebo (called a demon in the testimony) arranged for her by Eguiluz. The spirit was to assume her form and take responsibility for her tasks. In addition, the spirit would help her ward off the unwanted advances of a White Spaniard, Diego López Arias, which, as an enslaved woman, she could not resist without negative consequences.[155]

Regarding Blas de Paz Pinto, it is difficult to believe that Rufina and López were not aware of the ethnopolitical components of his commercial activities, even if they might not have known the details. In one audience, López claims a visiting Portuguese youth had told him that Pinto had come to the Indies "via the Kingdom of Angola" because various family members had been hounded and punished by the Inquisition.[156] Pinto himself had arrived from Angola, as a surgeon on a slaving ship, bringing with him several enslaved individuals whom he owned, who evidently died of smallpox.[157] According to López, Rufina had also told him that at one point there arrived in Cartagena "an important Jew / un gran Judio," whom Pinto and "all the Portuguese" went to visit. He had come "on a ship of slaves."[158] Beyond a merely biographical link to Angola, Pinto negotiated the sale of enslaved individuals who arrived from Guinea, among other goods.[159] He served as a physician to Blacks, but perhaps mostly in connection to his trade in sick slaves as an agent of Sebastião Duarte, partner and brother-in-law of Manuel Bautista Peres, one of the most active slave traders in the region.[160] From around 1628 on, it seems Pinto became more directly incorporated into the commercial network of Bautista Peres.[161] Pinto probably inspected the incoming enslaved people to determine which were healthy enough to be sold or distributed to their owners. In 1630 he tells the authorities that his work consists of "buying sick blacks and [those who are] rejected and that curing [them] he turns them over for sale." At this point he himself owned five enslaved people.[162] His work with non-Whites may have led to other forms of relationship with them. One Black woman named Ysabel de Ortega came to the authorities in 1636 to pay 90 pesos of 8 reales that she owed to Pinto.[163]

Maria da Graça A Mateus Ventura, basing herself on Bautista Peres' business letters, estimates that Bautista Peres treated his human merchandise relatively well (primarily for financial reasons?) and cites communications to Pinto in which he informs him of illnesses among the enslaved people in his charge, as well as of the diligence with which he cares for their well-being.[164] In his own, frequent letters to Sebastião Duarte, Pinto gives detailed updates on the health of the enslaved individuals in his own charge.¹⁶⁵ None of this alters the miserable conditions of the slaves' transshipment, which necessitated such medical care in the first place. In a letter to Duarte, Pinto celebrates Duarte's news in a previous letter regarding the good health of Bautista Peres and his household, mentioning in passing some deaths among the enslaved: "even though I feel the death of [the] blacks, certainly much less lamentable than [the death of] others / aunque siento la mortandad de negros si bien menos lastimado que otros." Pinto refers to the death of an enslaved man either named Brame or from the Bran nation — today's Senegal — (or both),¹⁶⁶ which, he writes, "I feel as my own the death of the Black brame, as sir captain Pedro Duarte [feels] that of the black girl but they are goods that have life and I beg God for life in order to serve it [Him?] / Siento como mio la muerte del negro brame y como del señor capitan Pedro Duarte la negrita pero son bienes que tienen vida yo la pido a Dios para servirlo."¹⁶⁷ Pinto's sentiments here hover between dismissal of the value of this human merchandise — better their death than one of "ours" — and recognition of their kinship as mortal beings, "goods" to be bought and sold but also people. The last phrase is obscure and could mean that Pinto prays to be able to make morally good use of his own life, the death of these slaves presenting him a kind of *momento mori*, or perhaps, less likely, even prays on behalf of the dead *negrita* that God should look out for her.

Pinto would seem to have been among the city's wealthier residents, though he claims to have arrived from Angola poor, with only two of his slaves surviving the transoceanic passage.¹⁶⁸ Among the goods deposited in his account after his arrest, either sequestered by the Inquisition from the inventory of his house or owed to him by others, were at least eight bars of gold and three of silver; a goblet, cruet and shaker of silver; a hair band of pearls; a smelted gold cross; some avocados of minute crystal with small shields each featuring an emerald; an avocado of crystal with a gold mount; a gold cross with white stones; gold shields, each featuring nine emeralds; a lamb of smelted gold with an image of Our Lady of the Rosary and Lady Saint Ana; three gold rings; a very small gold image of Our Lady and a green cross with an emerald back; and three strings of pearls.[169] The Inquisition also confiscated fourteen personal slaves.[170] According to the Cartagena tribunal's tabulations, Pinto's sequestered goods valued almost 22,000 pesos, while a 1638 letter from the tribunal's official receiver to the *Suprema* cites the confiscation of 50,000 pesos from the Portuguese surgeon/merchant.[171] Yet he clearly lived within physical proximity to the Mulata slave Rufina and the free Mulato López. Did they feel they could indulge desires for revenge against someone who had helped enslave their people? A murder that López attributes to one of Paula de Eguiluz's disciples, Maria Romero, had to do with "a Portuguese whose name he does not know because of jealousies she had regarding a mulata who lived in front of the house of the said Doña Maria Romero and the said mulata is Portuguese and has gone to and returned from Guinea."[172] Did this act evince an undertaking aimed at harming someone from a perceived higher social station, who yet lived within easy reach?

Though Rufina and López were allowed to participate in Eguiluz' "Whites-only" magical gatherings, both she and López seem aware of the exclusive nature of the White privilege operating there; the topic came up frequently enough, and they probably resented it. On one occasion another Mulata slave challenges how Rufina can attend if, as was rumored, Eguiluz admits "neither blacks nor mulatas" and Rufina and López offer to provide her a secret glimpse of the goings on. Similarly, a free Mulata and friend of Rufina's, conversing with her and López, relates how she stopped being a *bruja*, explaining how one time "my friend Rufina [a different woman] brought me in to [a gathering] and Paula says that she can't go with me because she goes with whites and Elena de Vitoria says that she can't admit me."[173]

Interestingly enough, Rufina never went to the Cartagena Inquisition with her painstakingly gathered information. Perhaps her store of data was to be put to use only in the event of need. However, unlike López or even Eguiluz, Rufina was never bothered by the local inquisitors, despite her serving, according to López, as Eguiluz's "aide." In his thirty-ninth *audiencia* (!) López recants what he has said against "a certain mulata," who must be our Rufina, "whom he named in order to avenge himself on her and have her brought a prisoner to this Holy Office."[174] The fact that Rufina was not tried makes it highly probable that López invented many of his charges against her and that it was actually López who instigated most, if not all of the activities he attributes to her inspiration. Douglas Cope, among other scholars, has noted the general reluctance of those from the plebian classes to inform on one another. Yet López also withheld his knowledge of people such as Pinto until he found himself a prisoner of the Inquisition.

Spilling One's Guts

It is readily noticeable that the accusations of López against Pinto differ in quality from anything divulged by the other witnesses, all Portuguese merchants and acquaintances, if not partners of Pinto's. From the similarities in content and wording, it seems clear that the unnamed witness whose charges are reiterated in August 1651 against a handful of Portuguese in Cartagena (João Rodrigues Mesa, Blas de Paz Pinto, Francisco Pineiro), is none other than our Diego López.[175] These charges seem to merely rehash the information López delivered years earlier. Hence it states at the end of each set of charges that they accord with those of the original trials.[176] Yet these accusations — each set relating to a Converso stem from a single, unnamed witness — bring a great amount of detail regarding Jewish practices not to be found in the testimony of López recorded for his own trial. Below I deal with whether it is possible that by 1651 López had learned enough from the Inquisition to deliver precisely what he thought his inquisitors wanted to hear or whether these charges were "polished" by one of the inquisitors.

If race was not a factor, the motivations of López remain obscure. In truth, specific motivations may have been of secondary importance when one was facing inquisitors and possible torture, knowing that one of the things they most wanted from you was the names of other sinners/criminals. López was supposed to be a friend of Pinto and both men were surgeons. As we have seen, the lives of López and Rufina were thoroughly intertwined with those on whom they spied, who were mostly their social superiors. López relates that the father of Rufina's mistress, Clara Nuñez, also a surgeon, "knows him from the time he was a slave at the hospital" as well as "after his liberty [sic]."[177] López claims that he never informed on yet another surgeon, Martín Sánchez, because "at the time he was his friend and was very poor and needy."[178] López himself was fairly well off for an ex-slave. Before his arrest, according to his own testimony, he possessed a Black enslaved woman named Luisa Dominguez.[179] In actuality, he owned several slaves, since during his imprisonment four were sold at auction (along with eight mules) in order to pay off his debts, which included 2,200 pesos that he owed to Maria de Esquivel, wife of the infantry captain Diego de la Torre.[180] Ceballos Gómez even cites our López as an example of the ambition and skill for economic ascent that characterizes many of the magical practitioners who found themselves in the Inquisitions' web.[181]

When asked by his inquisitors why he never came forward with the information regarding Pinto, López tells them that he feared doing so while being at the same time involved with the above-mentioned magical circles and conducting illicit relations with Rufina.[182] López may well have been telling the truth here. Perhaps López and Pinto shared a friendship, one not strong enough, obviously, to withstand the Inquisition that eventually came between them. Perhaps professional competitiveness or other more specific matters arose between them. Pinto, as was mentioned, dabbled in raising medicinal plants. His older colleague and fellow Portuguese, João Mendes Neto, a physician, treated individuals of all races with native medicines, which he describes in his *Discursos Medicinales* (1608).[183] As has been documented in recent studies, some of the botanical and medical knowledge used by European physicians in the Americas was gleaned from Amerindians and enslaved Afroamericans, the latter often versed in African expertise, though usually uncredited as sources.[184] Given López's involvement in magical circles as well as in medicine, perhaps he and Pinto discussed or shared professional knowledge. Finally, it is illuminating that Pinto faced feminizing charges from an anti-Jewish discourse that feminized Jewish men, while López seems to have been not only a womanizer but a man who enjoyed penetrating his masculine spirit companion. The two men, each from a marginalized and denigrated group, operated in different subject positions in relation to the dominant culture. Is it possible that the tensions between the psychological set of Pinto, declared "womanly" as a descendant of Jews, and that of López, opting for phallic dominance of others, might have contributed to López's willingness to inform on Pinto? Yet Pinto's entire career depended on the kind of dominance that his race and class made possible. It is easy to imagine between López and Pinto multiple relations of camaraderie, competition and animosity.

López may have been goaded into action by Rufina, though he never resisted or refused. Indeed, he seems to have been as intrigued as she by these investigations. It could well be that he feared her. After all, it had been she who introduced him to her "devil-worshipping" magical circle. In 1627, she had allegedly killed, through magical means, the newborn daughter of López and his wife, or at least so he believed (or pretended to believe).[185] Two years later, he claims to have told her not to come back to his house and to have given her the money to purchase her liberty (in an effort to buy her off?).[186] López also accuses Rufina of killing a free Mulata in whom he took an interest, and of whom Rufina became jealous, by magical means given her by Paula de Eguiluz.[187] He claims to have broken off their affair in July 1631 after he became ill, though he claims that even after this Rufina and Eguiluz beat his new lover, a Mulata from Jamaica, with clubs.[188]

López certainly makes efforts to convince his inquisitors that his denunciations, however belated, derived from sincere Christian piety. Even some of the witnesses who testify against him say that they "took him to be a good Christian and had seen him do works of charity."[189] He claims to have attended mass at the Convent of

San Augustin one time, when the father of Rufina's mistress pointed with a candle toward the Christ on the altar, saying "Doesn't this Christ have an evil face?" To which López responds, "He has nothing but a good face." The unnamed Nuñez goes on to say, "By God, he has such a villainous face." More explicitly defending the faith, or so he states, López retorts, "It is a great crime and sin to say this."[190] López claims to have been "scandalized" when he witnessed a Portuguese youth "gargle and spit" on an image of the Virgin and the infant Jesus in the Convent of San Augustin.[191] Suspiciously, all of these declarations come minutes after a few leading questions from his inquisitors, in which they explicitly challenge him on why he held back this information until now. In addition, as discussed above, López himself mentions conversations he has had while in prison with Juana Zamba and Rufina, among others, making it likely that he was being fed certain information. It does seem that he knows too concretely the terminology that the inquisitors want to hear, for instance that so-and-so is a "judaizer, observer of the Law of Moses," that so-and-so made a *"reniego ordinario"* at one of the magical gatherings, or that so-and-so adopted such-and-such an individual as her magical godmother (*amadrinarle*) "in order that she should become a *bruja*." Of course, it is quite possible that these terms are insertions of the inquisitorial scribe, seeking to "clarify" the testimony of the person deposing. López knows that Paula de Eguiluz and her alleged disciple Juana Zamba have already been arrested by the local inquisition.[192] Indeed, after investigation by the inquisitors, no fewer than eight prisoners confess to having "communicated under the doors of their cells."[193] It could thus well be that by this time López knows just what kind of things his inquisitors want to hear. The key question remains, obviously, whether he is inventing the contents of the various accusations he raises. It is hard to resist applying to López the general characterization formulated by Ceballos Gómez regarding the kinds of magical practitioners so frequently tried by the Inquisitions: "talkers, vivacious, often social climbers, capable and intelligent and astute;" "mulatos, zambos and mestizos, but above all most of them are free, for which reason they are not under the direct control of micropowers, which allows them more freedom of action; people "who fully believe that it is possible to modify destiny and the circumstances of life through extraordinary means."[194]

Benkos Biohó was born into a royal family that ruled what is today Guinea-Bissau. He was seized by a Portuguese slave trader, and transported to what is now Colombia. In 1599 he escaped into the marshy lands southeast of Cartagena, and organized an army that came to dominate all of the Montes de María region. He was referred to as the "king of Arcabuco."
On July 18, 1605, the Governor of Cartagena, Gerónimo de Suazo y Casasola, unable to defeat the Maroons, offered a peace treaty to Biohó, recognizing the autonomy of the Matuna Bioho palenque and accepting his entrance into the city armed and dressed in Spanish fashion, while the palenque promised to stop receiving more runaway slaves. (see page 45)

Trials and Errors

Over the course of his trial, López met with his inquisitors an astounding forty times.[195] Despite providing a plethora of evidence against others, he denied the charges against him through the thirty-ninth *audiencia*. A single turn on the rack at that point prompted him to admit his life as a *brujo*, that is, not merely a practitioner of herbalism or magic, but a practitioner of witchcraft, of the diabolical sort.[196] Evidently, various witnesses were interrogated regarding the seeming epidemic of magic that plagued Cartagena and often confirmed López's narratives of magically caused deaths around town.[197] After a three-year imprisonment, López appeared as a penitent in the *auto de fé* celebrated at the cathedral of Cartagena on 1 June 1636, wearing the special punitive emblem identifying him as a *brujo* and the required penitential habit, the sambenito, to receive a punishment of perpetual imprisonment and, on another day, two hundred lashes to be administered as he is led through the streets.[198]

About a month later, on 22 July, Blas de Paz Pinto was arrested by the Cartagena Inquisition. Of course, like most of the alleged judaizers, his heresy consisted of believing, despite being a Christian, that Judaism, the so-called Law of Moses, was better for his own salvation, perhaps even better in general, than Christianity and of acting on this belief. Beyond the Jewish practices Pinto supposedly carried out, that is, crimes of domestic cultural treason, the tribunal raised hints of crimes of political treason stemming from foreign provocation. Several of the local Portuguese merchants sentenced in 1638 — Juan Rodríguez Mesa, Manuel Álvarez Prieto, Manuel de Fonseca Enríquez, Fernando Suárez and others — were accused of having contacts with Holland, as members of the so-called Fraternity of Holland.[199] Fonseca Enríquez mentions seeing Pinto's firm in the group's logbook.[200] The members of the Fraternity of Holland were said to have contributed a great deal of silver in order to fund a Dutch fleet that would attack Pernambuco or even Cartagena itself.[201] Enriqueta Vila Vilar thinks the above-mentioned fleet consisted of the one formed by the Dutch West India Company (WIC) which attacked and conquered Pernambuco in 1630.[202] According to Maria Ventura, the fleet the fraternity members were alleged to be supporting might be one mentioned by a Portuguese captain tried by the Inquisition of Toledo, a "Company which the Portuguese Jews of there [Amsterdam] raised in order to go to Pernambuco against his Majesty and the Catholics who reside there," a group created in 1634 several years after the WIC Pernambuco attack.[203] Though the group's purpose and history shift from prisoner to prisoner, the alleged members supposedly considered it a vehicle for getting back at Spain and imagined this with relish, if not full accuracy. Duarte López Mesa, one of the Portuguese Conversos accused in Cartagena in 1636, claims that Manuel Álvarez Prieto once described being in Holland and learning the methods of the WIC: 24 powerful and wealthy directors gathered daily, with five Portuguese (Jews) joining the Dutch, English, Danish, French and other directors, all sitting on a fund of 1,800,000 ducats for the purpose of making war against Spain. López Mesa himself testifies that a Portuguese youth in the Canaries told him that in the WIC's first five years its directors earned enough money, not even counting what had been robbed and pillaged by Dutch soldiers, "that they would be able to set up forty thousand paid men in the Indies."[204] These statements constitute much wishful thinking. The one only loosely resembles what is known about the organizational structure of the WIC, which in fact was run by 19 directors, none of whom was ever a Jew, though some Spanish and Portuguese Jews became prominent investors in the company.

In addition, among the allegations against Pinto listed in 1651 is the following:

> And as a Jewish judaizer, observer of the Law of Moses, following the counsels contained in the letter of the Jews of Constantinople, [that they] wrote to those of Toledo, in which they say to profane the temples, and their images, a certain monk, from the convent of the discalced Carmelites of this city, making a profession that a certain person went to speak to the said Blas de Paz, who assisted in the hanging [of icons and art] and adorning of the church.[205]

While the monk's accusation that Pinto purposefully spat on the face of an image of Our Lady of the Conception comes straight out of López's testimony from 1634,[206] the matter of a letter from Turkish Jews that prompts attacks on Catholic property and sacred items is totally new. It is not clear whether Pinto's actions merely paralleled those called for in this letter or whether he was allegedly following its suggestions, but in any case, I have not seen any other reference to this letter in the records of the Cartagena tribunal. Somewhat surprisingly, the letter in question refers to a forged correspondence dating from the time of the expulsion of the Jews from Spain. The afflicted Toledan Jews supposedly wrote to their coreligionists in Constantinople, asking for advice. The response, from the "Chief of the Jews of Constantinople," urges the Spanish Jews to wreak revenge through a variety of patiently devious means: they should have their children become merchants, to slowly pilfer the goods of Spanish Christians, physicians, in order to take their lives, clerics and theologians, to destroy their churches from within, etc. Though not the last time the letter would be wielded by Iberian anti-Semites, it had been discussed and reprinted in an anti-Jewish work published in Madrid in 1614.[207] Daviken Studnicki-Gizbert suggests that the accusations of Jewish coordination with their Turkish leaders may be drawn from Quevedo's 1633 play, *Execración por la fe Católica*, which accused the Jewish Portuguese *asentistas* (contract holders) of "greater revenge than any of the machinations of the detestable rabbis of Constantinople," but it is more likely that the mythical correspondence influenced the playwright.[208]

It seems improbable that Diego López would have been aware of the tradition regarding these letters. It must be that it was Juan Ortiz, formerly the local tribunal's *fiscal* and now inquisitor, who "improved" the formulation of López's charges with such material. This might have been done as a response to the criticisms of the *Suprema* (the supervisory body that regulated the tribunals) leveled against the local tribunal for the flaws in several of their trials from the late 1620s and 1630s, criticism that led to a new trial for the Portuguese merchant in Cartagena, Luis Gomes Barreto, that began in 1652. Already in 1645, an investigative visit was conducted, under which numerous interviews turned up a great deal of inquisitorial abuse.[209] In 1648, a long list of accusations of irregularities by the Cartagena inquisitor and the *fiscal* Juan Ortiz, among others, were conveyed to the *Suprema*. Many of these transgressions revolve around favors that seemed to pass between the merchant Barreto and the inquisitor Juan de Uriarte, that is, around close relations between the commercial and religious elites, where the latter should have been superior to and supervising and guiding the former.[210] (Recall that Barreto told his inquisitors during his first trial that among those hosted by Blas de Paz Pinto on his ranch were the town's Senior Inquisitor and Archdeacon.) The inquisitor Uriarte was accused by Don Joseph de Bolibar, knight of the Order of Santiago and bailiff of the Cartagena tribunal, of receiving the payments owed to Pinto by other Portuguese merchants, not giving them any receipts that they had paid, and never remitting the payments to Pinto.[211]

Beyond hoping to distract attention from his own misdeeds, Ortiz no doubt wished to correct the bad impression of an incompetent and morally lax tribunal by emphasizing the prescience and sagacity of its sweeping and harsh treatment of the Portuguese New Christian merchants.[212] Several of the charges against Pinto from 1651 feature the kind of "improvements" that have been mentioned previously, mostly the addition of technical theological terms. Thus, where López merely describes the gatherings at Pinto's house, with enslaved individuals posted to keep out visitors, the new charges tack on "with which it is an evident thing that they have gatherings, of synagogues in contempt of the evangelical Law of our redeemer and savior Jesus Christ and falsely in their expired, condemned and dead law of Moses."[213] Where López merely depicts the low voices, pauses and seeming sighing of lamentation that lead him to believe that prayers are being conducted in Pinto's house, the later charges clarify that "without doubt [this] would be because they had neither temple nor King of the tribe of Judah, and because they did not sanctify and adore *in excelsis* [in the highest], as they have by custom, as obstinate and pertinacious, in their expired law."[214] It is here in the 1651 charges, more than a decade after his death, that Pinto is called "Rabbi of the said Law of Moses," and is considered by the other "Jews" "as a man learned and expert in the Law of Moses, and that he was a teacher of its ceremonies," is said to have observed various fasts "so that God should give them success and save their souls."[215]

The torture Blas de Paz Pinto underwent on 9 February 1637 (seven months after his arrest) produced contusions in his toes, nerve damage and caused him to go into shock. His right foot required amputation. He asked for a confessor, to whom he confessed, as well as for the administration of all the sacraments. Despite the attention of two surgeons, Pinto's condition worsened. The inquisitors gathered with their consultants, deciding that if the prisoner should live, he would go out in the next *auto de fé*, to be "reconciled" to the Church. His punishment would entail confiscation of all his goods, the wearing of the penitential habit and perpetual imprisonment. Given his state, however, the inquisitors saw fit to conduct a private ceremony of reconciliation in the jail, as Pinto himself desired. As the prisoner's condition deteriorated, his confessor, a priest serving as an officer of the Inquisition, was sent in to console him and offer him the last rites. In a fitting if unintended irony, the inquisitors asked that the priest be accompanied by Father Pedro Claver, whose ministrations to the enslaved and non-Whites would eventually earn him sainthood in the nineteenth century. Perhaps Claver and Pinto knew each other, had even been brought together by their different functions having to do with the population of the enslaved. Pinto died on 20 February 1637, without ever leaving the Inquisition jail.[216] Testifying in 1648, Gabriel de Uria Munguia, treasurer and judge of the royal court in Cartagena, recalls having heard that when Pinto died "they took him out [in the *auto de fé*] in state with a sambenito."[217] This would have been on 25 March 1638.[218] Because he died before the formal completion of his trial, Pinto was buried in a secret location, which would be revealed to his family only after the closure of the legalities. Hence those involved in his interment were sworn to secrecy, the sacristan, the gravedigger and the Blacks who carried his body.[219]

Appearing at the same *auto de fé* as the effigy of the defunct Blas de Paz Pinto was Paula de Eguiluz. She had evidently confessed to the accusations of her sorcery in her very first *audiencia*. She, too, was reconciled to the Church, and received as punishment the confiscation of her goods, two hundred lashes and perpetual incarceration. The *causa* or summation of her crimes and punishment could

An auto-da-fé of the Spanish Inquisition: the burning of heretics in a marketplace. Wood engraving by H.D. Linton after T. Robert-Fleury. Library of Congress Prints and Photographs Division, Washington, D.C.

not be read aloud to the assembled crowd, because of the great noise into which it erupted.[220] It is not clear whether the murmuring of the crowd signified an outcry against a detested and feared *bruja* or a protest by a mixed-race crowd against an unjust sentence and institution. At any rate, the imprisoned Eguiluz continued to be a requested healer in Cartagena, receiving permission to leave the Inquisition jail in order to treat patients, who included local inquisitors and the city's bishop. On these occasions she went out carried by enslaved individuals "in a sedan chair, without her penitential habit, wearing a little cloth with a gold border, and earned much money, part of which she distributed as alms between the rest of her prisoner companions."[221]

We do not know how many of the city's residents noticed the tragi-comic ramifications of Spanish racial politics. In the case of the individuals here, we ultimately know too little about their lives to fully explain the way their physical and social coexistence in the terrain of colonial Cartagena led them to get along, to understand one another or not. While the urban sphere and its daily exigencies in many respects led people of different classes to come together in an irenic manner, the inquisitorial mentality, class differences and the racial caste system that seeped into the consciousness of those high and low all too often generated quite contrary, agonistic results. In 1675, the Rev. Elias al-Mûsili, an Arab Christian from Baghdad, visited Cartagena for forty days. With himself in mind as a tourist, he described the city's inhabitants as "Catholic, true Spaniards who love foreigners."[222]

In a final irony, once the inquisitors satisfied themselves that Pinto had died a good Christian, he was described in the report of the *auto de fé* at which he was posthumously displayed in effigy as having been "esteemed and beloved by all for being very interested in and enthusiastic for repairing altars and decorating churches."

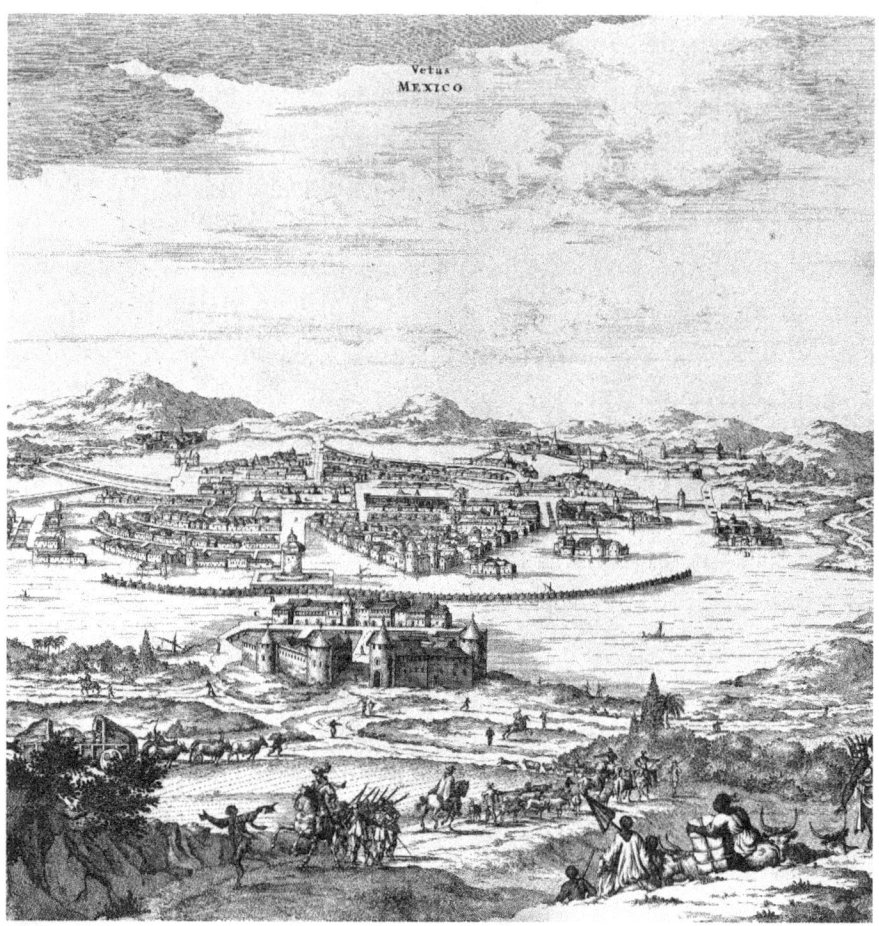

Map of Mexico City in the 17th century.
This unsigned view of the city of Mexico was probably published as a book illustration in Amsterdam ca. 1700, Netherlands. Its engraver is unknown.
Library of Congress Geography and Map Division, Washington, D.C. 20540

Esperanza Rodríguez:
A Life In-between

I turn now to the case of Esperanza Rodríguez, "a mulata, dark, born in the city of Puebla and resident of Mexico City, widow of Juan del Bosque, of the German nation, deceased, ... 50 years old, more or less, tall, aged, greying," who was tried as a judaizer by the Mexican Inquisition in the mid-1640s.[223] She and her three daughters were arrested in the summer of 1642, along with numerous other alleged Crypto-Jews, many of whom knew and associated with one another. In fact, the Inquisition-based information on her birthplace is mistaken; Rodríguez was born in Spain. For an age of incipient globalization and ethnic-racial intermingling, her story is both remarkable and typical.

When her second owner, Doña Catalina Enríquez, emigrated from Seville to Veracruz, Rodríguez came along with Catalina to the Americas, residing in Cartagena, Havana, Veracruz, Guadalajara and Mexico City. Having won her freedom as a teenager, Esperanza worked as a dressmaker, as did her daughters.[224]

After her arrest, when pressed for her genealogy by the inquisitors, Esperanza insists she has no knowledge of it: "as she does not know who her father was, neither does she know who her grandparents were."[225] But her silence does not last. She eventually reveals that her father had been Francisco Rodríguez, a New Christian of Seville, accused of judaizing.[226] Francisco Rodríguez was the brother of Esperanza's owner Catalina. Esperanza Rodríguez's mother, Isabel, a

Black/*negra* from the West African region called by the Spanish "Guinea," had died in Seville when Esperanza had been six or seven. Esperanza asserts that her mother died a free woman.[227] Whether this was true or not, her mother's freedom did not result in her own liberty.

Isabel, Esperanza's mother, seems to have been unmarried, along with some 80 percent of the enslaved women in Seville.[228] In the late 16th century, the city hosted the second highest population of Africans in Europe (after Lisbon). Yet despite an extremely high rate of endogamous marriages among the enslaved and free Afroiberians, a growing population of Mulatos developed, making Rodríguez a typical child of a common, unofficial and clearly tolerated White-Black, free-enslaved kind of concubinage.

The husband of Esperanza's owner was Pedro Arias Maldonado, first cousin of Antonio Rodríguez Arias — called "the famous Jew" by the Mexican inquisitors. Arias Maldonado conducted trade with partners in Mexico City and Havana. Esperanza remained in Seville in the house of her mistress Catalina Enríquez until the age of seventeen or eighteen. She then spent a year in a convent with the nuns of Nuestra Señora de Socorro (Our Lady of Help) along with her mistress Catalina because Arias Maldonado had gone to Havana. The convent was one of four such institutions in Seville founded by the Franciscan Order of the Immaculate Conception. According to its 1522 founding deed, the convent was to follow the constitution of the Hieronymite order. Many scholars have noted the attraction of Conversos to and their prevalence in the Hieronymite order, with its more internal, Pauline approach to religiosity.[229] This affiliation led the order to ban New Christians in 1489.

Arias Maldonado was killed in Havana, and soon after Catalina left with Rodríguez for the Caribbean in order to recover his estate. Rodríguez claims that they arrived in Cartagena de Indias around 1602 and shortly thereafter left for Havana.[230] Whether she simply

Panorama of La Habana (Amsterdam, 17th century).
Engraving 17th century in Amsterdam +1650, Atlas Baedeker. British Library, London.

does not remember accurately or is intentionally changing the date, a travel license was issued to Catalina Enríquez to travel to Cartagena in December 1607.[231] Rodríguez says she married Juan Baptista del Bosque in Havana around 1606.[232] The couple remained together in Havana for about a year, at which point she accompanied Baptista del Bosque back to Cartagena, where he worked as a sculptor for around five years. Her former owner, Catalina, also seems to have remained in Havana during this time. Rodríguez and her husband then left Cartagena and met up with Catalina in Veracruz, but after fifteen days left for Mexico City, where the couple resided for four or five years. In Mexico City Rodríguez ran a shop as a seamstress. At some point Bautista del Bosque got work in the port city of Acapulco and Rodríguez went to be with him. After two and a half years, they returned to Mexico City. After another four or five years they transferred to Guadalajara, where Rodríguez lived for ten or twelve years and where she again operated a store.²³³ Baptista del Bosque died around 1629 in Guadalajara, about five years after their arrival there.²³⁴ Their long marriage, terminated only because of Del Bosque's death, seems to reflect an impressively stable relationship. Rodríguez moved back to Mexico City with all her children sometime between 1634 and 1636.²³⁵ Joan Bristol rightfully suggests that Rodríguez made this move in order to reunite with her extended clan from Seville, foremost among them Blanca Enríquez.²³⁶

Map of Colonial Mexico.
Engraved map of New Spain (colonial Mexico) in 1599: Girolamo Ruscelli, "Nueva Hispania tabla nova, Library of Congress Geography and Map Division, Washington, D.C.

An Extended Family of Fervent Crypto-Jews?

According to the inquisitional testimony of many witnesses, the Enríquez family matriarch Blanca comes across as a fervent Crypto-Jew, knowledgeable about crypto-Jewish practices, possibly even capable in Hebrew. According to the son-in-law of Blanca Enriquez, Thomas Nuñez de Peralta (married to her daughter Beatriz), Rodríguez "was brought up with" Blanca, the matriarch of the extended Enríquez clan.[237] A close family friend of Blanca Enriquez, Blanca Mendez de Rivera, from the same generation as Esperanza and Blanca, says that she "knew [Esperanza] from the city of Seville."[238] In fact, although the full genealogy remains unclear, Ynes Lopez, the woman Rodríguez claims brought her to Judaism in Seville, and the Mexico City Enríquez clan were related to one another, while Rodríguez also shared blood ties, not to mention long-standing familiarity, with various members of the extended set of families. Intriguingly, Blanca, her husband, their five children, her mother and Blanca's three sisters were issued permission to travel to New Spain (Mexico) in 1608, the year after Catalina and Esperanza received their license to sail to Cartagena.[239] Ynes Lopez's first cousins included the daughters of clan matriarch Blanca Enriquez. Pedro de Espinosa, husband of Ysabel de Silva (Blanca's sister), was the son of the merchant Simon Rodríguez, who was the brother of Esperanza's father, Francisco Rodríguez.[240] The husband of Esperanza's owner was the merchant Pedro Arias Maldonado, first cousin of Antonio Rodríguez Arias, Blanca's husband. Antonio and Blanca were married at Arias Maldonado's house in Seville, and Antonio may have been the son of Simon Rodríguez, the brother of Esperanza's father Francisco. Maria de Rivera, daughter of Blanca de Rivera, both supposedly involved in the Enriquez clan's judaizing activities, had married

Manuel de Granada. Manuel's father had been Antonio de Granada (or at least so Rodríguez thinks she recalls his name), who passed away in Seville. Rodríguez's mother had cooked for him. Rodríguez states that these Granadas are relatives of hers through her father, Francisco Rodríguez.[241] Esperanza's son, Diego, was married to Geronima de Miranda, whose cousin was Gaspar de Robles, another accused judaizer in the Enriquez family circle.[242] Other ties also existed.

Ysavel de Silva testifies that Blanca's mother, Juana Rodríguez, had been imprisoned by the Inquisition already back in Seville.[243] Also supposedly tried by the Seville tribunal were Francisco Rodríguez, Esperanza's father, Ynes Lopez and her sister Ana Enríquez, and Blanca Enríquez. Ysavel de Silva testifies that Blanca Enriquez had been imprisoned, along with the slave Isabel, by the Seville tribunal "for six or eight months. And that all that the inquisitors said was that they should tell the truth and that [Blanca] had said to [Ysavel de Silva] as well that from the beginning to the end she had defied [the truth, i.e., denied all allegations]. And that they had put her to the torture and she signified the arms on which they had given it to her, with signs that this confessant saw. And how much better was it to suffer that than to lose honor and estate."[244] Others also had seen Blanca's scars, such as Blanca Méndez de Rivera and Isabel Duarte.[245] Inquisition sources confirm the accuracy of these clan memories and legends. Ynes Lopez was sentenced as a judaizer by the Seville tribunal in 1604, earning the punishment of wearing the penitential habit and perpetual imprisonment.[246] Blanca Enríquez's parents were both arrested, tried and sentenced by the Seville tribunal, her father Diego Núñez Batoca in 1593 and her mother Juana Rodríguez in 1595 and again in 1599.[247] Blanca herself was arrested in 1599 at the age of 17, denied everything and survived being tortured, such that the case was ordered suspended ("estubo negativa y vencio el tormento y visto en consulta se mando suspender").[248] Other members of the interlocking network of families also appear to have been active judaizers back in Spain and Portugal as well, while some lived as open Jews in Italy.

Blanca Enríquez is alleged to have instructed various family members in religious matters. Beatriz Enríquez states that when she was around the age of twelve, her mother Blanca told her that "she should believe in the one sole true God and should observe the law of Moses" and that she has also taught the law to all her other daughters.[249] Pedro Tinoco testifies that his grandmother Blanca advised him to observe the Law of Moses, "in which it is necessary to be saved" and which "was better than that of my lord Jesus Christ which this confessant observed."[250] Isabel Tinoco, Pedro's sister, tells the inquisitors that she observed the Law of Moses because her grandmother Blanca taught it to her when she was a girl.

Blanca and her daughters are said to have fasted on Fridays.[251] Before fasts, Blanca would bathe and put on clean clothes.[252] Pedro Tinoco describes to his inquisitors how his grandmother Blanca once called him alone to her and had him prepare bread, following her instructions, such as using a new knife. But this was bread unlike "the ordinary bread that the catholics eat," and she explained to him that this was "the bread of bitterness that the Israelites ate in the desert" and that now must be eaten by those who observe the Law of Moses, clear allusions to matzah and Passover.[253] In addition to making matzah with her daughter Beatriz several times, Blanca gave her as well an extended explanation of the history and meaning of this bread "without yeast nor salt," which the ancient Israelites "ate together with much parsley and many herbs and which in memory of this the observers of the Law of Moses have to eat three days before the Passover of the Resurrection that the Christians celebrate." Blanca's ritual punctiliousness was stronger than her faulty and syncretistic conception of Passover. She used only new utensils when preparing her matzah — a traditional precaution of Jews to ensure complete *kashrut* for Passover. Blanca (and Beatriz) even knew some of the terminology involved, as well as the *halakhic* requirement of removing and burning a bit of the dough: "having burned [?; *açetado*] the sacrifice of the *Jala* [challah bread], which was that little piece of *massa* [matzah] that she removed from the middle of what she had in the new saucepan." Blanca made from her dough only the three *tortitas* ritually required for the central Passover *seder* plate.[254]

In his testimony, Pedro Tinoco recounts one occasion when all those present "got on their knees, the said Blanca Enríquez, standing and putting her hands over their heads, recited the blessing of Abraham, Isaac & Jacob," also saying "other words that this confessant did not understand well."[255] Beatriz Enríquez relates that after the blessing "each asked forgiveness of the other, the younger ones then embracing the elders."[256] According to the testimony of one witness, one year 13 members of the clan plus 6 other intimate associates observed the fast of the Queen of Esther, a popular crypto-Jewish "festival" in honor of this ancient proto-Conversa heroine.[257] While the deceased Blanca Enríquez was burned only in effigy at the 11 April 1649 *auto de fé*, her daughter Catalina — not Esperanza Rodríguez's former mistress but her cousin — was burned alive.

Becoming a Crypto-Jew

Various permutations of the same basic story about Rodríguez's coming to Judaism circulated. Ysavel Antunes, a close associate of the Enríquez family, imprisoned as a judaizer by the Mexico City tribunal, confesses that Rodríguez told her "how she had been taught it by them in Seville," that is, how she had been taught the Law of Moses by members of her family.[258] Clara de Rivera also relates that when Rodríguez and her daughters visited the house of Clara's mother, Blanca Mendez de Rivera, Rodríguez told them "that she had been taught [the Law] in Seville."[259] Blanca Mendez de Rivera claims that Rodríguez had told her that she had been taught the Law of Moses in Seville by a Portuguese widow named Ynes Lopez. Later, Blanca deposes that Ynes Lopez had told her herself about teaching Rodríguez.[260] According to Raphaela Enríquez, daughter of Doña Blanca Enríquez, Rodríguez was taught the Law of Moses by "a mistress of hers, the mother of a Doña Catalina who is in Veracruz."[261] Ysavel de Silva thinks she heard from Blanca Enriquez that Rodríguez's mother Isabel "also knew of the said law. And had been a prisoner in the Inquisition of Seville three days."[262] In their summary of the case and sentencing, the inquisitors make no mention of Isabel's judazing, however.[263]

Esperanza Rodríguez's first encounter with a "judaizer," as far as she tells it to her inquisitors, was striking. It took place more than thirty years earlier, in Seville, yet her memory of it seems fraught with emotion still. The incident only emerges in her response to the charges read to her by her inquisitors, that is, relatively late in her trial. She says that an old Portuguese woman, Maria Hernandez, lived right next door and the young Rodríguez could see into her house through the kitchen window. Rodríguez watched her conduct

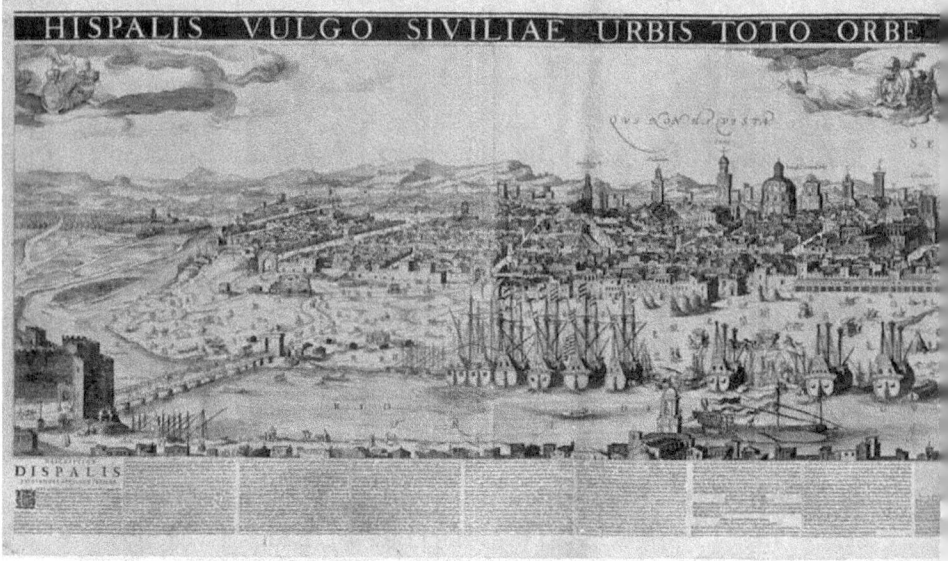

Panoramic view of Seville. [Amsterdam] : [Johannes Janssonius], 1617. Etching and engraving. Library of Congress Prints and Photographs Division Washington, D.C. 20540

fasts at nighttime, or so she claims. One day Hernandez asked her to give an afternoon snack to her son, about seven years old. The young Rodríguez gave him a piece of bread with a slice of ham. Discovering this, Hernandez smacked it away, knocking it to the ground, shouting at her son not to eat pig. Offended, Rodríguez said that she must be a Jewess if she is not allowed to eat pig meat. Hernandez "made her cry," Rodríguez tersely reports. All of this seems to have caused Rodríguez's masters amusement ("they laughed to/among themselves").[264] The manner in which Rodríguez recounts the episode reveals the deep and confusing emotions caused to this young slave girl by the contradictory religious dictates motivating the different individuals, herself included, and by her relatively powerless position resulting from her less than full knowledge in a situation in which she is still expected to know how to act.

Rodríguez, finally giving information (accurate or not) to the inquisitors after a few months in prison, relates that Ynes Lopez, seemingly her father's mother, began teaching her the Law of Moses when she was about twelve or thirteen. One afternoon, says Rodríguez, Lopez called the young enslaved girl over and tried to persuade her not to believe in Christ nor in his mother Maria, nor to make anything of the sacred images of the religion built around them. The latter attack aimed at various images of Mary that Rodríguez possessed (*carrosas estampadas* [...] *de bulto*). Rodríguez was told that one should believe only "in a single God who was called aDonay." If she were to accede to these requests, her mistress "would give her freedom, she would be very happy, and greatly fortunate." The young Rodríguez supposedly "replied to them with the art of confusion that she would look into this," but their importunities and promises of benefits, combined with Rodríguez's young age, ignorance and vulnerability led her to yield, which caused them "particular joy."[265] Catalina Enríquez, her owner, "also showed pleasure," said that "with her husband Pedro arrias she would do it [so that Rodríguez] would be given liberty."[266] In testimony given after having heard the charges against her and responding to them, Rodríguez says that it was actually a cousin, Margarita Enríquez, who had promised her liberty, "a thing greatly desired by slaves," and at the time she had been "between nine and ten years old."[267]

Because of the testimony of Rodríguez and others, Ynes Lopez was "relaxed" (Inquisition-speak for execution) in absencia at the 11 April 1649 *auto de fé* in Mexico City.[268] Ynes Lopez's daughter Catalina, Rodríguez's former mistress, also appeared at the same *auto*, aged 80 years old, where she was reconciled with a formal abjuration. Her goods were confiscated at her arrest. She is accused of having judaized continuously since the age of twelve. In her confessions, she claims that after her incarceration she saw in her dreams a crucified Christ surrounded by innumerable lights and resplendent glories. This, she asserts, indicates her good intentions. Her many confessions and desperate pleas for mercy did not prevent her from dying while still in prison. Though the inquisitors granted that she died "with signs of penitence," her goods were nonetheless confiscated.[269]

Esperanza Rodríguez seems to have been active as a judaizer and known as such by many. She is said to have made and attended various fasts, including those devoted to Queen Esther, which lasted three days, the number of days the biblical Esther fasted before calling on King Ahasuerus to beg the king to save the Jews from the wicked Haman, who plotted their destruction.[270] Many witnesses testify to gathering for fasts at Rodríguez's house or going there simply to pass the fast day. Rodríguez was also present at Blanca

Enríquez's final hours.[271] Catalina Enríquez (Blanca's daughter), Ysavel de Silva and Beatriz Enríquez relate separately to the inquisitors that after Blanca's death, Rodríguez was among the women who washed the body, dressed it in a new shirt set aside for this purpose and arranged the deceased on the bed.[272] This honorific role reflects intimacy and trust. Juana Enríquez claims to have been told by her mother Blanca before her death "to buy four or five yards of Ruan [fabric]," which she sent "to the house of Esperanza Rodríguez so that she would make a shroud for her said mother."[273] Rodríguez was present at the gathering of the Enríquez clan that took place the day Blanca Enríquez was buried (in the Carmen convent).[274]

In her own depositions, Rodríguez confirms many of the above allegations and adds details of her own.[275] She testifies that she and Blanca Enríquez declared themselves to one another as followers of the Law of Moses many times back in Seville. In both Seville and in Mexico City, Rodríguez "saw" Blanca Enríquez conduct so many fasts of the Great Day, fasts of Queen Esther and ordinary fasts that she cannot count them all.[276] Rodríguez and Blanca were clearly close to one another. Rodríguez testifies that Blanca would visit her house in Mexico City.[277] According to Rodríguez, Blanca's mother, a Portuguese "Jewess" named Juana Rodríguez, a relative, "was very happy to see this confessant [i.e., Rodríguez] become Jewish."[278] This statement reflects either this woman's great desire to see this Mulata slave girl join the family religion, perhaps because of special qualities she recognized in her, perhaps because of Rodríguez's New Christian paternal blood (or both), or it might reflect Rodríguez's great desire to be wanted. Rodríguez was present at the "Jewish" wedding of Maria de Rivera and Manuel de Granada (in Seville?), and she confesses that she and Maria de Rivera declared themselves to one another "various times and that they did fasts together many times, that she couldn't come up with a definite number of these fasts because they were so many."[279] Not only did Rodríguez and Juana Enríquez (daughter of Blanca) declare themselves to one another "very many times," but Juana, from whom Rodríguez frequently received dress work, was her godmother (*comadre*) in the realm of their Catholic existence.[280] Rodríguez claims that when she married Juan Bautista del Bosque, her coreligionists Blanca Enríquez and her former mistress Catalina Enríquez held it to be a bad thing, as "he was not Jewish but German."[281]

The testimony of Juan de León/Salomón Machorro (if accurate), provides a glimpse into the social network of Esperanza Rodríguez. One day he went to visit the elderly Blanca Enríquez, with whom he maintained close relations. He found there with them "an old mulata named doña Esperanza Rodríguez." In the presence of this Mulata, Blanca Enríquez narrated to De León/Machorro some things about his grandfather, Rodrigo Rodríguez, who had died in Antequera, Spain or Nueva Granada (it is not clear which town of this name is meant). Thus, Blanca Enríquez

> came to tell the said Esperanza Rodríguez who this confessant [León/Machorro] was and that he kept the said Law of Moses, to which the said Esperanza Rodríguez responded that she had heard about or [had] known the said Rodrigo Rodríguez, grandfather of this confessant, and then the said Doña Blanca told him how the said Esperanza Rodríguez was an observer of the said Law of Moses, and the said Esperanza Rodríguez said that it was indeed true that she kept the said Law.[282]

It must be noted that Rodríguez, like so many New Christians and acculturated Africans, knew how to cross herself and say the Pater Noster, Ave Maria, Credo and Salve Regina well in Spanish. She also insists that she heard mass and confessed regularly.[283] Before her two youngest daughters began observing the Law of Moses, Rodríguez would spend entire days on which she was fasting at the church of Santa Clara with them, "in order to dissemble and distract herself" from her hunger.[284]

From her teachers, Rodríguez seems to have learned much and well. She is accused of explaining to her daughter Ysavel that when one fasts "one should not be menstruating but be very clean" and that one should observe the sabbath — on Saturday of course — by not working. Rodríguez allegedly knew enough to inform Ysavel de Silva regarding the burning of candles on the fast of the Great Day — Yom Kippur — "that she never had burned them because it was an invention." In other words, that burning candles in this manner was borrowed from Catholic practice.[285] In fact, Jews light candles at the evening entrance of the holy day, so perhaps Rodríguez was referring to burning candles over the duration of the fast day. Rodríguez is said to have told her daughters that on fast days "one must not enter the churches of the Christians" (though she allegedly frequently did exactly this, as was just mentioned).[286] Supposedly, Rodríguez taught her two youngest daughters, Ysavel and Maria, the following prayer, to be said daily:

> With the weapons of Adonai
> I go armed.
> With the cape of Abraham
> I go covered.
> With the faith of Ishmael
> in my prayer,
> wherever [God?] wants that I go and come
> Good and bad people I will meet.
> The good should come to me

The bad should be intimidated by me
that I not fear the rod of justice
neither the jailer nor the [Inquisition] agent
that he will not be able to harm me
nor initiate evil
nor [do] more evil than that which
Haman did to Mordechai.

Con las armas de Adonai
ando armadas.
Con la capa de Abraham
ando couijada.
Con la fee de Ysmael
en mi oracion.
por donde quiera que fuere y Viniere
Buenos y malos encontrare.
Los Buenos se me llegaran
Los malos se me arredraran
que no temere bara de justiçia
ni alcalde ni familiar
que no me podra maleçer
ni mal empeçer
ni mas mal de lo que passo
Aman sobre Mordocheo.[287]

This prayer contains some intriguing features. For instance, the line referring to meeting good and bad people and being kept safe from the latter vaguely echoes a prayer from the morning service, the *Yehi Ratzon*, that derives from the ancient sage, Rabbi Yehuda HaNasi, while the general tenor of the prayer vaguely resembles other morning prayers said by other ancient sages, all listed in the same Talmudic passage (BT Berakhot 16b-17a).[288] Rodríguez's prayer obviously refers explicitly to functionaries of the Inquisitions, whose malevolent powers God is asked to avert. Rodríguez sees herself here as Mordechai, persecuted by the powerful servant to the Crown, Haman, who represents the Inquisition. Through the surprising appearance of the figure of Ishmael, the prayer reminds us of the importance of Moorish or Islamic tropes in anti-establishment Iberian discourse. This Crypto-Jew seems to envision herself and her group as downtrodden in the same way as Ishmael, the son from the "wrong" side of the family. Many scholars have pointed to the symbolic importance of the Moriscos in the Iberian imaginary. Irene Silverblatt mentions that *Moriscas* were "commonly held to be experts in occult matters."[289] A Mexican Mulato, Francisco Ruíz de Castrejon, who was accused in 1597 of witchcraft and making a pact with the devil, was allegedly called by his Amerindian acquaintances Mahoma, that is Mohammed.[290] The imprisoned priest Francisco de la Cruz characterizes part of his own anti-establishment mysticism, including a one-time dialogue with God against Rome, as one in which both De la Cruz and God speak "in the way that moriscos who are not very *ladinos* [i.e., acculturated] pronounce the Castilian language."[291] As far afield as the Philippines, a festival of "Moors and Christians," re-enacting and celebrating the triumph of *reconquista* was regularly held into the seventeenth century.[292] Both of these features — anti-Inquisition rhetoric/magic and Morisco/Muslim symbology — percolate through the religious-magical practices of Afro Iberians. That they surface in a prayer of a Mulata judaizer in New Spain, whose African mother might have worshipped according to the Law of Moses in the formerly Muslim city of Seville, not only makes perfect sense, but adds poignant nuance to the heritage of her religious discourse.

Testifying to Rodríguez's parental pedagogy, her daughters also

Palace of the Inquisition, Mexico City.

In front of this place was the quemadero (burning place) of the 1596–1771 Inquisition.

seem to have been involved to some degree in the Enríquez clan's Judaizing activities, especially the oldest, Juana. Juana's husband, Blas Lopez, allegedly told Blanca Enríquez that he married her because "she was of a good heart," in other words, that she was an observer of the Law of Moses.[293] Juana herself testifies that she learned the Law of Moses from her spouse and his family around 1632, over the course of a period of about fifteen days.[294] Isabel Antunes offers a similar story, saying that Juana "was taught [the Law] by Blass Lopez her husband, being in Guadalaxara, where she married him."[295] Rodríguez "showed great joy that this confessant [Juana] observed" the Law and that "her husband had taught it to her."[296] Shortly after this, Juana and Blas Lopez celebrated their first "fast of the great day" together.[297] In this same deposition Juana makes it sound as if until this point she was unaware that her mother also observed the Law of Moses, but it seems likely that Rodríguez had ensured that Juana marry a Crypto-Jew. The next September Juana and Rodríguez celebrated the Great Day fast together, washing their heads, putting on clean clothes and supping that evening on eggs and vegetables. The next day they fasted at home through the afternoon.[298] Juana confesses to attending suppers with her mother after her first Great Day fast, at which she, her husband and her mother all declared themselves to one another.[299]

When Rodríguez finally taught her daughters Ysavel and Maria the Law of Moses, she conveyed to them exactly what she had learned from Ynes Lopez: "that they should not believe in the most holy Virgin nor in Christ nor should they adore the Images."[300]

The nature and extent of the three Rodríguez del Bosque sisters' crypto-Jewish knowledge does not seem particularly vast. Juana knows that certain things are ceremonies of the Law of Moses: fasting on the Great Day until nightfall; eating hard-boiled eggs after a death; fasting after a death; the closest friend(s) or relative(s) of the new widow/er send food; and to pour out the water at the house of the deceased. For reasons not clear to me, neither of Rodríguez's two sons, Juan and Diego, the latter a carpenter, seem to have been connected to crypto-Judaism. The sisters evince certain theopolitical interests, at least do so as their situation deteriorates. After their imprisonment, some of the Rodríguez del Bosque sisters and Enríquez sisters carry on extended conversations from their cells. Among the many topics they discuss is a mysterious man, a gentleman of illustrious lineage (*muy hidalgo*) from Bragança who is present in the kingdom to liberate them. He is in contact with the king of France and of Portugal, and even has orders from the Spanish king to remedy the ongoing abuses. The women talk about God giving long life to the king of Portugal, that the kingdom should thrive; that of all places they could only live safely in Portugal.[301] I was not able to determine the identity of this mysterious savior, but he would seem to be connected, whether in the sisters' minds or in reality, with the Duke of Bragança and his secession from Spain.

Within the Bosom of the Clan: From Slave to Elder

According to Blanca Mendez de Rivera, just after Blanca Enríquez passed away (in late 1641), Rodríguez told her that Blanca Enríquez's daughter Beatriz gave her 70 pesos for her and her daughters to observe fasts in honor of the soul of Blanca Enríquez. Rodríguez also allegedly told Blanca Mendez de Rivera some days later, at the latter's house, how after having received the seventy pesos, she had instructed her two younger daughters, Ysabel and Maria, in the Law of Moses in order that they be able to carry out the necessary fasts along with their older sister Juana, who evidently was already inside the judaizing circle. According to Beatriz herself, she gave Esperanza 70 pesos.[302] Rodríguez's daughter Juana testifies that Beatriz gave Esperanza "eighty or ninety pesos," which she saw the former bring.[303] Beatriz's sister, Catalina Enríquez, was given by their mother Blanca the key to a trunk containing money, from which Catalina distributed 400 pesos as alms to various individuals, including Rodríguez. Beatriz herself says that the alms were to go to observers of the Law of Moses.[304] According to her daughter Juana, Rodríguez "fasted three or four Mondays" for the sake of the soul of Blanca Enríquez.[305]

The fact that Beatriz Enríquez offered Rodríguez money to perform a spiritual favor sheds some light on the latter's relationship to the crypto-Jewish community. On the one hand, leaving money for the reciting of certain prayers or psalms on behalf of the dead comprised standard practice within both Judaism and Catholicism. Blanca Enríquez also left money so that masses should be said on her behalf in at least two local churches.[306] Beatriz asserts that paying people to perform fasts is a "custom" among observers of the Law of Moses.[307]

Blanca de Rivera states that Beatriz Enríquez asked other daughters and grandchildren of Blanca Enríquez to observe similar fasts, offering them a mere peso or a few, openly given and accepted as alms.[308]

On the other hand, Rodríguez, as both a beloved former slave and a Mulata, may have stood unclearly defined in relation to this clan. Despite the many attestations of familiarity cited above, the intimacy of relations does not seem to have been consistent among all members of the extended family. The husband of Beatriz Enríquez, Thomas Nuñez de Peralta, for instance, claims never to have communicated with Rodríguez, while Raphaela Enríquez fails to include her in the list of those present after the burial of Blanca Enríquez.[309] Beatriz Enríquez herself testifies that though she knew from others that Rodríguez was an observer of the Law of Moses and that Beatriz had had various interactions with her, the two women had never declared themselves to one another until the death of Beatriz's mother, Blanca.[310] Raphaela Enríquez says that though she knew Rodríguez, the two never spoke about judaizing matters.[311] Blanca Mendes de Rivera, who knew Rodríguez already in Seville, claims that neither "she nor her daughters ever did a fast in [Rodríguez's] company, but when they declared themselves to one another, they said that they had done the fasts."[312] Ysavel de Rivera allegedly asked Ysavel Rodríguez del Bosque whether her two brothers were Jews. When Ysavel Rodríguez del Bosque replied in the negative, Rivera exclaimed that "Esperanza Rodríguez was worthless and that they would have to take away the demons because she had not taught [her sons] / era para poco, y se la auian de llevar los diablos porque no los auia enseñado."[313]

Even within these ostensibly tight-knit crypto-Jewish circles, race or social status appears to have surfaced as a factor. Though her father was a Judeoconverso, almost every witness for the Inquisition who refers to her mentions her status as a Mulata. In other words, they choose to highlight her mother's Afroiberian lineage (just as I do, I must confess). Beatriz Enríquez says, seemingly distantly, that she also distributed monies to "a mulata called esperanza Rodríguez." Others, such as Blanca and Clara de Rivera, identify her as "a mulata called Esperanza Rodríguez," putting her racial status before her personal name, while Catalina Enríquez (Blanca's daughter) says merely "an old mulata." Though this marker might have been inserted in order to aid the inquisitors in identifying the person being discussed, perhaps even to provide psychological distance between the witness and the person being denounced, one cannot help but wonder if and how the consciousness of this racial difference affected the everyday relations between the involved parties.[314] On two occasions it appears that race became an issue within this crypto-Jewish community itself. According to one unnamed witness, Rodríguez and her daughter Juana once visited Blanca Enríquez, who was speaking openly of "Jewish" matters with her daughter Beatriz and them. When Antonio Caravallo (Ysavel de Silva's husband) entered and understood the topic of conversation, he asked Beatriz "in secret [...] how they dared to speak such things in front of the said Esperanza Rodríguez." Beatriz assured the new guest that Esperanza and her daughter were trustworthy, were "our people" ("que segura era la gente"), but it is quite possible that his initial reaction was based on the assumption that a Mulata only could have been an outsider, not to be included in discussion of such dangerous subjects.[315] In the final publication of the charges, Antonio Caravallo's complaint bears even more distance: "how did they speak in such a manner in the presence of these three people?" Similarly, one day, testifies Manuel Nuñez Caravallo, he went to visit his relatives, the sisters Elena and Ysavel de Silva. Rodríguez was there with one of her daughters. The two "acted familiarly / trataban familiarmente" with the Silva sisters. After Esperanza and her daughter left, he asked, "who were those people with whom they acted with such familiarity. They responded that they were from mine [i.e., of my people / de los mios], which is the same as saying that they were observers of the Law of moses."[316] In their summary of the case and issuing of the sentence, the inquisitors fill in what they think went unsaid, stating that Caravallo's perplexity arose from the Rodríguezes "being a few mulata dogs / siendo unas perras mulatas."[317]

Paying Rodríguez so much money for the service of conducting fasts on behalf of the late Blanca Enríquez might signify that Rodríguez held a marginal status within the community; in other words, family members did not require such an amount, as they acted on an unquestionably personal level. Rodríguez's poverty may also have moved Beatriz Enríquez to offer her such a sum of money as an act of charity, unless Blanca had specified the amount. Indeed, according to Maria de Rivera, also accused of judaizing, and other witnesses, Blanca had ordered before her death the distribution of some 400 pesos to the poor among the crypto-Jewish community (as already mentioned) and these witnesses list Rodríguez explicitly as one of the recipients.[318] The de Riveras together received 60 pesos. Yet, according to Beatriz Enríquez, and Rodríguez confirms this independently, it is Rodríguez who showed up at Beatriz's house to ask for 70 pesos, indicating that Beatriz was unaware of the arrangement. Beatriz even queried Rodríguez, who had to explain why she wanted such an amount.[319] When Blanca Enríquez died, various clothes of hers were distributed to poor observers of the Law of Moses, including a mattress that was given to Rodríguez.[320] One unnamed witness told someone else that one could send alms to Rodríguez, as he/she had "sent alms several times to the said Esperanza Rodríguez as a poor observer [of the Law]."[321] According to Juana Rodríguez del Bosque, the payment from Beatriz was only "one of the times that the said Esperanza Rodríguez her mother took money" from the

Enríquez women. Raphaela Enríquez claims that "she has given various alms" to Rodríguez from the money Raphaela received from Manuel Albarez to distribute to poor observers of the Law of Moses, so that they would fast on his behalf. Juana Enríquez testifies that she gave alms to Rodríguez three times, later adding that after the death of Blanca Enríquez she gave Rodríguez at different times eight or nine pesos.[322] One unnamed witness sums up the relationship bluntly: "because the said Esperanza Rodríguez, and her daughters, profess [the Law of Moses], all the rich observers of [the Law] give them alms, and do them much kindness ("las hazen mucho bien").[323] At any rate, the fact that Rodríguez told Blanca Mendez de Rivera that she had been given 70 pesos on the occasion of Blanca's death to conduct these fasts with her daughters shows that it meant a great deal to her.[324]

Rodríguez's poverty is easy enough to deduce. When she and her daughters were arrested by the Mexico City tribunal, their goods are inventoried together. Among these goods is "an ordinary guitar."[325] Perhaps one of the women or Rodríguez's deceased husband knew how to play. Like a fair number of her goods, it is listed as broken. The inquisitional inventory deems many of the items belonging to her to be old.[326] As free urban mixed-race individuals, the Rodríguez women lived in the multicultural American world; hence their possession of "nine small, old pictures of different saints, painted by indians," an "old turkish woman of black damask," "three small measures of silk from China," various skirts, muffs and cloths from Rouen, and "a little desk from Japan."[327] The only enumeration of the value of the Rodríguez estate, or at least of some of its items, yields a total of 17 pesos.[328] When deposing in connection with the trial of Beatriz Enríquez, Juana Rodríguez del Bosque describes with seeming excitement how her mother Rodríguez spent the money she received for the above-mentioned fasts, retrieving, for instance, a little rug that she had had to pawn.³²⁹ Their stark financial situation lends motivation to Juana's exaggeration of the amount her mother received to fast for Blanca Enríquez. It also makes understandable how on two occasions Rodríguez sent one of her grandsons "to request from [Juana Enríquez] three pesos for her household, and the other time two pesos which she sent her said grandson to request, saying that [Rodríguez] would pay it in sewing. But [Juana Enríquez] sent to her saying that she did not want it paid in sewing but rather that [Rodríguez] should commend her said mother [Blanca] to God."³³⁰

In fact, there was more to the relationship between Rodríguez and the other judaizers than mere charity. One unnamed witness deposes that Esperanza was given money on different occasions by a judaizer who was having an extramarital affair, so that Rodríguez would fast for the sake of his/her gaining forgiveness for this sin ("por la intençion de la dha persona").³³¹ On another occasion, Rodríguez claims, Blanca Enríquez herself sent her a peso (again, through Pedro Tinoco) to fast "for the peace of her house."³³² According to Rodríguez herself, Ana Xuarez one time sent her two pesos by means of Pedro Tinoco (her aunt Catalina's son) so that Rodríguez (and her daughter/s? — the language is plural) would fast on her behalf, "that God should enlighten her [*la alumbrasse*] because she was about to give birth." The use of the term *alumbrar* here is intriguing. Rodríguez uses it elsewhere in her depositions, but as far as I could see, it is rarely mentioned by any of the judaizers associated with the Enríquez clan. Is Xuarez requesting divine illumination in order to teach her future child properly? Enríquez's request might well contain an allusion to the messianic beliefs that some family members attached to certain newborn children, who were hoped or expected to become the new savior, such as the son of Juana Enríquez and Simón Váez Sevilla. Perhaps she is referring to the mystical understandings of the Virgin Mary's annunciation from Gabriel and the light it produces.³³³ It is likely, therefore, that Rodríguez was considered a particularly powerful spiritual presence because of her age, knowledge and close connections to Blanca Enríquez and the fonts of their collective heritage in Seville. The inquisitors themselves are convinced of the high esteem in which she was held. In their summary of the case and sentencing, they state that Rodríguez was "held to be a holy Jewess" or "Jewish saint" ("tenida por sta judia"), "was esteemed as a perfect Dogmatizer / perfecta Dogmatiçadora" and they speak of "the respect with which she was treated among the Jews," indeed pointing to the alms given to Esperanza as evidence.³³⁴

In a circle of White merchants, some of a prominent and even internationally recognized stature, Esperanza Rodríguez stands out as an anomaly in terms of both economic status and race. It is understandable if she had aspirations for a better life and more secure social status. Unusual for a woman and a half-White, she knew how to read and write, having been taught during her year at the convent in Seville.³³⁵ When discussing her grandchildren — having been prompted by the inquisitors to do so — some of her strong character and worldliness shines through the usually dry language. She offers seeming apologetics when mentioning that her eldest daughter Juana had children by different men. Yet Rodríguez notes proudly that the father of Juana's son was "Don Nicolas de Alarcon, son of the former governor of Soconusco," a region in southern Mexico near Guatemala, and that the father of her daughter was "Hernando Cassado, servant of Don Franco de Arevalo Suazo," clearly emphasizing the high social connections.³³⁶ When relating the story of her youth and arrival in Mexico to the inquisitors, she points out, as if the social connections rebound to her credit, that she arrived in the Americas (at Cartagena) on a fleet led by "general Juan de Sulas de Valdes nephew of the Señor Inquisitor Don Juan de Llaro y Valdes who was the godfather or companion [*compadre*] of the said Doña Catalina her mistress. And by her order the said general brought her until Cartagena."[337] When relating her husband's work experience, she states that one of his employers in Acapulco had been "the third Marquesa of Guadalcaçar."[338]

Unlike most of the Mexico City judaizers, especially the younger generation, Rodríguez tends to use in her testimony the term "Jewish" rather than "observer of the Law of Moses," whether applying it to herself or to others. People teach others "to be Jewish," before some men are permitted to marry into the family they were "made to be Jewish," which most likely refers to being taught some of the tradition rather than to being circumcised. Rodríguez seems to regard herself self-consciously as "a Jew," an upholder of a significant and legitimate tradition rather than a follower of a cowering, subterranean cult. An indication of what all this meant to her can be gleaned from a moralistic tale told one night at her house by Diego Tinoco, who grew up as an open Jew somewhere outside of Spanish territories, when Rodríguez, her daughters, and he had been discussing the Law of Moses:

> In an ossuary in a certain place where Jews live in freedom, a Spanish catholic stayed in order to sleep. he saw rising up two deceased Jewesses, discussing how the following day another Jewess had to die from a fall. The said catholic, making an inquiry in the city after the said woman and seeing that she had not died that day, returned to sleep in the same place, and turned to see the same Jewesses who spoke, saying that the [other] Jewess did not have to die from the fall for having given alms to another Jew, from which it resulted that the catholic became a Jew.[339]

In this story, related by a group of Crypto-Jews to bolster their own faith and practice, Judaism is figured as the embodiment of ancient statements repeated around and on Rosh HaShana, the Jewish New Year, and Yom Kippur, the Day of Atonement, that charity saves one from death (Proverbs 11:4; BT Bava Batra 10a). The death which charity can stave off is, as the Talmud exhorts, the spiritual punishment meted out in the afterlife. In Tinoco's tale, Judaism comprises the possibility of escape from a punishing fate, a path for transcending strict judgement through goodness and good deeds.[340]

Such sentiments likely had an even more particular resonance for a woman such as Esperanza Rodríguez who was part Afroiberian and a former enslaved person. When asked regarding her maternal grandparents by the inquisitors, she retorts that "her said mother being a black woman born in Guinea, she therefore has no notice of who her parents were."[341] Her emotions here might be both sarcastic defiance and genuine sadness. Accepting the Judaism urged on her by her owners-relatives closed a gap in social status that separated her from them. She recounts how after she had acceded to believing in Adonay "she sat down with Ynes and her cousins to have a light meal with special foods that these Jews ate before fasts – fish, salad, and beans. [...] they gave her 'a lot because she had condescended to [take] their advice.'"[342]

Another insight into the motivating factors of her devotion to her new religion might be obtained from the statement made to her by Ynes Lopez and Lopez's cousins when they tried to convince her around age thirteen that "whoever believes in that which they say [i.e., the Law of Moses] cannot be a slave / no podia ser esclaba."[343] The reasoning Rodríguez relates is not merely an effort at manipulation of a young enslaved girl. It constitutes a form of cognitive self-liberation, a stance of symbolic marronage wielded by those who so often historically were constrained by external circumstances. It also finds expression within "normative" Jewish circles before and during Rodríguez's own lifetime. Commenting on the commandment to bore a hole into the ear of a Hebrew slave who chooses not to go free after the sixth year (Exod. 21:6; Deut. 15:17), the ancient *Mekhilta* (parshat Bo) explains that this is a fitting punishment for the ear that heard at Mt. Sinai God announcing, "for the children of Israel are slaves to me and not slaves to slaves [i.e., other people]," and the one possessing the ear, who refuses to act on this epiphany. The fifteenth-century Isaac Abravanel cites this midrash in his commentary to Deut. 15:17. Rabbi Ishac Athias of Amsterdam, a contemporary of Esperanza Rodríguez, concludes his discussion of why Jews use non-Jewish servants with a nod to this and another biblical statement [Lev. 25:44-46]: "He commanded you that pagan servants serve you in perpetuity, in order that your own brothers don't serve you, who are the children of Israel, all elected for My service, and as such it is necessary to be unoccupied [that is, unemployed, available, free to serve divine needs and seek holiness]. And whoever serves such a Master needs not serve humans."[344] How attractive such a rhetoric of overturning must have appeared to someone who managed to escape a fate of servitude.

The Attraction of the Other

Rodríguez was born to a New Christian father. Even for those Afroiberians without New Christian blood, however, "Jews" often played a significant rhetorical role. Solange Alberro adduces many cases which, she argues, prove that "the Jewish-Christians," i.e., Judeoconversos, came "to constitute the valued and admired reference" for "these pariahs who are the slaves and the free men of African origin," linked by them "to the Portuguese rebels [against Spain], victims of oppression like the blacks and mulatos, but who participate without room for doubts in the splendor which confers prestige and social power."[345] These cases hint at the range of possible attributes Jewishness or Judaism might have held for these exiled, destitute Africans: wealth, power, the capacity of defiance.

A few months after a wave of *autos de fe* in 1651 Mexico City, one slave, Diego de la Cruz denounced himself to the Holy Office, declaring "that he had desired to adopt the Old Law in order to be rich since 'this was the cause by which the Portuguese [i.e., perceived Jews or judaizers] had so much money.' "[346] Such views of material reward had many adherents among non-Blacks as well, of course, and constituted a popular vestige of ancient anti-Jewish rhetoric among non-Jews and of a redemptive logic of *resentiment* among Jews.[347] Such class consciousness among Judeoconversos themselves arises occasionally in Inquisition sources. Testifying against the Mexican Conversa Rafaela Enriquez, an unnamed witness relates the following conversation: Rafaela was chatting at her house with a female friend one day. In walked another acquaintance, someone who "had not wanted to help [fund] by means of a charitable donation the wedding of someone very close to the woman who spoke" with Rafaela. So Rafaela's friend commented pointedly "that God

100   The Underground World of Secret Jews and Africans

An auto-da-fé in New Spain, 18th century in the Town of San Bartolomé Otzolotepec. Museo Nacional de Arte (MUNAL) of Mexico City.

did not have to give goods to the Portuguese because they did not know how to act well toward" one another. The newcomer responded, in resoundingly theological language, that "he did not want to give his *hazienda* and remain poor, for no one poor is able to be saved."[348] On the other hand, another Mexico City New Christian, Maria de Rivera, supposedly taught another alleged judaizer a prayer that included the following lines:

> Give me honesty
> Against the dishonesties of this world
> Don't give me riches
> That I should grow haughty [*me ensoberbesca*]
> Nor poverty that brings me down
> Only an alm with which to serve you [God].[349]

Toward the end of the fifteenth century, Pedro de Villanueva of Quintanar, Castile, denied to the inquisitors that his grandfather, Fernán Sánchez de Villanueva, who had converted to Catholicism, had said that "like a good Jew his only wealth was the Law of Moses."[350]

As Alberro suggests, wealth was not the only attraction the Law of the Jews held for downtrodden Afroiberians. The hopes of poor slaves for material ease need no explanation, but the rhetorical use of "Judaism" by slaves operated on more ideational levels as well. In the 1650s, a slave in Mexico, the Mulato slave Sebastián de los Reyes, wielded the already martyred judaizer Thomas Treviño de Sobremonte as an exemplar.[351] Sobremonte, a wealthy merchant, had become renowned for his defiance and even mockery of the Inquisition, up to and including at his dramatic public execution. When drunk, the Mulato slave Sebastián would rave: "I'm not a Christian, I am Treviño."[352] Even years later, another slave in

Mexico, a Black woman named Maria de la Cruz or Maria de Armijo, spat out, among other statements deemed to be heretical blasphemies, "that if she had not confessed her crime, it would have been worse than [it was with] Tremiño." The legend of Treviño's life (and/or death) obviously made quite an impression. Maria was said to be over twenty-five years old, and might actually have seen Treviño's martyrdom firsthand.[353] Such sympathetic glances at the fate of Crypto-Jews came from non-Afroiberians as well. The Carmelite Ana de Guillamas, tried in Mexico in 1598 as a "false" visionary (an *alumbrada*), stated that while she prayed one time "the devil had spoken to her [...] and said, 'Poor Carvajal who was killed without guilt.' "[354] Guillamas was probably referring to Luis de Carvajal, executed the year before, and it is not surprising that she dissociates herself from having originated this thought. New Christians, obviously, were those who most fervently upheld the notion that the victims of the Inquisitions were martyrs.

Some Afroiberians, like others, could not help but be influenced by the riveting fates of Judeoconversos: insiders often persecuted as outsiders, insiders who yet might challenge and even defy the powers-that-be. Hence the disgust with which one mid-seventeenth-century inquisitor described one such scene of cultural contamination:

> Certain Portuguese judaizers presented a Comedy in this city [Mexico City], the author of which was this evil man [whom Blanca Enriquez praised as a "great Jew"], and he gave the foremost seats to two jews who had been reconciled by this H[oly] Office, standing were many other Catholics, and honored, having waiting for those two reconciled to begin the Comedy. After it finished he took them to his house and entertained them, an action so evil

that it caused admiration in one Black *boçal*, slave of one of the Presenters [Actors?], who said (though a barbarian) that they had been at the Comedy in such beautiful seats, just as those seated men had been taken out [as penitents in the *auto de fé*] in S. Domingo [cathedral] with green candles and yellow caps [*capisayos*]. Such is the rupture [*rotura*] and shamelessness with which this infamous jewish people proceeds."[355]

Jews or Judaism, then, sometimes appeared "good for thinking with" (Lévi-Strauss) as a means of needling Afroiberians' Christian overlords.[356] One wonders, for instance, exactly what was meant by the Mulata servant of a New Christian in Pernambuco, who in 1599 "extolled the New Christians."[357] A startlingly explicit formulation of the logic at work here can be found in the twentieth-century family memoirs of an Afro-American woman from Philadelphia. Her mother, she writes, would fight prejudice by claiming to belong to whatever group was being denigrated.

> [H]er strategy is usually confined to strangers or people who do not know her very well. Her strategy is to counteract prejudice against any group by immediately informing the speaker that she is a part of whatever group is under attack. If it is the Jews, she is a Jew; if it is the Italians, she is an Italian; if it is the Catholics, she is a Catholic. And there are *no exceptions*. One day I asked her about Native Americans, and she said, "Well, I just say that my grandfather was one, or my daughter is married to one, or something like that."[358]

A similar tendency manifested itself among *Moriscos*, Muslims forcibly converted to Christianity during and after the Spanish Reconquista. The slaves Brianda and Andrés Cano, both punished by the tribunal of Córdoba, Andalucía, between 1575 and 1576 for performing Muslim ceremonies, both proffered the transparent provocation "that the Christians are Jews / que los cristianos son judíos."[359] Blanca Becerra, "black in color," slave of Jorge Becerro from Ubeda near Córdoba, probably had something similar in mind when she repeated even after being castigated that "the better law was that of the Jews and not that of the Christians." Being a minor helped this slave escape with no penalty other than a light abjuration of her delinquencies sometime between 1571 and 1572. In addition, variance between the testimony of the witnesses injured the prosecution's case, with "most of them saying that she said that the Jews were better people and more charitable than the Christians," a perhaps more pointed statement, whether she believed it or not.[360]

Utterances like these must be seen in a comparative light. Insulting the dominant religion entailed a tack taken by a variety of individuals. In the mid-sixteenth century at least eight Muslim Africans who had been imported to Lisbon found themselves arrested and tried by the Inquisition. Most had asserted "the superiority of Islam over the religion of their Catholic masters, pointing out, among other things, that Christians did not bathe before prayers. Several others expressed the belief that God had no son and that Jesus was the servant of Mohammed."[361] Though here the religion wielded rhetorically was their own, mistreated slaves often put comparative polemics to good use in self-defense. In 1661, one Black slave in Mexico, Nicolás Bazán, begged the inquisitor to ignore the blasphemy he had uttered while enduring a horrific, if altogether common torture administered by his master, assuring him that his suffering as a Christian " 'redeemed by Christ's blood at the hands of fellow Christians' was so painful that 'not even among Turks and Moors was a comparable martyrdom endured.' "[362] This appeal was meant to include the slave within the Catholic body politic, as he should have been according to theology, and to remind the inquisitor that Christians were supposed to behave better than "barbarian" non-believers. White Christians also wielded such polemics when critiquing what they saw as problems within the Christian body politic. A Mexican *alumbrado* of the sixteenth century, Juan Núñez de León, was accused of having publicly announced that "the Jews kept their God better than the Christians."[363]

Certain cases show how the various facts or fantasies about "Judaism" were picked up from the environment and came to be put to use. The fifty-year-old Francisca de Carvajal, slave of Doña María de Carvajal, "dark black," was apprehended by the Inquisition of Córdoba, Andalucía, sometime in 1598 or 1599 for blasphemy.[364] Because of variations in her testimony, the inquisitors held several audiences with her. In the third one she confessed that on an occasion other than the one pertaining to her crime, when quarreling with some women, they asked her why she did not attend mass, to which she replied "that she did not want to go, that the law of Moses was better than that of God, which she said with the rage that she had because she had heard the law of Moses named in the *autos* without knowing what it was and without having the intention of following it."[365] Her reference indicated the recent *autos de fe* in Córdoba aimed at extirpating the alleged conspiracy of judaizing in the area, in which numerous "judaizers," real or otherwise, had appeared (25 March 1597: 71 "judaizers" reconciled, 1 burned at the stake; 8 March 1598: 32 "judaizers" reconciled, 1 burned in absentia). Such a confession notwithstanding, in the heat of an argument, the Law of Moses served this slave well and spontaneously as a tool with which to belittle the Christianity that, for whatever reasons, so frustrated her. Regarding Francisca de Carvajal, as with many of the Afroiberians mentioned above, there is no question of knowledge of Judaism; it simply stands for the anti-norm, which the powerless wield against the norm disempowering them.

Sincere non-White judaizers must have perplexed and enraged Christian ecclesiastical authorities. Such a reaction erupted in 1579, when a Spaniard from Córdoba visiting in Venice sighted in the Ghetto a young Black boy wearing the yellow Jew's cap. Rebuking him, the good Christian visitor, Don Ferdinando de las Infantes, became further exercised on hearing from a local Jew how slaves bought in Constantinople were circumcised, "made of their own law," and brought West (the quote and paragraph are brought in the previous chapter). Don Fernando informed the local Inquisition, which arrested several people, though they could not find the Black youth in question. One of those whom they did interrogate was the

> dark-skinned Samuel Maestro, [who] appeared to be the child of a well-to-do Jew by a middle-aged servant of Ferrara who was "neither white nor black", and was said to be Jewish herself. [....] "Are you not ashamed," the pious Spaniard remonstrated, "you were born black, you have this grace given you by God to be able to turn Christian, and you have become a Jew?"[366]

Christianity, seen as a remedy for Blackness, became conveniently confused with Whiteness. Not surprisingly, such a confusion proliferated in this era. The Jesuit Alonso de Sandoval, in his 1627 tract on Africans and Christianity, argues that given their treatment at the hands of Europeans, most Africans would never voluntarily consent "to receive that water [of baptism] and be like whites."[367] An incident from early New France, i.e., Canada, then very much Jesuit territory, reflects similar notions. One minister to the natives, Father LeJeune, wrote the following back home in 1632:

> I have become a teacher in Canada: the other day I had a

little Savage on one side of me, and a little Negro or Moor on the other, to whom I taught their letters... The little Negro was left by the English with this French family which is here. We have taken him to teach and baptise, but he does not yet understand the language well; therefore we shall wait some time yet... His mistress asking him if he wanted to be a Christian, if he wanted to be baptized and be like us, he said "yes," but he asked if he would not be skinned in being baptized. I think he was very much frightened, for he had seen these poor Savages skinned. As he saw that they laughed at his questions, he replied in his patois, as best he could: "you say that by baptism I shall be like you: I am black and you are white, I must have my skin taken off then in order to be like you" (this comment followed by general laughter).[368]

The boy's imputation that the priests encouraged the belief in the whitening power of baptism was not false. The famous António Vieira stated in his Epiphany Sermon of 1662: "An Ethiope if he be cleansed in the waters of the Zaire is clean, but he is not white; but if in the water of baptism he is both."[369]

From the Catholic perspective, Judaism, a deviation from Christianity, turned logically into a deviation from Whiteness. The ostensibly separate discourses of "religion," "race" and "politics" become entangled, revealed in their entanglement. Conversion "upward" meant entrance into the circle of those "chosen" for acceptance, recognition and citizenship, or so went the rhetoric.[370] In both senses, from the Christian point of view, not only did Judaism not offer non-Whites salvation — terrestrial or celestial — but it stood as a diversion, distraction and mirage for them on their path to the Christian city of heaven.

The Tragic Sense of Humor of the Cosmos

Perhaps it was the women of the Rodríguez del Bosque family who resorted to the dealer in cocoa, Luis Núñez Pérez, a fellow prisoner who "not only was a Jew, but rather a superstitious prophet," who, among other suspect practices, "promised safety from imprisonment to certain Jewesses. He also later assured them "that he hadn't denounced them another time when he was a prisoner, but rather a man or a Black woman [had]; what was certain was that hardly had he separated from them when they were immediately arrested by this Holy Office."[371] In jail, Esperanza claims to have suffered from delirium, giving this as the reason in late September 1644 that she did not confess immediately upon her imprisonment. It is not clear whether this illness, as she calls it, is identical with the rational fear she then describes having experienced that if she confessed she would be burned or gravely punished, a fear she says was put in her by the devil.[372] In light of what struck the inquisitors as Rodríguez's willful observance of Jewish practices, they decided to apply "the most serious penalties established by the law, relaxing her person to justice and to the secular arm," — Inquisition-speak for death by burning.[373] In her later meetings with the inquisitors, however, Rodríguez repeatedly expresses repentance for her judaizing and remorse for having shunned "the Law of Our Lord Jesus Christ," begging the Inquisition for mercy. Evidently, the inquisitors were convinced of the sincerity of her remorse. According to the 1646 summary of that year's *autos de fé*, Rodríguez

> was imprisoned as a Jewess, observer of the law of Moses, with confiscation of goods. Was negative a long time and, becoming tightfisted [i.e., not giving the information that

was wanted], pretended to be crazy, allowing herself to eat lice; saying and doing actions and words with which she pretended to be taken for such [crazy], like the gathering of her shirts and tearing them up, making a large doll, with her *mantilla* [a lace scarf], girdle, stuffed arms and *capillos* [cloths used in Mexico as a hat or mantilla] on the head; and kissing it, making as if she gave it the breast, saying it was her baby, and that they would look after him and they would not kill him; and other times, hiding it herself deliberately, she implored and cried that he should return; thinking, by this route so beyond reason, to escape from confessing her grave sins and speaking against the many accomplices who she knew kept the said law of Moses.[374] Ultimately, becoming more agreeable, she admitted being a Jewess judaizer and begged mercy.

Was admitted to reconciliation and sentenced to the *auto* in the form of a penitent; green candle in the hands; confiscation of goods, which she did not have; formal abjuration; sambenito, and perpetual imprisonment,[375] and in public humiliation and in perpetual banishment from all the West Indies and from the city of Seville and town of Madrid, Court of His Majesty.[376]

Like all those "reconciled," Rodríguez was to leave Mexico on the first available fleet to Spain and present herself to the Inquisition in Seville within a month to be assigned the place elsewhere where her sentence was to be served. A former enslaved girl who had sought to improve her lot, she was forbidden now to wear or possess "gold, silver, pearls, nor precious stones, nor silk, camlet [*chamelote*, a strong, impermeable woven fabric that originally might have been made of camel or goat hair], nor fine cloth, nor to ride on horseback."[377]

Rodríguez's eldest daughter, Juana Rodríguez del Bosque,

> was imprisoned as a Jewess, observer of the law of Moses, with confiscation of goods. She confessed to being a Jewess judaizer and begged mercy. Before her imprisonment she agreed with certain Jews and her mother and sisters not to speak against accomplices in the Inquisition, and after imprisonment she communicated in the jails with many of the prisoners, in order to know what they had deposed against her and whether it was contrary to what she had confessed.[378]

Juana was also reconciled, with a sentence slightly different than her mother's, a rope around the throat at the *auto*, only six months imprisonment, and 100 lashes. She too had no goods to be confiscated. Juana's sister Isabel found herself accused of the same crime of judaizing and likewise begged mercy.[379]

> She herself, of her own will and cause, made application to Esperanza Rodríguez, her mother, that she teach her the law of Moses, having heard said that a certain famous Jewess [Blanca Enríquez], deceased, had left money so that another Jewess, her daughter [Beatriz Enríquez], would dispense it in order to make abstinence for her soul, taken away from the avarice that is innate in the Hebrews and their descendants. And being a prisoner, she feigned revelation from the Heavens and that she had heard a voice which exhorted her to confess and discharge her conscience, and the revelation was the communications of the jails which she had with other prisoners, under false names, discussing and confirming among themselves about their lawsuits, laying out the way in which they had

behaved in them; threatening with notable temerity a certain minister [of the Inquisition?], that she, through the hand of a Jew, would have his face cut.[380]

Isabel also had no goods to confiscate. She received the same sentence as her sister Juana of a rope around the throat at the *auto*, only six months imprisonment, and 100 lashes.

María Rodríguez del Bosque, the youngest sister, likewise confessed to the same crime of judaizing, received the same sentence as her older sisters, and likewise had no goods to be taken from her.[381] Of María we read that

> she had notable rebelliousness in confessing her sins, and with threats of denouncing her said mother to this Holy Office for what she had seen her do in the observance of Judaism, she obliged her to teach her the law of Moses [!]. Making up, when she judaized, with some famous Jewesses, she and they made mockery and ridicule of the processions of the Catholics, speaking ill of them. And all that she got out of her apostasy and of the monies she received for making fasts of the said law of Moses was but a damask doubloon of China, blue and red, which she brought to the jails, so that, as a witness, it would convince her of her evildoing. And in them [the jails], stubborn and rebellious, she communicated with her sisters and other Jews and Jewesses, using false names and serving as intermediary, giving assurances from some prisoners to others, that they shouldn't confess, and if they should, it should be about what they had arranged.[382]

Esperanza Rodríguez delivered the renunciation required of her by the Inquisition, stating formally that she understands the proceedings and promises to live as a good Christian. All in all, she denounces more than 70 individuals in order to appease her inquisitors.[383] On 29 October 1646, still imprisoned after some four years, she pens a note to the inquisitors begging to be allowed to serve life imprisonment together with her daughters. The same day, she is granted this permission, as well as to leave the place of her incarceration on holidays to hear mass with the other penitents.[384] It is not clear what happened to the inquisitors' allowance of perpetual imprisonment instead of banishment from the Americas and Seville. A Relation of the Mexico City Tribunal from 1647 lists Rodríguez among other prisoners who are to embark for Spain, where they are to present themselves to the tribunal of Seville.[385] Not surprisingly, given what she had endured, Rodríguez is described in this document as appearing older than her age and greying (avejentada, enttrecana). She seems to have set out for Spain as ordered, since an undated Inquisition list of those sentenced in Mexico City to banishment states that she died in the city and port of Veracruz.[386] In the cases of the Rodríguez del Bosque women, one sees at work some of the various forms of resistance and mutual cooperation taken up by those caught in the Inquisitions' net, however fruitless.

With perhaps little choice, Rodríguez opted to identify herself as a daughter of her Judeoconverso father, though little surfaces regarding their relationship. It is possible that her mother, Isabel, had already chosen to throw her lot in with crypto-Judaism. These choices may have reflected positive affection for this religious complex or mere efforts to escape an enslaved status or both. All in all, the story of Esperanza Rodríguez, at least insofar as it can be gleaned from Inquisition documents, offers a glimpse of a rich if idiosyncratic example of how a part-Afroiberian went about forging the kind of "new kin-like ties" that helped remake the "natal network of kin" lost in enslavement.[387]

Conclusion

"The woman who knows giving birth will not feel the [Inquisition's] torture." ("La muger que sauia parir no sentia el tormento.")[388] So proclaimed Blanca Enriquez to her young relative Ysavel de Silva when recounting her months-long imprisonment by the tribunal of the Seville Inquisition and displaying the marks of the torture she had received at its hands. To give birth in this imperfect world is to become familiar with pain. To make life is to come to know the handiwork of decay, of degeneration, of death. To generate the future, to have felt its powerful potential, to have seen that creation is not only possible but survivable, is to become — to varying degrees — inured to the forces trying to prevent that future. To a large extent, trust in the future may well be nurtured best through a connection to a past that will be met on the road to that future. We see in the narratives about Diego López, Rufina, Blas de Paz Pinto and Esperanza Rodríguez some of the power subaltern cultural traditions lent to Judeoconversos and Afroiberians: community, substitute family, strength, hope, strategies, self-knowledge, and a sense of belonging.

Early modern "race" stands as a significant bridge for scholarship between the "raceless" culturally oriented medieval world and the "scientific" racism of the more modern world. Like its later progeny, early modern race was both biological and cultural, essentialist and situational, rigidly defined and permeable, political and theological. The Inquisitions maintained and stoked anti-Jewish stereotypes, just as various European/White institutions and individuals maintained and stoked anti-Black prejudices, in order "to relegate" each group "to being 'objects of phobia,' " as Marie Theresa Hernández notes.[389]

Social constructs — ethnic, religious, racial — were used by groups other than the dominators. Belonging to a collective, real or imagined, held out powerful identity-forming possibilities, both for negative, external, ascriptive purposes regarding others as well as for positive, internal purposes for oneself. Diego López, Rufina, Blas de Paz Pinto and Esperanza Rodríguez stand among many examples of individuals who wielded tropes about other groups as a means toward their own well-being, advancement and survival.

New Christians of Jewish and African origin suffered for centuries from being positioned by the dominant majority and other minorities as "in-between" (Certeau, *The Mystic Fable*) yet also cultivated on their own such in-betweenness as a defensive barrier, a privileged space, an unsharable uniqueness. To borrow terminology from Hernández, they were "maybe" Christians, "maybe" Spaniards, "maybe" Whites.[390] Though many, perhaps even most individuals from these groups no longer practiced many or any particulars of their traditions, the entire group remained, seemingly permanently, "designated" as Jews or Africans. Some New Christians expressed skepticism toward religious and political orthodoxies.[391] Many individuals also expressed egalitarian views in opposition to dominant ethnic and/or racial hierarchies. I have not found, however, that most Judeoconversos voiced distinct urgency for tolerance other than for themselves under the tyranny of the Catholic Inquisitions, nor that most Afroiberians argued for an end to anti-Converso/Jewish state-church activities.

Many parallels attend these Judeoconverso and Afroiberian efforts at separate survival. Just as the enslaved and "colored" sought in their get-togethers a means of escaping misery, as María Méndez of Cartagena, also known as María Quelembe, put it in her 1634

Inquisition trial,[392] so too might Judeoconversos have seen in judaizing practices and beliefs a mode of being true to themselves and their past. While those of African origin might have sought an escape, literally or figuratively, back to their homeland from which they had been wrenched, for Judeoconversos, on the other hand, flight from Iberian territories, which was often achievable, likely entailed an undesired self-exile from the homeland in which they continued to live but that had in a deep sense been wrenched away from them by the rise of militant Catholic xenophobia. Many Judeoconversos and Afroiberians therefore sought, "through the use of specific knowledges, liberty, goods…to oppose slavery,"[393] though the kind of slavery that members of each group faced differed.

While in this book I do not dwell on the martial efforts of slaves to undo their captivity, Judeoconversos also at times attempted to make use of more normative forces, diplomacy, wealth and even physical/military resistance to "free" themselves from oppression, with perhaps less success. Yet each group had at its disposal mostly the weapons of the weak (a term from James C. Scott). For many Afroiberians or Judeoconversos, the most they could hope to do might involve casting a spell over one's master or doing violence to a crucifix. Symbolic marronage may well have permitted psychic survival, even if it did not undo the objective conditions of oppression.

From the perspective of the dominant elite, the advances of globalization birthed a shadow realm of magic and resistance where the Other took on exaggerated dimensions. Hence in Peru, as Irene Silverblatt shows, "Jewish symbols and the insights of *moriscas* […] were common ingredients in devilish brews," and the same women who wielded them "were also experimenting with indigenous lore." Magical practitioners made purposeful use of the bones of Amerindians, who "never [had been] baptized," who "had never been touched by the Christian world," or chanted incantations to and used the bones of "men who had been either hanged or decapitated."³⁹⁴ Dislocated and fragmented in family and culture, the Afroiberians Diego López and Rufina participated in this invocation of things Native American as a strategy of coping and empowering themselves. Esperanza Rodríguez, knowingly or not, made use of Muslim and Morisco wisdom.

Cultural and discursive mixing was not a neutral commingling. The borrowings by the subaltern sought a renegotiation of the terms.³⁹⁵ As simultaneous insiders and outsiders, these groups shared certain perspectives of the dominant majority but from a dissonant position. Fuchs calls it the "deliberate enactment of imitation as a strategy for inclusion."³⁹⁶ This is not to say that they questioned or opposed the prejudices of the mainstream, which would be little more than a retrojected romantic hope, but that such imitations might take positive or negative forms. When in 1566 Felipe I prohibited Moriscos from owning Black slaves, various fifteenth-century Morisco noblemen, such as Don Francisco Núñez Muley, protested their right to do so and the importance of doing so in order to protect Morisco society from the erosion.³⁹⁷ One scholar finds that in sixteenth-century Santiago de Guatemala, "[m]arginal individuals, in particular, foreigners such as Portuguese, were likelier to recognize mulatto children than were those in a better social position."³⁹⁸ On the Caribbean island of Montserrat, the Irish immigrants who made up two thirds of the population by the late seventeenth century were relegated to second-class status by the English elite. Yet by the early eighteenth century, the Irish constituted the island's primary sugar producers and slaveholders.³⁹⁹ Michel de Certeau notes how "users make (*bricolent*) innumerable and infinitesimal transformations of and within the dominant cultural economy in order to adapt it to their own interests and their own rules."⁴⁰⁰ James C. Scott famously illuminated the modes of resistance taken by those in a position of weakness in relation to the larger structures of domination: within certain limits, all subaltern "human actors fashion their own response, their own experience of class, their own history."⁴⁰¹ Here is the prolonged, persistent struggle between the dominant cultural system and the groups and individuals under and within it, each with its own forms of weaponry, each ceaselessly attempting to make use of, to seduce, to exert control over the other. The dominant sociocultural system is never totally homogeneous though this may not prevent its being received as a monolith.

It must also be remembered that Europeans in the Americas — Blas de Paz Pinto and the clan of Mexico City Crypto-Jews, for instance — were "strangers in a strange, often dangerous, and hostile world" where "European power and control was often weak, especially during the early, most crucial stages of culture formation."⁴⁰² From a different context and perspective, Mieke Bal underscores that "[i]nsecurity is not a prerogative of the dominated. The burden of domination is hard to bear. Dominators have, first, to establish their position, then to safeguard it. Subsequently, they must make both the dominated *and* themselves believe in it."⁴⁰³ Subaltern self-fashioning can be decidedly reactionary, mirroring, consuming and wielding empire's most exclusionary and divisive aspects. Who "wins" is perhaps not clear until long after the struggles subside; perhaps not even then, as contestation continues over the re-presentation of the struggles.

All this points to ways of reading the recurring violence against Christian images (the crucifix, images of Christ, the Virgin, etc.) often attributed to Judeoconversos and Afroiberians. The same goes for the range of magical acts wielded by slaves and downtrodden minorities against their masters. We saw such behaviors in our two narratives. These acts seem difficult to believe for moderns, who are inclined to take all this supernatural stuff less than seriously. In a recent study of Purim and Jewish violence, Elliott Horowitz offers the first extended scholarly treatment of recorded Judeoconversos violence against Christian icons.[404] Such alleged violence, at one and the same time physical and semiotic, may be part of a larger issue. For one thing, given the intertwining of body and spirit in the pre-modern world, physical violence constituted a legitimate avenue for problem-solving in the judiciary and religious systems. Discussing the matter of the treatment of Amerindians, Anthony Pagden points out that most of the *encomenderos* in the New World "had come from a stratum of society where violence was endemic, and where religious beliefs frequently assumed highly unorthodox forms in which outbursts of frustration might easily express themselves by physical attacks on holy images."[405]

In a world highly determined by religious matters, encompassing much of what today would fall under politics, seemingly minor differences could take on disproportional symbolic importance. Readers need only recall the intense physical violence wreaked in Europe by Protestants against Catholic churches, their statuary and imagery, or "idols," in particular.[406] Calvinists effected similar destruction in Pernambuco after they conquered it from the Catholic Portuguese/Brazilians in the early seventeenth century. In the Iberian orbit, William Monter notes that "[o]utrages to the crucifix were often alleged against Jews, but [were] more often practiced by Moriscos."[407] Playing out their own issues regarding gender and femininity through a ritual semiotics, a number of the *ilusas* or *alumbradas* in colonial Mexico were accused of desecrating "religious sites and symbols — altars, hosts, and crucifixes — with sexual acts."[408] Among enslaved Afroiberians, the semiotics of ritual went from the suffering caused by slavery, a beating by a master for instance, to a pointed renunciation of the master's religion; in other words, it became a denunciation, a challenge, an undoing of the discourse that insisted on such injustice as part of the logic of its own maintenance. In many cases, similar and sometimes even the exact same kind of charges are made against Afroiberians as Crypto-Jews: denying Christ or the power of the priests, desecrating the host, mocking, abusing and even destroying sacred images.[409] Around 1608, two Mexican Mulatos who "kept company with Indians" and had spent time in an isolated region that served as a destination for runaway slaves were "accused of removing from a church sacred images that they then spit on and stepped on."[410]

For accused Afroiberians and Crypto-Jews, it is fair to ask whether their actions were misunderstood. For instance, Afroiberians may not have intended mockery or attack on Catholic icons but merely to Africanize them for the sake of their own spiritual lives. At the same time, it is clear that minorities and dominated groups, while politically dependent, were not necessarily timid about self-expression. With some colorful examples, Horowitz shows the frequency and unselfconsciousness of early modern Jewish responses to (perceived) Christian domination, responses that were often physical and violent.[411]

Horowitz is misleading, however, in characterizing violence against Christian icons as "part and parcel of what [Cecil] Roth memorably described as 'the religion of the Marranos.' "[412] For one thing, Roth takes a particularly romantic and maximalist stance regarding Judeoconverso/Marrano religiosity, one that lends it far more coherence than might be warranted. For Horowitz to quote Roth here betrays a desire to establish a persistent and homogeneous tradition of violence.[413] There is no such thing as "*the* religion of the Marranos," but rather numerous variants produced by individual families, groups of individuals, and even isolated individuals. Some Judeoconversos may have seen fit to act out their well-earned hostility toward the Catholicism imposed on them by twisting the mandated adoration of crucifixes and other icons into its opposite, a psycho-theologically mandated denigration. Many other Judeo-conversos, most of them in fact, were never accused of such behavior. Horowitz cites Gitlitz, who reasons that since allegations of violence against Christian icons were so widespread and often based on firsthand reports, they must have had some truth to them.[414] This logic does not hold up and returns us to the crux of the hermeneutic conundrum of the Inquisitions. A *priori* acceptance of accusations because of their ubiquity cannot be sustained as a rule. Blood libels against Jews were also a widespread allegation, but this does not mean that they were true. Gil Anidjar argues convincingly that late medieval accusations of desecration of the host by Jews had more to do with Christian fixations on the blood of Christ and projection onto the Jewish Other.[415] As Catherine Gallagher and Stephen Greenblatt note: "For a Jew to attack the Host seems strange, since there would appear to be no reason to attack something you believe to be a mere piece of bread."[416] It is possible that the anti-Christian violence reported to the Inquisitions and "documented" by them reflects a kind of collective wish-fulfilment. Again, Gallagher and Greenblatt: "The Jews are inevitably guilty in such stories because they do not believe and because at the same time they are made to act out, to embody, the doubt aroused among the Christian faithful by eucharistic doctrine."[417]

This is not to suggest that the extremity and perversity of oppression from above could not have generated such subaltern anti-establishment hostility. Subversive intent and refashioning are not hard to see, for in whipping crucifixes or similar acts, the individual may have been refashioning the intense, inner, emotional life that monastic Catholicism insisted on into anti-normative ritualized emotional behavior. Another plausible Christian source for the practices in question can be found in the medieval monastic practice of ritual humiliation of saints' relics as part of prayers to God for help against an enemy (known as a "clamour"). This inversion ritual included placing relics and a crucifix on the floor on a hair shirt, thus in some sense punishing the relics/saints for not having done their duty as intercessors. In the hands of laypeople imitating the monkish rite, the clamour included actual striking of the altar supporting the relics.[418] These scenarios offer mental circumstances remarkably similar to the incidents involving Judeoconversos and other aggrieved subalterns.

My insistence on maintaining the possibility that such violence happened but was also imagined/projected stems from a desire to uphold the cogency of both logics. The violence of the dominators produced violent reactions as well as the imagination/projection of violent reactions. Both occurred; subaltern violence was real at times and also absent at times yet projected.

Recent scholarship of Amerindian and Afroamerican responses to colonization recognize the post-traumatic symptoms manifested in these societies and cultures over the course of the following centuries. The emotional and psychic consequences of slavery for Afroamericans has long been a staple of scholarship. There is a tendency in scholarship regarding Judeoconversos to treat only the religious ramifications of the group's similar but peculiar post-traumatic situation. Hardly alone in this, Norman Simms is right to highlight the individual and familial pathologies to emerge as a consequence of the continued non-integration of personality and culture forced onto devoted Crypto-Jews and even frequently onto religiously disinterested New Christians.[419] Given Crypto-Jews' situation, it is noteworthy that compensatory anti-Black racism, an easy place to channel displaced anger, was not more evident (as is true of the relative lack of anti-Jewish or anti-Judeoconverso prejudice among Afroiberians), just as the frequency of melting into a quiet

Catholic life is noteworthy.

When Afroiberians denounced their masters or others as alleged judaizers, they played on the empire's theo-politics, whether they shared it or were just manipulating it to their advantage. Other utterances seem to reflect a world view less specifically religious if at all. When Juan de León/Salomón Machorro laments that colonial Blacks receive better treatment than "honorable" men, we must ask whether he is referring to New Christians or Whites in general.[420] Even if the former, whether this is a statement of ethnocentrism that is "secular" or "religious" may depend on a variety of factors. The distinction may not be particularly important, given the ways religious and secular discourse overlapped in what Kathryn Burns calls a "spiritual economy."[421]

Both Catholicism and Judaism sought a "maximalist" unity, where "there could be no radical disjunction between outer behavior and inner motive, between social rituals and individual sentiments, between activities that are expressive and those that are technical."[422] In distinct opposition, those Judeoconversos and Afroiberians who resisted their own Christianization all to some degree made a virtue of necessity, that is, made the modalities that were necessary for their survival into new virtues — splitting their subjectivity into inner and outer; refashioning the symbols of the dominators into usable symbols for themselves, the dominated; foregrounding elements of their religious culture that aided, encouraged and glorified the avoidance, subversion or even destruction of "false" Catholicism. One prominent Converso tack comprised a subjectivization or relativization of truth claims. Spinoza expresses this possibility of overturning the purportedly natural modalities of domination when he declares goodness to flow from subject position rather than the other way around: "We neither strive for, nor will, nor want, nor desire anything because we judge it to be good; on the contrary, we judge something to be good because we strive for it, will it, want it, and desire it."[423] Spinoza's proposition relativizes belief on both subjective and institutional levels, as was done by numerous Judeoconversos, Afroiberians and others. Following this precept means that no one religious system, no matter how dominant or imposed on people, can claim absolute truth.

Spinoza's allegedly Judeoconversos relativism reminds us, however, not to mistakenly think that all pre-modern individuals lived exclusively by or in religious discourse and practice; or, alternatively, religious discourse and practice by no means prevented cognition and experience of the world that today we would distinguish as secular. What is, I think, remarkable about many of the individuals who appear in the preceding pages is the lucidity of their understanding of their situation from the perspective of what today we would call sociology or politics. Perhaps this lucidity stems from the improvisational skills developed by so many Judeoconversos and Afroiberians in order to survive the very mobility foisted upon them by the incipient modernity of the European empires: "the ability both to capitalize on the unforeseen and to transform given materials into one's own scenario."[424] Perhaps most importantly, their capacity for mutation, for self-metamorphosis — into pretend faithful Catholics, into pretend well-behaved slaves, into pretend Whites — carried with it the threat of the kind of difference and distance that could transform into satanic opposition yet was also a sign that such rebellion had already transpired.[425]

Tying up Toxic Loose Ends

What at first glance appears to be a distant and obscure history of the seventeenth century turns out to persist into the present. Standing as a near constant is the tension between two competing visions: the homogeneity of collectives and their internal non-coherence. Can an identity — singular, the same as itself — be multiple, that is, many and different from each other? The many scholars of Jewish matters since the nineteenth century who have mentioned Afroiberian judaizers, treat them as little more than something exotic, that is, aberrant and, therefore, insignificant, on the one hand, or use them to signify the obvious attractions of Judaism even in the bowels of Christendom particularly to those who have "nothing." Many scholars of the African diaspora have been too busy focusing on the supposedly exclusive victimization of Afroiberians to recognize Afroiberian religious collusion as Catholics against those seen as Jews.[426] Both groups of scholars fail to remind us that there is no "disposition" for members of a group to respond to their group's persecution or oppression in a given manner.[427] Yirmiyahu Yovel uses studies of Judeoconversos to explain the philosophy of Spinoza. Yovel's thesis imagines that Judeoconversos display "a this-worldly disposition; a split religious identity; a metaphysical skepticism; a quest for alternative salvation through methods that oppose the official doctrine; an opposition between the inner and outer life, and a tendency toward dual language and equivocation."[428] Historically, given the hermeneutical and epistemological difficulties of dealing with Inquisition records and the extreme situations that produced the Converso problem, I believe Yovel's thesis is simply inaccurate, as new historical studies make increasingly clear. On another level, the danger of such theses lies in the ease with which they become generalized into essentialist understandings about the group under discussion. Many Judeoconversos evince none or few of the above characteristics, while many non-Judeoconversos of the era, New Christian or otherwise, do manifest them. Similarly, Afroiberians showed a wide range of reactions to their captivity, mistreatment and exclusion.

Irene Silverblatt sees the rise of "race thinking, nationalist sentiments, bureaucratic rule, colonialism — and the nascent capitalist order girding them" in the sixteenth- and seventeenth-century Spanish empire.[429] I fully agree, though I would include Portugal. Yet the truth of this does not mean that subaltern populations and their individual members did not also collude, wittingly or not, in the perpetuation and manipulation of prejudices, as I hope to have shown. Indeed, some dominated groups willingly allied with dominating groups against other dominated groups, some members of every dominated group willingly aided, served or joined the forces of domination, either on specific occasions or for life.[430] Bourdieu comments on this perhaps disappointing propensity:

> The deadly passions of all racisms (of ethnicity, sex or class) perpetuate themselves because they are bound to the body in the form of dispositions and also because the relation of domination of which they are the product perpetuates itself in objectivity, continuously reinforcing the propensity to accept it, which, except in the case of a critical break (that performed by the "reactive" nationalism of dominated peoples, for example), is no less strong among the dominated than the dominant.[431]

Characterizing "Black-Jewish" relations in the seventeenth century, therefore, almost inevitably retrojects today's socioeconomic and political tensions. Yet, despite some significant and vast differences between the two eras and situations, it is hard not to recognize similarities. As two groups of intermediaries or go-betweens that served vastly different purposes for the empires, Judeoconversos and Afroiberians stood very much in conflict, often quite direct, with one another. Added to this was a very real religious and theopolitical divergence. Nonetheless, it is difficult to detect much, if any, particular animus between members of the two groups.

Analysis must be able to free itself from structuralist binarisms, attentive to the different modes in which power circulates from above to below, from bottom against top, attentive to the multiplicity, partial awareness and even uncertainty that might characterize personal motivation, self-consciousness and self-justification.[432] Discussing "the *range* of experiences of indigenous women in [colonial] Potosí," Jane Mangan highlights how one finds women "who suffer, manage, and thrive," and she insists that the object of her inquiry can be understood "only by treating this complexity."[433] Walter Mignolo has proposed approaching colonial situations with diatopical or pluritopical perspectives.[434] Pointing with condemnation at "empire" and harping on "asymmetries of power" erects the dominators and their instruments as metaphysical principles, totalizing and incontestable. It erases through negativity the agency and efficacy of those who resist or oppose from below or from within, and seemingly seeks to absolve resisters and opponents from moral standing. On the one hand, even if, as Michel Foucault and others have argued, power circulates diffusely, this does not mean that its local forcefulness and effectiveness cannot be measured and described. Agency and responsibility continue to exist even where power is curtailed. The agency of those "under" power's sway and the circulation of power do not make up a zero-sum game. This is the tension laid out by Talal Asad between history from the perspective of the dominant power and the "active" subaltern history favored by anthropologists.⁴³⁵ It would seem self-evident that neither pole can exist in isolation. Asad himself concludes with a query: "People are never only active agents and subjects in their own history. The interesting question in each case is: In what degree, and in what way, are they agents or patients?"⁴³⁶

On the level of hermeneutics, many scholars continue to operate as if there must be a single explanation for historical events, as if one must choose between ideological or materialist readings. Here too, I would suggest, mutual exclusivity should not hover like a specter. Some acts of violence might be acts of resistance, while some might be efforts to improve the life of the actor. Some might be neither. Some might be both. Judeoconversos or Afroiberians might well have been torn between both of these motivations as well as others, such as romance, hatred, jealousy or unpremeditated impulse. The same multiplicity holds even for explanations of group behavior or complex phenomena such as colonization, racism or resistance to domination. Generalizations should make us wary however well-intentioned or rationalized as necessary for the production of "digestible" historiography.

One modern scholar, introducing a new translation of a seventeenth-century Spanish chronicle about the discovery and conquest of Nueva Granada, concludes that "all history, at bottom, is a study in human nature."⁴³⁷ If by "human nature" we mean something both cultural and natural, both constructed and real, something meaningless enough to extend to any number of conditions/situations yet meaningful enough that most of us use the term on occasion, then I might well agree. This human nature operates within a real world whose parameters are concretely given. The heterogeneity of individuals and groups does not result in a simple symmetry of equal and equally free players. Rather, the variety of forces and claims need to be deconstructed with their origins, vectors and effects in mind. We are more in-between than we imagine.

Final Thoughts

> If I press my nose to someone's window, it isn't to see everything in his house. There is much that would not satisfy my curiosity enough to repay the effort. The privacy I want to invade is that which allows me to learn the denouement of some story about which I have my own psychological urgency, and for which I lack an ending.
> — Janna Malamud Smith, *Private Matters*

I confess to having been significantly influenced by scholars, particularly feminists, who meditate on the meanings of anger in scholarship and wonder what the scholar who feels it is to do with it.[438] Studying seventeenth-century Judeoconversos and Afroiberians inevitably leads to anger over the ubiquitous instances and systemic use of denigration, mistreatment, cruelty and homicidal violence again Others. (It can be asked to what degree a lack of responsive anger or its dismissal signifies a desire for histories "purified" of "our" own transgressions.) Yet looking mostly for historical examples of resistance to domination, to oppression that will mirror the scholar's own tendencies, often leads to romanticization and a blindness to the ways in which subalterns willingly acquiesce and submit to the systems in which they find themselves. I have tried to overcome this blindness, to intentionally face it, while not forgetting the very real power of the dominators, of the empire-builders, and the abuses to which their power leads.

Early modern Iberian political and religious triumph and expansion brought about its own tarnishing: immense wealth that barely improved the lives of most citizens if at all; a "pathological fear of uncleanness — of pollution by secret Judaizers, but also of Protestant 'heretics,' 'demoniac witches,' and sexual 'perverts' — underlay almost everything in Spanish life"; a rampant and justified paranoia regarding denunciation by others for the slightest deviation, real or imagined, and a concomitant internal paranoia concerning whether one was deviating from the norms oneself; a fetishistic obsession with reputation, honor, glory, that is, with how one was seen by others.[439] The seemingly society-wide depths of projection of problems onto Others, of endless, obsessive-compulsive self-scrutiny, of willful obfuscation and denial stand in ironic proportional contrast to the very heights of victory, conquest, domination achieved by Spain and Portugal, achievements which should have brought about mostly security, confidence and satiety but did not.

– Notes –

Preface

1. www.blacksandjews.com. The now dated site is/was possibly affiliated with but certainly adulates Louis Farrakhan and the Nation of Islam. It is anti-Jewish because it goes beyond justifiable critical appraisals of Jewish involvement in slave trading and Jewish participation in colonial domination over and control of Black populations to indulge in unjustifiable attacks — on Jews as almost innate capitalists and anti-Black racists, on Zionism and Israel — and extreme partisan apologetics, such as denying that Muslims had anything to do with the bombings of 11 September 2001.

Introduction

2. This perspective may have been expressed first in writing by Benedict (alias Baruch) Spinoza, in his *Theologico-Political Treatise*, trans. Martin D. Yaffe (Newburyport, MA: Focus, 2004), 64.
3. Studies of the Jews of medieval Sepharad — a biblical toponym retroactively applied to Spain — are too numerous to mention. Also too many to list are treatments of the experience of the New Christians or Judeoconversos, of whom Crypto-Jews comprise a subset, which inevitably intertwines with the story of the Sephardic communities beyond Iberian lands with which Conversos had family and commercial relations and into which many later reintegrated; some recent and classic surveys include: Renée Levine Melammed, *A Question of Identity: Iberian Conversos in Historical Perspective* (New York: Oxford University Press, 2004); Pier Cesare Ioly Zorattini, *L'identità dissimulata: giudaizzanti iberici nell'Europa cristiana dell'eta moderna* (Firenze: L.S. Olschki, 2000); David M. Gitlitz, *Secrecy and Deceit: The Religion of the Crypto-Jews* (Philadelphia: Jewish Publication Society, 1996); Norman Roth, *Conversos, Inquisition, and the Expulsion of the Jews from Spain* (Madison: University of Wisconsin Press, 1995); José Faur, *In the Shadow of History: Jews and Conversos at the Dawn of Modernity* (Albany: State University of New York Press, 1992); Haim Beinart (ed.), *Moreshet Sepharad: the Sephardi Legacy*, 2 vols. (Jerusalem: Magnes Press/Hebrew University, 1992); Julio Caro Baroja, *Los judíos en la España moderna y contemporánea*, 3 vols. (Madrid: Istmo, 1986); Antonio Dominguez Ortiz, *Los judeoconversos en España y América* (Madrid: Istmo, 1971); B. Netanyahu, *The Marranos of Spain: From the Late 14th to the Early 16th Century According to Contemporary*

Hebrew Sources (New York: American Academy for Jewish Research, 1966); João Lúcio de Azevedo, *História dos cristãos novos portugueses* (Lisbon: Clássica Editora, 1921).

4. Among many other sources: the economic essays in Richard L. Kagan and Philip D. Morgan (eds.), *Atlantic Diasporas: Jews, Conversos, and Crypto-Jews in the Age of Mercantilism, 1500-1800* (Baltimore: Johns Hopkins University Press, 2009); Daviken Studnicki-Gizbert, *A Nation upon the Ocean Sea: Portugal's Atlantic Diaspora and the Crisis of the Spanish Empire, 1492-1640* (New York: Oxford University Press, 2007); *Familia, religión y negocio: El sefardismo en las relaciones entre el mundo ibérico y los Países Bajos en la edad moderna*, ed. Jaime Contreras, Bernardo J. García García, and Ignacio Pulido (Madrid: Fundación Carlos de Amberes/Ministerio de Asuntos Exteriores, 2002); several essays in *The Jews and the Expansion of Europe to the West, 1450-1800*, ed. Paolo Bernardini and Norman Fiering, European Expansion & Global Interaction, Vol. 2 (New York: Berghahn Books, 2001); Daniel M. Swetschinski, *Reluctant Cosmopolitans: The Portuguese Jews of Seventeenth-Century Amsterdam* (London: Littman Library of Jewish Civilization, 2000), 102-64; Jonathan I. Israel, *Diasporas Within a Diaspora: Jews, Crypto-Jews and the World Maritime Empires (1540-1740)*, Brill's Series in Jewish Studies, 30 (Leiden: Brill, 2002); idem, *European Jewry in the Age of Mercantilism, 1550-1750*, 3rd ed. (London: Littman Library of Jewish Civilization, 1998); José Alberto Rodrigues da Silva Tavim, *Os judeus na expansão portuguesa em Marrocos durante o século XVI: Origens e actividades duma comunidade* (Braga: Edições APPACDM Distrital de Braga, 1997), 253-374; Stephen Alexander Fortune, *Merchants and Jews: the Struggle for British West Indian Commerce, 1650-1750* (Gainesville: Center for Latin American Studies/University of Florida Press, 1984); Gedalia Yogev, *Diamonds and Coral: Anglo-Dutch Jews and Eighteenth-Century Trade* (New York: Holmes and Meier Publishers, 1978).

5. Albert Memmi, *The Colonizer and the Colonized* (Boston: Beacon Press, 1967 [1957]); Jonathan Boyarin, *Storm from Paradise: the Politics of Jewish Memory* (Minneapolis: University of Minnesota Press, 1992). The same is true for the first African slaves used by the Spanish in the Americas. Writing in the historical mode of recuperation of the 1960s, James Lockhart cites their contributions: "[t]hey were an organic part of the enterprise of occupying Peru from its inception," Blacks "were for the main part the Spaniards' willing allies... And this willingness is understandable. Though Negroes were subordinated to Spaniards, they were not exploited in the plantation manner; except for mining gangs, Negroes in Peru counted as individuals." Lockhart's assessment is quoted, in turn, by Herman Bennett, un-self-consciously, as a still under-appreciated facet of the African origins of the western hemisphere (James Lockhart, *Spanish Peru 1532-1560: A Colonial Society* [Madison:

University of Wisconsin Press, 1968]); Bennett, *Africans in Colonial Mexico*, 2, 199-200, n. 9). Using the tactic of ethnic diversity among subaltern populations that goes back at least to Plato, in both New Spain and Perú, Ladino Afroiberians served *encomenderos* as "intermediaries and supervisors over indigenous laborers' (Bennett, *Africans in Colonial Mexico*, 21).

6. Diana Luz Ceballos Gómez, "Grupos sociales y prácticas mágicas en el Nuevo Reino de Granada durante el siglo XVII," *Historia Critica* 22 (Jul.-Dec. 2001): 54-5; Anidjar, "Blood Works."
7. Jonathan Israel, "Menasseh ben Israel and the Dutch Sephardic Colonization Movement of the Mid-Seventeenth Century (1645-1657)," in *Menasseh ben Israel and his World*, ed. Yosef Kaplan, Henry Méchoulan and Richard H. Popkin (Leiden: E.J. Brill, 1989), 146.
8. New Christians were allowed to emigrate to the colonies of Spain and Portugal only in 1601, after "the payment of the enormous bribe of 200,000 ducats to Phillip III, [...] the king promising that [the prohibition on emigration] would never again be enforced. [...] This 'irrevocable' permission was canceled in 1610 [...and again] restored in 1629" (Cecil Roth, *A History of the Marranos*, 4th ed. [New York: Hermon Press, 1974], 197) Oddly enough, before all this, beginning in 1548, "one of the penalties imposed by the tribunals of the mother-country upon convicted but 'penitent' heretics was that of deportation — generally across the Atlantic" (ibid., 283).
9. Gomes Solís, *Memoires*, 12, 16; cited in Israel, *European Jewry*, 57.
10. Salo W. Baron, *A Social and Religious History of the Jews*, 18 vols. (New York/Philadelphia: Columbia University Press/Jewish Publication Society of America, 1952-83), 15:301; Dominguez Ortiz, *Judeoconversos*, 136; Israel, *Diasporas Within a Diaspora*, 135; Green, "Masters of Difference." The prominence of "Jewish" slavers seems to lead Maria Ventura to claim that in old Veracruz, Mexico, "one of the principle destinations of the slaving routes, there existed a river named *Espanta Judios* [Scare off the Jews]" (Ventura, *Negreiros portugueses*, 37). One wonders whether similar considerations led to the naming of the "Jewess' shoal / Baixo da Judia" off of the Cape of Good Hope mentioned in at least one Portuguese shipwreck narrative (Blackmore, *Manifest Perdition*, 45-6). On the other hand, these toponyms could be wielding Jews as either (1) a demonic force whose animating hostility is attached to dangerous nautical passages or (2) as a metaphor for those too cowardly to face a difficult nautical situation.
11. Novinsky, *Cristãos novos na Bahia*, 59.
12. See, among other studies, Alencastro, *Trato dos viventes*, 77-116; Ventura, *Negreiros portugueses*; Vila Vilar, *Hispanoamerica y el comercio de esclavos*.
13. The best treatment remains Seymour Drescher, "Jews and New Christians in the Atlantic Slave Trade," in Bernardini and Fiering, *Jews and the Expansion of Europe to the West*, 439-70.

14. Gwendolyn Midlo Hall, *Slavery and African Ethnicities in the Americas: Restoring the Links* (Chapel Hill: University of North Carolina Press, 2005), 20.
15. David G. Sweet, "Black Robes and 'Black Destiny': Jesuit Views of African Slavery in 17th-Century Latin America," *Revista de Historia de America* 86 (July-December 1978): 105-6.
16. Cope, "Limits of Racial Domination," 4; Jack D. Forbes, "Africans and Native Americans: The Language of Race and the Evolution of Red-Black Peoples" (Urbana: University of Illinois Press, 1993), chs. 4 and 8.
17. On the "invention" of the Mulato, see Luiz Felipe de Alencastro, *O trato dos viventes: formacao do Brasil no Atlantico Sul* (São Paulo: Cia das Letras, 2000), 345-53; Martínez López, María Elena, "The Spanish Concept of *Limpieza de Sangre* and the Emergence of the 'Race/Caste' System in the Viceroyalty of New Spain," (PhD Dissertation, University of Chicago, 2002), 211-17 (now María Elena Martínez, *Genealogical Fictions: Limpeza de Sangre, Religion and Gender in Colonial Mexico* [Stanford: Stanford University Press, 2008]); Forbes, *Africans and Native Americans*, chs. 5 and 6.
18. Stuart Hall, "Pluralism, Race and Class in Caribbean Society," in *Race and Class in Post-Colonial Society* (Paris: UNESCO, 1977), 158, 162.
19. Javier Villa-Flores, " 'To Lose One's Soul': Blasphemy and Slavery in New Spain, 1596-1669," *Hispanic American Historical Review* 82,3 (2002): 435-68; Palmer, "Religion and Magic." Palmer, citing Philip Curtin and K. A. Busia, compares the blasphemous oaths uttered by slaves during beatings or mistreatment, with an Ashanti oath meant to prevent bodily harm from others and/or to secure the intervention of the central authority (ibid., 318).
20. Lewis, *Hall of Mirrors*, 32.
21. Iosef Fernandez, Apostólica y penitente vida de el V.P. Pedro Claver, de la compañía de Jesús. Sacada principalmente de informaciones juridicas hechas ante el Ordinario de la Ciudad de Cartagena de Indias. A su religiosísima provincia de el Nuevo Reyno de Granada. Por el padre Iosef Fernandez de la Compañía de Jesús natural de Taraçona (Zaragoça: Diego Dormer, 1666), 222.
22. Bowser, *African Slave in Colonial Peru*, 28; Jonathan I. Israel, *Race, Class and Politics in Colonial Mexico, 1610-1670* (Oxford: Oxford University Press, 1975), 66. Bennett, *Africans in Colonial Mexico*, 49, agrees with Bowser, while Alberro, *Inquisición y sociedad en México*, 26, calls Africans neophytes.
23. David Eltis, "Identity and Migration: The Atlantic in Comparative Perspective," in *The Atlantic World: Essays on Slavery, Migration, and Imagination*, eds. Wim Klooster and Alfred Padula (Upper Saddle River, NJ: Pearson/Prentice Hall, 2005), 111.
24. Gil Anidjar, "Blood Works: The Fluidity of the Bio-Political c. 1449," paper, conference on Cultural Mobility, Wissenschaftskolleg, Berlin, May 2004, 11; idem, "Lines of Blood: *Limpieza de Sangre* as Political Theology," in *Blood in*

History and Blood Histories, ed. Mariacarla Gadebusch Bondio (Firenze: Sismel Edizioni il Galluzzo, 2005).
25. María Elena Martínez, *Genealogical Fictions: Limpieza de Sangre, Religion and Gender in Colonial Mexico* (Stanford: Stanford University Press, 2008).
26. Latour, *We Have Never Been Modern*, 40.
27. Latour, *We Have Never Been Modern*, 40. And not, therefore, a "phantasm," as Silverblatt has it (*Modern Inquisitions*, 18). Without wanting to enter into an enormous and dangerous topic, my perspective is that race/ethnicity is real, i.e., "natural," insofar as different population groups often manifest different biological conditions: immunities to particular diseases or lack thereof, manifest specific patterns of disease (lactose intolerance, Sickle Cell Anemia, Tay-Sachs disease, etc.). Different population groups might also manifest statistically notable somatic uniquenesses: eye shape, particularly light skin, height, etc. The problem — racism — arises from, itself entails a socio-cultural response to such axiologically meaningless natural differences.
28. Jorge Cañizares-Esguerra, *Puritan Conquistadors: Iberianizing the Atlantic, 1550-1700* (Stanford: Stanford University Press, 2006).
29. Judaizing refers to the teaching or promulgating of Jewish beliefs and/or practices, and thus carried a heavier penalty than merely maintaining such practices oneself.

The Inquisition: The Clash of Two Surgeons and a Slave

30. Descripción del Peru, 121; for an English translation of the text, see "Anonymous Description of Peru (1600-1615)," in Irving A. Leonard (ed.), *Colonial Travelers in Latin America* (New York: Alfred A. Knopf, 1972), 97-117.
31. Antonio Vázquez de Espinosa, *Compendio y descripción de las islas occidentales* [1629], the original manuscript transcribed by Charles Upson Clark, Smithsonian miscellaneous collections, 108 (Washington, D.C.: Smithsonian Institution, 1948), 220.
32. Descripción del Peru, 121-2.
33. C. R. Boxer, *The Portuguese Seaborne Empire, 1415-1825* (London: Hutchinson, 1969), 337; Gonzalo Aguirre Beltrán, *La población negra de México: Estudio etnohistórico* (Mexico City: Fondo de Cultura Económica, 1989), 45-6.
34. On the slave trade and economy in Spanish South America, see Herbert S. Klein and Ben Vinson, *African Slavery in Latin America and the Caribbean*, 2nd ed. (New York: Oxford University Press, 2007); Bowser, *The African Slave in Colonial Peru*; Leslie Rout, *The African Experience in Spanish America, 1502-present* (New York: Columbia University Press, 1976); Rolando Mellafe, *La*

introducción de la esclavitud negra en Chile: Trafico y rutas (Santiago de Chile: Universidad de Chile, 1959); Maya Restrepo, *Brujería*, 64-213.
35. Descripción del Peru, 122.
36. Walter Rodney, "Portuguese Attempts at Monopoly on the Upper Guinea Coast, 1580-1650," *Journal of African History* 6 (1965): 309; cited in Philip D. Curtin, *The Atlantic Slave Trade: A Census* (Madison: University of Wisconsin Press, 1969), 108.
37. Cited in Ventura, *Portuguese no Peru*, 1:57.
38. Iosef Fernandez, Apostolica y penitente vida de el V.P. Pedro Claver, de la compañia de Iesus. Sacada principalmente de informaciones juridicas hechas ante el Ordinario de la Ciudad de Cartagena de Indias. A su religiosisima provincia de el Nuevo Reyno de Granada. Por el padre Iosef Fernandez de la Compañia de Iesus natural de Taraçona (Zaragoça: Diego Dormer, 1666), 105.
39. Quoted in Medina, *Inquisición de Cartagena*, 139.
40. Translated by H. P. Salomon, "The Portuguese Background of Menasseh Ben Israel's Parents as Revealed through the Inquisitorial Archives at Lisbon," *Studia Rosenthaliana* 17,2 (July 1983), 113.
41. Enriqueta Vila Vilar, "Extranjeros en Cartagena (1593-1630," *Jahrbuch für Geschichte von Staat, Wirtschaft und Gesellschaft Lateinamerikas* (Koln Wein, 1979): 155, 175-76. The most comprehensive analysis of the Portuguese presence in the adjacent and perhaps most prosperous Spanish colony is Ventura, *Portugueses no Peru*.
42. The quote is from Ceballos Gómez, *Hechicería, brujería, e inquisición*, 141.
43. A list of foreigners in Cartagena, compiled in 1630, calls him forty years old (reprinted in Ventura, *Portugueses no Peru*, 3:40). The list, *Relación y abecedário de los estrangeros que se hallan en la ciudad de Cartagena...*, is reprinted in ibid., 3:31-77.
44. Letter to Manuel Bautista Perez from Simon Dias Pinto, 17 April 1634, AGN Peru, Inq., Leg. 34, fol. 173r.
45. Studnicki-Gizbert, *Nation Upon the Sea*, 57.
46. Ventura, *Portugueses no Peru*, 1:171, 208, 400-1. Bautista Peres and Duarte established their firm in Lima in 1627 (ibid., 1:287). Further details on Bautista Peres and his trade network, including Pinto, can be found in Linda A. Newson and Susie Minchin, *From Capture to Sale: The Portuguese Slave Trade to Spanish South America in the Early Seventeenth Century* (Leiden: Brill, 2007).
47. Ventura, *Portugueses no Peru*, 1:296.
48. I ic Croitoru Rotbaum, Documentos coloniales originados en el santo oficio del tribunal de la inquisición de Cartagena de Indias (Contribución a la historia de Colombia [vol. 2]) (Bogota: Tipografia Hispana, 1971), after p. 136.
49. Ventura, *Portugueses no Peru*, 3:41.

50. Ventura, *Portugueses no Peru*, 1:337, 401-2.
51. According to Spanish legislation of the colonies, Portuguese were considered foreigners (Lewis Hanke, "The Portuguese in Spanish America with Special Reference to the Villa Imperial de Potosí," *Revista de Historia de América* 51 (June 1961), 10 n. 34).
52. Álvarez Alonso, *Inquisición de Cartagena*, 118-9.
53. AHN Inq. 1021, fols. 1-4v., Relación del auto de fe que los señores inquisidores licenciado Don Martín de Cortázar y Azcárate y Doctor Damián Velázquez de Contreras, celebraron a 25 del mes de Marzo de 38 años, a honra y gloria de Dios y exaltación de la fe católica y extirpación de las herejías, en la ciudad de Cartagena de las Indias; reprinted in Anna-María Splendiani, Cincuenta Años de Inquisición en el Tribunal de Cartagena de las Indias, 1610-60, 4 vols. (Bogotá, 1997), 3:39.
54. The Cartagena tribunal's summary of the charges against Pinto appear in the *Relación de la causas de fé* from 1636; AHN Inq. 1020, fols. 503r.-507v.; reprinted in Splendiani, *Tribunal de Cartagena*, 2:438-43.
55. AHN Inq. 1020, fol. 504r.; Splendiani, *Tribunal de Cartagena*, 2:439.
56. AHN Inq. 1020, fol. 504r.; Splendiani, *Tribunal de Cartagena*, 2:439.
57. AHN Inq. 1021, fol. 28r.-v., Relación de las causas de fe del santo oficio de la inquisición de Cartagena, que este año de mil y seiscientos y treinta y ocho remite a su alteza el licenciado Juan Ortiz, fiscal de dicha inquisición, reprinted in Splendiani, Tribunal de Cartagena, 3:63-4.
58. AHN Inq. 1021, fol. 32v., Relación de las causas de la fe; Splendiani, Tribunal de Cartagena, 3:68.
59. The text pertaining to Judaism is reprinted in Medina, *Inquisición de Cartagena*, 52-5.
60. AHN Inq. 1020, fol. 504r.; Splendiani, *Tribunal de Cartagena*, 2:439.
61. AHN Inq. 1620/18, fol. 265-67; reprinted in Croitoru Rotbaum, *De Sefarad*, 283.
62. Croitoru Rotbaum, *De Sefarad*, 283.
63. AHN Inq. 1620/15; reprinted in Croitoru Rotbaum, *De Sefarad*, 308-12.
64. AHN Inq. 1020, fol. 503v.; Splendiani, *Tribunal de Cartagena*, 2:439.
65. Green, "Masters of Difference," 219, citing AHN, Inquisición, Legajo 1608, Expediente 24, folio 25v: "...*alavo a Dios para server a VM*..." and see Green's notes for the other examples of the expression.
66. AHN Inq. 1620, fol. 505r.; Splendiani, *Tribunal de Cartagena*, 2:440.
67. AHN Inq. 1620, fol. 505v.; Splendiani, *Tribunal de Cartagena*, 2:441. The time of the torture session appears on fol. 506r.
68. AHN Inq. 1620, fol. 505v.; Splendiani, *Tribunal de Cartagena*, 2:441. The weekday fasts of Crypto-Jews comprised a rather flexible system, some fasting on Tuesdays and Thursdays, some one day a week, others any day(s) they chose (see Gitlitz, *Secrecy and Deceit*, 396-7).

69. AHN Inq. 1620, fols. 505v.-506r.; Splendiani, *Tribunal de Cartagena*, 2:441.
70. See, for instance, AHN Inq. 1021, fols. 1-48r., reprinted in Splendiani, *Tribunal de Cartagena*, 3:39-85.
71. Jairo Solano Alonso, *Salud, cultura y sociedad: Cartagena de Indias, siglos XVI y XVII* (Bogota: Fondo de Publicaciones de la Universidad del Atlántico/ Colección de Ciencias Sociales Rodrigo Noguera Barreneche, 1998), 71, 75-6.
72. Concerning Santiago de Guatemala, see Herrera, *Natives, Europeans, and Africans*, 90.
73. Ceballos Gómez, *Hechicería, brujería, e inquisición*, 70. The author does not describe the nature of her sources.
74. Solano Alonso, Salud, cultura y sociedad en Cartagena, 103-15, 119-231; Ceballos Gómez, Hechicería, brujería, e inquisición, 71.
75. *Testimonio de Diego López*, AHN Inq. 1620/7/1, fols. 1-3r. All reproduced in Tejado Fernandez, *Vida social en Cartagena*, 307-23 (Appendix 3, "Testimonio de las confesiones del mulato Diego Lopez").
76. A full treatment of Eguiluz, born on the island of Santo Domingo to a Biafran mother, and her circle is offered by Maya Restrepo, *Brujería*, 599-615, 623-5, 629, 647-9, 704.
77. Maya Restrepo, *Brujería*, 590-4.
78. *Testimonio de Diego Lopez*, AHN Inq. 1620/7/1, fols. 3v.
79. *Testimonio de Diego Lopez*, AHN Inq. 1620/7/1, fols. 32v-33r.
80. *Testimonio de Diego López*, AHN Inq. leg. 1620/7/1, fol. 51.
81. *Testimonio de Diego Lopez*, AHN Inq. 1620/7/1, fols. 13v.-14r.; quoted in Tejado Fernandez, *Vida Social en Cartagena*, 316.
82. On "knowing other people's lives" in the inquisitional context, see Joseph H. Silverman, "On Knowing Other People's Lives, Inquisitorially and Artistically," in Mary Elizabeth Perry and Anne J. Cruz (eds.), *Cultural Encounters: the Impact of the Inquisition in Spain and the New World* (Berkeley: University of California Press, 1991), 157-75.
83. *Testimonio de Diego Lopez*, AHN Inq. 1620/7/1, fols. 14r., 17v.; quoted in Tejado Fernandez, *Vida social en Cartagena*, 316, 319-20.
84. Ceballo Gómez, "Grupos sociales y prácticas mágicas," 54.
85. Sánchez, seeing what López is doing, and knowing "that the accused [López] was a friend of the said Blas de Paz, asked him if he came to speak with his friend."
86. *Testimonio de Diego Lopez*, AHN Inq. 1620/7/1, fols. 17v.-18r.; quoted in Tejado Fernandez, *Vida social en Cartagena*, 320.
87. *Testimonio de Diego Lopez*, AHN Inq. 1620/7/1, fols. 16v.-17r.; cited in Tejado Fernandez, *Vida social en Cartagena*, 318-9.
88. AHN Inq. 1021, fol. 3r.-v., *Relación del auto*; Splendiani, *Tribunal de Cartagena*, 3:39.

89. Daviken Studnicki-Gizbert, "*La Nación* among the Nations: Portuguese and Other Maritime Trading Diasporas in the Atlantic, Sixteenth to Eighteenth Centuries," in Richard L. Kagan and Philip D. Morgan (eds.), *Atlantic Diasporas: Jews, Conversos, and Crypto-Jews in the Age of Mercantilism, 1500-1800* (Baltimore: Johns Hopkins University Press, 2009), 88-90.
90. Willis Johnson, "The Myth of Jewish Male Menses," *Journal of Medieval History* 24 (1998): 273-95; John L. Beusterien, "Jewish Male Menstruation in Seventeenth-Century Spain," *Bulletin of the History of Medicine* 73,3 (1999) 447-56; Sander L. Gilman, *Jewish Self-Hatred: Anti-Semitism and the Hidden Language of the Jews* (Baltimore: Johns Hopkins University Press, 1986), 64-5. Elliott Horowitz cites Irvin Resnick to argue that the myth first appeared in the thirteenth-century work of Jacques de Vitry, *Historia orientalis* (Elliott Horowitz, *Reckless Rites: Purim and the Legacy of Jewish Violence* (Princeton: Princeton University Press, 2006), 194). Johnson emphasizes that "medical theorists, from Galen (130-199) to Arnold of Villanova (1240-1311), described menstrual and haemorrhoidal bleeding as interchangeable. This bleeding was part of a natural process in which the body rid itself" of unhealthy humors ("Myth of Male Menses," 288; see also Thomas Laqueur, *Making Sex: Body and Gender from the Greeks to Freud* [Cambridge: Harvard University Press, 1990], 107).
91. Johnson, "Myth of Jewish Male Menses," 275. On the symbolic potency of Judas, see, for example, Othlon de Saint-Emeran (11th cen.): "these things that have been said concerning Judas the traitor extend to the entire Jewish people" (David Nirenberg, *Communities of Violence: Persecution of Minorities in the Middle Ages* [Princeton: Princeton University Press, 1996], 62, n. 79).
92. Johnson, "Myth of Jewish Male Menses," 275.
93. Juan de Quiñones, Memorial de Juan de Quiñones dirigido a Fray Antonio de Sotomayor, inquisidor general, sobre el caso de Francisco de Andrada, sospechoso de pertenecer a la raza judía, discutiendo sobre los medios de conocer y perseguir a ella (Madrid: Biblioteca Nacional, VE, box no. 16, 1632); translated in Georgina Dopico Black, Perfect Wives, Other Women: Adultery and Inquisition in Early Modern Spain (Durham: Duke University Press, 2001), 3; on Quiñones and his tract, see also Yerushalmi, From Spanish Court to Italian Ghetto, 122-33.
94. Toward the end of the fifteenth century, Torquemada had convinced Ferdinand and Isabella to reinstate a 1412 statute forbidding the employment of Jewish physicians. In Mallorca, Conversos had been prohibited from practicing medicine, pharmaceutics or phlebotomy in 1488 (Antonio Contreras Mas, *Los médicos judíos en la Mallorca bajomedieval: Siglos XIV-XV* [Palma de Mallorca: Miquel Font Editor, 1997], 105).
95. *Discurso contra los judíos traducido de lengua portuguesa en castellano por el Padre Fray Diego Gavilán Vela* (Salamanca, 1631); cited in Dopico Black, *Perfect*

Wives, 218, n.2. This text is discussed and excerpted at length in Josette Riandère La Roche, "Du discours d'exclusion des juifs: Antijudaïsme ou antisémitisme?" in *Les problèmes de l'exclusion en Espagne, XVI-XVII siècles*, ed. Agustín Redondo (Paris: Sorbonne, 1983), 51-75. The original Portuguese version is Vicente da Costa Mattos, *Breve discurso contra a heretica perfidia do iudaismo, continuada nos presentes apostatas de nossa sante Fe, com o que conuem a expulsao dos delinquentes nella dos Reynos de sua Magestade, co suas molheres & filhos: conforme a Escriptura sagrada, Santos Padres, Direito Ciuil, & Canonico, & muitos dos politicos* (Lisbon: P. Craesbeeck, 1622); for Jewish menstruation, see 131r-v. The translator to Spanish, Gavilán Vela, was the Bishop of Lugo. According to Yerushalmi, the same accusation later appeared in Francisco de Torrejoncillo, *Centinela contra judíos* (Pamplona, 1691), 174 (*From Spanish Court to Italian Ghetto*, 128). Franco da Piacenza, a Jewish convert to Christianity, included in his 1630 catalogue of "Jewish maladies" the charge that Jewish men and women of the lost tribe of Simeon menstruated four days a year. "In placing the menstruating male Jew in the exotic world of the lost tribes (the New World), he substantiated the charge of Jewish difference while freeing himself from the stigma of difference" (Gilman, *Jewish Self-Hatred*, 75). See also Pedro Aznar Cardona, *Expulsión justificada de los moriscos españoles* (1612), cited in Beusterien, *Jewish Male menstruation*, 451-2. Even the English member of Parliament Edward Spencer used such notions. Arguing that the Jews should only be readmitted to England if they repent for their crucifixion of Christ, he asked rhetorically: "have not all of you a bloody issue about your bodies, [...] and doe not the Italians say, *they smell a Jew before they discerne him with their eyes?*" (Edward Spencer, *A Briefe Epistle to the Learned Manasseh Ben Israel. In Answer to his, Dedicated to the Parliament. September. 6* [London: John Downame, 1650], 10).

96. T. Malvenda, *De Antechristo* (Rome, 1604), 513; quoted in Henry Méchoulan, *El honor de dios: Indios, judíos y moriscos en el siglo de oro* (Barcelona: Editorial Argos Vergara, 1981), 158.
97. David B. Ruderman, "The Community of Converso Physicians: Race, Medicine, and the Shaping of a Cultural Identity," in David B. Ruderman, *Jewish Thought and Scientific Discovery in Early Modern Europe* (New Haven: Yale University Press, 1995), 290; Méchoulan, *Honor de dios*, 138-41. Neither Méchoulan nor Yerushalmi gives the date of Huarta's proposal, though it might stem from his *Problemas filosóficos* (Madrid: Iuan Goncalez, 1628), 12 and following. Physicians from other suspect minorities suffered from growing Iberian intolerance as well. By the late sixteenth century, Morisco physicians were being accused of poisoning and maiming their Old Christian patients, as often had been alleged regarding converso doctors, and there was a growing demand that Moriscos be excluded from medical schools (Stephen Haliczer, *Inquisition and Society in the Kingdom of Valencia, 1478-1834* [Berkeley: University of California Press, 1990], 258).

98. Shlomo ibn Verga, *Shevet Yehuda*, ed. A. Shochat (Jerusalem: Mosad Bialik, 1947 [orig. 1554]), 129; cited in Yosef Hayim Yerushalmi, *Freud's Moses: Judaism Terminable and Interminable* (New Haven: Yale University Press, 1991), 32.
99. AHN Inq. 1020, fol. 503r.; Splendiani, *Tribunal de Cartagena*, 2:438; AHN Inq. 1601/18, fols. 40-43v.; Croitoru Rotbaum, *Documentos*, 231-4.
100. I surmise Rufina's illiteracy from the fact that, according to Diego López, she several times asked him to spy on Paz Pinto for her by trying to determine the book from which the people in the latter's house seemed to be praying, "since you know how to read," i.e., *she* did not (*Testimonio de Diego Lopez*, AHN Inq. 1620/7/1, fol. 19v., see also fol. 20r.).
101. In 1777, the Inquisitors of Cartagena complained that the Edicts of the Faith needed to be copied by hand because the city's only press had been sold by its desperately poor owner (Letter of the Inquisitors José Umeres and Juan Félix de Villegas, 11 October 1777; Medina, *Inquisición de Cartagena*, 378, n.1). Medina's history of printing in Cartagena thus begins only in 1809, without mention of any early modern publishing in the city (J. T. Medina, *La imprenta en cartagena de las indias 1809-1820* [Santiago de Chile: Imprenta Elzeviriana, 1904]).
102. Maya Restrepo, *Brujería*, 602, 612. According to a 1622 letter, consignment to the "general hospital" to serve the patients alongside the Capuchin brothers seems to have been the punishment meted out to four other Afroiberian practitioners of magic, because "nowhere [else] did they want to receive them" (Medina, *Inquisición de Cartagena*, 122).
103. Solano Alonso, Salud, cultura y sociedad en Cartagena, 65-6; Pedro López de León, Pratica y teorica de las apostemas en general y particular. Questiones, y praticas de cirugia, de heridas, llagas, y otras cosas nuevas, y particulares (Sevilla: Luys Estupiñan, 1628). The idea of Jewish male menstruation does not appear in the most oft-used text of surgery, Juan Fragoso, Cirugia universal (Madrid, 1581), reprinted and expanded in several editions.
104. Ceballos Gómez, "Grupos sociales y prácticas mágicas," 55.
105. Ceballo Gómez, *Sociedad y prácticas mágicas*, 465. Maya Restrepo, on the other hand, convincingly argues that Eguiluz was familiar, as were other Black or Mulata Caribbean *brujas*, with the magical recipes and incantations proffered in the Mediterranean/European magical discourse attributed through the centuries in a variety of ever-morphing texts to King Solomon (*Brujería*, 615-38).
106. *Testimonio de Diego Lopez*, AHN Inq. 1620/7/1, fol. 16v.
107. Croitoru Rotbaum, *Documentos*, 232, who reproduces all of the charges against Pinto, 231-234.
108. Ina Johanna Fandrich, *The Mysterious Voodoo Queen, Marie Laveaux: A Study*

of Powerful Female Leadership in Nineteenth-Century New Orleans (New York: Routledge, 2005).
109. Ceballo Gómez, Sociedad y prácticas mágicas, 299.
110. *Testimonio de Diego Lopez*, AHN Inq. 1620/1/7, fol. 15r.
111. *Testimonio de Diego Lopez*, AHN Inq. 1620/1/7, fol. 15r.
112. "[S]iempre dixo la dcha Rufina con admiraçion que si tocaba en esta materia que de Ruina ha de aver" (*Testimonio de Diego Lopez*, AHN Inq. 1620/1/7, fol. 10r.).
113. *Testimonio de Diego López*, AHN Inq. 1620/1/7, fol. 25r.
114. *Testimonio de Diego Lopez*, AHN Inq. 1620/1/7, fol. 22r.-v.
115. *Testimonio de Diego Lopez*, AHN Inq. 1620/1/7, fol. 22r.-v.
116. "y aviendole dho que no le dixo que se baxasse abaxo que no querian estos hombres que nadie viesse sus qtas en dhos libros dando Con esto a entender a este que era Libro donde estaban Armadas quentas Con lo qual aquel dia no se effetuo La Compra de las liquidas que yba a Comporar por el alboroto que se avia Caussado Con el Libro, si bien tubo effecto de alli a un mes sin volver a su cassa" (*Testimonio de Diego Lopez*, AHN Inq. 1620/1/7, fol. 22v.-23r.).
117. *Testimonio de Diego Lopez*, AHN Inq. 1620/1/7, fol. 24v.
118. Ceballos Gómez, Hechicería, brujería, e inquisición, 141-42.
119. Ceballos Gómez, Hechicería, brujería, e inquisición, 131-32, but see the whole section on this episode, 125-54. All of the above motivations came into play with many forms of African magic used by slaves; on the Portuguese world, see Sweet, *Recreating Africa*, 164-88.
120. Ceballos Gómez, Hechicería, brujería, e inquisición, 135.
121. Ceballos Gómez, Hechicería, brujería, e inquisició, 132.
122. Sweet, *Recreating Africa*, 14, 171.
123. *Testimonio de Diego Lopez*, AHN Inq. 1620/1/7, fol. 32v.
124. Silverblatt, "Colonial Conspiracies," 263.
125. Michael Taussig, *Shamanism, Colonialism, and the Wild Man: A Study in Terror and Healing* (Chicago: University of Chicago Press, 1987), 218.
126. Maya Restrepo, *Brujería*, 503-4; on the Portuguese world, see Sweet, *Recreating Africa*, 134-7, 145-59. Maya Restrepo shows, for instance, how Eguiluz utilized ritual gestures, verbal and otherwise, drawn from the Yoruba-influenced traditions surrounding the spirit/diety Exu (*Brujería*, 647-9). White admiration of African spiritual/magical powers was widespread. At the beginning of the eighteenth century, one poor Mexican *castiza* (half White, half Mestizo), Marta de la Encarnación, told an acquaintence that "she had traveled 'in spirit' to a sinful man she knew, 'transformed as if she were a black woman [*negrita*] and told the man the story of his whole life and sins, warning him that he must amend his ways' " (cited in Jaffary, *False Mystics*, 48). This woman's subliminal desire to be Black (she herself may

have had some African ancestry) likely is connected to a positive perception of the relevant African prowess. Two other accused Mexican mystics shared similar visions/fantasies (ibid., 103-4).
127. *Testimonio de Diego Lopez,* AHN Inq. 1620/1/7, fol. 2r.
128. *Testimonio de Diego Lopez,* AHN Inq. 1620/1/7, fol. 32v.
129. Sweet, *Recreating Africa,* 175. Much of the magic practiced by Whites also pertained to romance and sexuality; see Behar, "Sex and Sin."
130. *Testimonio de Diego Lopez,* AHN Inq. 1620/1/7, fol. 37v.
131. Maya Restrepo, *Brujería,* 605; for examples of "politically" motivated attacks by members of other groups (*juntas*) of magical practitioners, on domestic slaves, for example, see 556-62. Similarly, Lutz, *Santiago de Guatemala,* 43, reads the frequent larcenies committed by non-Whites of Santiago de Guatemala as acts targeting the city's Spanish elites.
132. "Los mios no lo son sino los de Paula que nos anima a Todas y de semejantes cassos" (*Testimonio de Diego Lopez,* AHN Inq. 1620/1/7, fol. 35v.). Maya Restrepo reads the frequent acts of infanticide as resistance to enslavement and the slave system, and the use of various body parts of the dead as a component of African medico-magical practice (*Brujería,* 697-705; see also Sweet, *Recreating Africa,* 67).
133. "no fiarsse la dha Paula de ningna negra sino de sua zamba" (*Testimonio de Diego Lopez,* AHN Inq. 1620/1/7, fol. 36r.). Ultimately, Eguiluz was sentenced twice by the Cartagena tribunal, the second time in 1642, in trials that produced some 405 folios of documentation (Maya Restrepo, *Brujería,* 506).
134. *Testimonio de Diego Lopez,* AHN Inq. 1620/1/7, fol. 6r.-v., 26r. A free Black woman, Potenciana de Abreu, also of Cartagena, describes a nearly identical mark in her own 1635 inquisition trial — ritual scarification? a marriage pledge? a pact of resistance? (AHN Inq. 1020, fol. 467v.; Splendiani, *Tribunal de Cartagena,* 2:420).
135. The Dominican friar Francisco de la Cruz also claimed to receive visits from a demon who appeared in the guise of an Amerindian (Castelló, *Francisco de la Cruz,* 1:517). In the 1620s, Juan de Mañozca y Zamora, one of the founders of the Cartagena tribunal in 1610 and inquisitor at Lima from 1624-1639, complained that the viceroyalty's many magical practitioners who were not themselves Amerindian "were immersed in the customs and knowledge of the colony's natives" (quoted in Silverblatt, "Colonial Conspiracies," 261). This cultural interchange is traced in Silverblatt, "Colonial Conspiracies," esp. 261-8; Garofalo, "The Ethno-Economy of Food, Drink, and Stimulants, 400-67. Maya Restrepo, *Brujería,* 659, reads the exchange of botanical and psychopharmacological expertise between Afroamericans and Amerindians as being more reciprocal, as does Gonzalo Aguirre Beltrán for Mexico (*Medicina y magia: El proceso de aculturación en la estructura colonial*

[Mexico City: Instituto Nacional Indigenista, 1963]). Of course, the symbolic importance of things Amerindian for non-Amerindians entailed a continuation of the more basic cultural adoption of Amerindian comestibles, including coca or the native Andean alchoholic beverages, known to the Spanish as chicha, which was drunk and even sold by Africans and Spaniards alike (Jane E. Mangan, *Trading Roles: Gender, Ethnicity, and the Urban Economy in Colonial Potosí* (Durham: Duke University Press, 2005), 83-6). The inquisitor Mañozca y Zamora seems to have been of New World origin himself, having graduated from the University of Mexico in 1596 before studying canon law at Salamanca (Medina, *Inquisición de Cartagena*, 114). Due to irregularities, he was eventually removed from his position as inquisitor in Lima.

136. *Testimonio de Diego Lopez*, AHN Inq. 1620/1/7, fol. 6v. This particular spirit, Taravira, was in all other cases assigned to *women* (Maya Restrepo, *Brujería*, 569). Rufina's accord with her demon, Huebo, includes her having to permit it/him to penetrate her anally (*Testimonio de Diego Lopez*, AHN Inq. 1620/1/7, fol. 34r.). For an interpretation of these companion spirits as a reconfiguration of personal sexuality, among other aspects of personhood, independent from the slave/racial economy, see Maya Restrepo, *Brujería*, 564-71. The repeated appearance of anal penetration suggests a counter-rhetoric of overturning, opposition and reversal. On the other hand, Sweet argues that same-sex relations were both common in Central African cultures and a response to the lack of available women in many slave settings, the latter clearly not the case here (Sweet, *Recreating Africa*, 50-8).

137. *Testimonio de Diego Lopez*, AHN Inq. 1620/1/7, 33r. Is this merely another name for the spirit Huebo or another spirit?

138. Ventura, *Portugueses no Peru*, 1:138.

139. Nathan Wachtel, *La Foi du souvenir: Labyrinthes marranes* (France: Editions du Seuil, 2001), 83; Boyajian, *Portuguese Bankers*, 122. Bautista Peres stood among the wealthiest New Christian merchants of the Americas, estimated, along with Simon Váez Sevilla of Mexico City, to possess a fortune of over 200,000 pesos (AGN Inq. 409, fol. 381; Israel, *Diasporas Within a Diaspora*, 98; according to Boyajian, *Portuguese Bankers*, 124, Bautista Peres' estate was "valued at about 650,000 ducats"). Pinto traded with Bautista Peres and Duarte through two brothers of the latter, Pedro Duarte and Paolo Rodrigues (Maria da Graça A. Mateus Ventura, "Los Judeoconversos portugueses en el Perú del siglo XVII: Redes de complicidad," *Familia, religión y negocio: El sefardismo en las relaciones entre el mundo ibérico y los Países Bajos en la edad moderna*, ed. Jaime Contreras, Bernardo J. García García and Ignacio Pulido [Fundación Carlos de Amberes/Fernando Villaverde Ediciones, 2002], 400), as well as directly. On the African connections of Bautista Peres and Duarte, see Green, "Masters of Difference," 223-7, 230-1. One of the New Christians

who traded slaves and other commodities with Pinto and Sebastián Duarte was Tomás Rodrigues Barassa, associate and relative of Diogo Barassa, "one of the most powerful Portuguese residents in Cacheu," on the West African coast (ibid., 217). According to Green, Pinto was so well known in Guinée that in 1637 "4 people testified in Cacheu that they recognized his handwriting" (ibid., 226).

140. Green, "Masters of Difference," 226.
141. Green, "Masters of Difference," 231, n. 305.
142. Salo W. Baron, *A Social and Religious History of the Jews*, 18 vols. (New York/Philadelphia: Columbia University Press/Jewish Publication Society of America, 1952-83), 15:301; Dominguez Ortiz, *Judeoconversos*, 136; Israel, *Diasporas Within a Diaspora*, 135; Green, "Masters of Difference."
143. Israel, *Diasporas Within a Diaspora*, 102. Elsewhere he cites a 1608 tract by the Spaniard Pedro de Avendaño Villela which claims that it was the Portuguese New Christians "who navigate the coast and rivers of Guinea to ply the trade in negros" (135-36). The fact is that many slavers, even among the Portuguese, were not Conversos.
144. Israel, *Diasporas Within a Diaspora*, 104; see the following pages, including the many individuals who had been in/through Angola, 106-7. Here Israel's terminology is unfortunately vague; it remains the case that credible scholarship has yet to delineate the ethnic or religious loyalties of most of these slave traders.
145. Relación y abecedário de los estrangeros que se hallan en la ciudad de Cartagena, reprinted in Ventura, *Portugueses no Peru*, 3:31-77.
146. Jonathan Israel cites Eva Uchmany to the effect that Angola and Guinea were places where "many Portuguese New Christians were inducted, 'converted' or confirmed in Crypto-Judaism" (Israel, *Diasporas Within a Diaspora*, 106; Eva A. Uchmany, "The Participation of New Christians and Crypto-Jews in the Conquest, Colonization and Trade of Spanish America, 1521-1660," in Bernardini and Fiering, *Jews and the Expansion of Europe to the West*, 198; Toby Green, "The Role of the Portuguese Trading Posts in Guinea and Angola in the 'Apostasy' of Crypto-Jews in the 17th Century," in *Creole Societies in the Portuguese Colonial Empire*, eds. Philip J. Havik and Malyn Newitt (Bristol: Bristol University Press, June 2007), 25-40.
147. Lewin, *Singular Proceso de Salomón Machorro*, xii-xviii.
148. Printed in Tejado Fernández, *Vida social en Cartagena*, 186.
149. Israel, *Diasporas Within a Diaspora*, 105, citing Lucía García de Proodian, *Los judios en America: Sus actividades en los Virreinatos de Nueva Castilla y Nueva Granada s. XVII* (Madrid: Instituto Arias Montano, 1966), "Appendice documental," 287. Irene Silverblatt brings more such examples in "New Christians and New World Fears in Seventeenth-Century Peru," *Comparative Studies in Society and History: An International Quarterly* 42, no. 3 (July 2000): 545, n. 71.

150. Green, "Masters of Difference," 146.
151. Testimony of an unnamed witness; AGN Mexico, Inq. 402, exp. 1, leg. 2, fol. 364r. It is unclear whether the term *Capitanes de negros* refers to mere masters of slaves or actual ship captains.
152. *Testimonio de Diego Lopez*, AHN Inq. 1620/1/7, fol. 33v.
153. "Vino a ver a este en Compañia de Germa sobrina de Juo Tellez que tambien era bruja y este la dixo que aguardas mulata como no buelles a mi cassa pues tienes alla los quatroçientos pessos que te he dado pa tu libertad a que La susodcha Respondio no tengas pena que yo tengo trazado Con que amansar a mis amos Y porque lo heches dever tu lo Veras Y este La dixo pues conque y ella le Respondio Yo Te embiare una [...] seña [?] porque Paula de Eguiluz me ha enseñado un conjuro de doña Maria de Padilla quieres oyr le Y este dixo que no Y el dia sigte suçedio que la dcha Rufina le embio un Razimo de ubas a este y fue Assi que sus amos Se aquietaron" (*Testimonio de Diego Lopez*, AHN Inq. 1620/1/7, fols. 33v.-34r.). This may or may not refer to the time Eguiluz offered to give Rufina a bit of eucharist to mix in a chocolate drink in order to tame her mistress (ibid., 47v.-48r.).
154. The inconsistency of López's claims is difficult to resolve. Did she prefer her relatively secure slave condition under "tamed" masters? Did López really give her the funds as he claims? Did she prefer to spend the money on other things? For example, she is said to have paid Eguiluz six pesos to teach her the above-mentioned spell, while later she supposedly paid one Black slave of Catalina de Castro, in silver, to put certain herbs at the threshold of the house of the Black Juana de Hortensia in order to kill her (ibid., 34r., 45v.).
155. "Rufina le dixo avia hecho un conçierto Con otro diablo que le avia traydo Paula de Eguiluz llamado Huebo y era El dho Conçierto que el dho diablo avia de Tomar La figura de la dha Rufina Y en ella avia de asistir en su cassa a todos los actos pa en que fuesse llamada assi para El serviçio de La cassa Como para asistir con diego lopez Arias su amo quando La fuesse a buscar para sus torpezas Y que enpago desto avia de Comer cal La dha Rufina y dexarse conoçer carnalmte por el vaso trasero Con el dho demonio huebo y que avia venido en el dho Contrato por poder mas Libremte salir de su Cassa quando quisiesse" (*Testimonio de Diego Lopez*, AHN Inq. 1620/1/7, fol. 34r.). Such magical means of coping with one's servitude as cited here are attested throughout the Americas; see Palmer, "Religion and Magic, 322-3; Sweet, *Recreating Africa*, 164-71.
156. *Testimonio de Diego Lopez*, AHN Inq. 1620/1/7, fol. 20v.
157. Ventura, "Judeoconversos portugueses en el Perú," 405, n. 21; idem, *Portuguese no Peru*, 1:171, 3:40.
158. *Testimonio de Diego Lopez*, AHN Inq. 1620/1/7, fol. 20v.
159. He sold pearls to Simon Rivero and through him (AHN Inq. 1601/8, fols. 20-21; cited in Croitoru Rotbaum, *Documentos*, 148).

160. Ventura, *Portugueses no Peru*, 1:398-99. On Duarte, see Mellafe, *Introducción de la esclavitud*, 169-81.
161. Ventura, *Portugueses no Peru*, 1:396. On Bautista Peres's life, career and commercial activities, see ibid., 1:347-457, 2:16-93; Wachtel, *Foi du souvenir*, 79-101; Studnicki-Gizbert, *Nation upon the Ocean Sea*, throughout; Boyajian, *Portuguese Bankers*, 122-4; Silverblatt, *Modern Inquisitions*, 47-53, 132-5, 145-8, 152, 157 and elsewhere. Inquisition sources allow Studnicki-Gizbert to surmise that Bautista Peres's residence in Lima was "a good-size manse" housing, among others, "close to two dozen adult African slaves and their children: servants, maids, cooks, liverymen, porters, and stable hands." Besides trading in slaves, he ran a general store in town and a hacienda outside of Lima at which worked 50 slaves that he had imported (*Nation upon the Ocean Sea*, 77, 109, 200, n. 45). Mentions of Pinto in the business letters between Peres, Duarte and others reprinted by Maria Mateus Ventura can be found in *Portugueses no Peru*, 3:138, 142, 145-6, 148, 151, 163, 166-7, 185, 294, 296, 302-3; letters to/from Pinto: 3:170-2, 179-82.
162. Ventura, *Portuguese no Peru*, 1:171, 3:41. Among the items Pinto fed his sick slaves were wine, oranges, grains and sugar. These were not cheap commodities but also did not guarantee the recovery of the slaves' health (letter of Brás de Paz Pinto to Sebastião Duarte, 13 January 1634, AGN Inq., S.O., Co. caja 30, exp. 299, fols. 251-2; Ventura, *Portugueses no Peru*, 1:431 and 3:172). Rolando Mellafe draws on a *Memoria de las medicinas que han llevado para los negros del capitán don Sebastián Duarte*, in the Archivo Nacional de Santiago, that offers a detailed glimpse of the kinds of treatments Pinto might have used (Mellafe, *Introducción de la esclavitud*, 177).
163. AHN Inq. 1601/8, fol. 21; cited in Croitoru Rotbaum, *Documentos*, 148.
164. Ventura, *Portugueses no Peru*, 1:381; see also Mellafe, *Introducción de la esclavitud*, 174. The biographer of Pedro Claver, on the other hand, provides a harsh depiction of the general mistreatment of the slaves in the interest of increasing profits (Fernandez, *Apostolica y penitente vida de el V.P. Pedro Claver*, 105-7).
165. Ventura, *Portugueses no Peru*, 1:399.
166. On the Branes, several groups living around the Casamance River in West Africa (today's Senegal), see Alonso de Sandoval, *Un tratado sobre la esclavitud*, Intro., transcription and translation [of *De instauranda aethiopum salute* (1647)] by Enriqueta Vila Vilar (Madrid: Alianza Editorial, 1987), 107-8, 119.
167. Letter of 13 January 1634, AGN (Peru) Inq., S.O., Con., box 30, exp. 299, fol. 251r.; reprinted in Ventura, *Portugueses no Peru*, 3:170.
168. Ventura, *Portuguese no Peru*, 1:171, quoting the Relação e abecedário dos estrangeiros que se acharam na cidade de Cartagena.
169. AHN Inq. 1601/8, fol. 21-26v.; cited in Croitoru Rotbaum, *Documentos*, 149-55.

170. Ventura, *Portugueses no Peru*, 2:541.
171. AHN Inq. 4822/8, fol. 217; cited in Álvarez Alonso, *Inquisición en Cartagena*, 321; Medina, *Inquisición de Cartagena*, 230.
172. *Testimonio de Diego Lopez*, AHN Inq. 1620/1/7, fol. 41v.
173. See, for instance, AHN Inq. 1620/1/7, fol. 29r.-v., 32r.-v.
174. AHN Inq. 1020, fol. 420v., Splendiani, *Tribunal de Cartagena*, 2:377.
175. AHN Inq. 1601/18, fols. 31-7, 40-4; Croitoru Rotbaum, *Documentos*, 223-9, 231-6. The date is given on AHN Inq. 1601/18, fol. 46r. The unnamed witness states that "he has been brought to this *audiencia* various times" (AHN Inq. 1601/18, fol. 43v.; Croitoru Rotbaum, *Documentos*, 234).
176. AHN Inq. 1601/18, fols. 30, 37, 46r.; Croitoru Rotbaum, *Documentos*, 223,229, 236. The official presiding over these sessions, the prosecutor (*fiscal*) of the local tribunal, the *licenciado* Juan Ortiz, summarizes that the accused have been "reconciled in their trials of faith which remain in the secret chamber of the Inquisition of the city of Cartagena de Indias to which I refer, Done in said secret chamber on five august one thousand six hundred and fifty one years." This is why these sessions are inserted with material from 1636 and thereabouts, the period of the earlier trials.
177. *Testimonio de Diego Lopez*, AHN Inq. 1620/1/7, fol. 24r.
178. *Testimonio de Diego Lopez*, AHN Inq. 1620/1/7, fol. 23v. This is the same Sánchez who complains that the Inquisition does not arrest judaizers such as Pinto.
179. *Testimonio de Diego Lopez*, AHN Inq. 1620/1/7, fol. 30v.
180. According to Esquivel's testimony, 1649 (AHN Inq. 1601/3/8, fol. 46v.; Croitoru Rotbaum, *Documentos*, 327). He owed her the money for "*escritura*," which could mean letter-writing, though he was himself literate, or for some kind of notarial service.
181. Ceballos Gómez, "Grupos sociales y prácticas mágicas," 57.
182. *Testimonio de Diego Lopez*, AHN Inq. 1620/1/7, fol. 23r.
183. Solano Alonso, *Salud, cultura y sociedad en Cartagena*, 251-3; Ventura, *Portuguese no Peru*, 1:208-9. Neto's work was recently published, for the first time: Juan Méndez Nieto, *Discursos Medicinales* (Salamanca: Universidad de Salamanca/Junta de Castilla y León, 1989).
184. For instance, the royal physician Luis Mercado (1525–1611) published *De la facultad de los alimentos y medicamentos yndianos*, no longer extant, while Pedro López de León cites Amerindian cures, the practices of Blacks and American medicinal plants (Alonso, *Salud, cultura y sociedad en Cartagena*, 130, 179, 200-9). Natalie Zemon Davis, *Women on the Margins: Three Seventeenth-Century Lives* (Cambridge: Harvard University Press, 1995), 184-89; Sweet, *Recreating Africa*, 145; Jonathan Schorsch, "American Jewish Historians, Colonial Jews and Blacks, and the Limits of *Wissenschaft*: A Critical Review," *Jewish Social Studies* 6,2 (Winter 2000): 111; James

Delbourgo, "Slavery in the Cabinet of Curiosities: Hans Sloane's Atlantic World," www.thebritishmuseum.ac.uk/the_museum/news_and_debate/news/hans_sloanes_atlantic_world.aspx, 16; Lawrence Levine, "The Sacred World of Black Slaves: The Quest for Control, Slave Folk Belief," in *Black Consciousness* (Oxford: Oxford University Press, 1977), 65; Michel Laguerre, *Afro-Caribbean Folk Medicine* (South Hadley, Mass.: Bergin and Garvey Publishers, 1987); Karol K. Weaver, *Medical Revolutionaries: The Enslaved Healers of Eighteenth-Century Saint Domingue* (Campaign, IL: University of Illinois Press, 2006).

185. López testifies that one night Rufina created a late-night ruckus outside his house, causing him and another man to go out to investigate. Coming across her, López asks what she is doing there. "That's a good question," she responds, "as you have not seen me in some time." He explains that his wife just gave birth and, being the first time, he is helping. "Your Honor will be very content because he has a daughter, but before much time you will not have her," states Rufina in a mixture of sarcasm and threat. "By your life, leave her be," replies López. "There is no remedy, because my devil *Rompe sanctos* has thrown the three stones [a method for trying to determine a desired outcome?]," Rufina concludes the conversation and leaves. Minutes later he catches her in his arms, though this time she is flying through the air with her devil. López summarizes for the inquisitors: "Within two days, as the above-mentioned transpired, the infant died" (*Testimonio de Diego Lopez*, AHN Inq. 1620/1/7, 33r.).
186. *Testimonio de Diego Lopez*, AHN Inq. 1620/1/7, fol. 33v.
187. *Testimonio de Diego Lopez*, AHN Inq. 1620/1/7, 36r.-v.
188. *Testimonio de Diego Lopez*, AHN Inq. 1620/1/7, fol. 52v.
189. AHN Inq. 1020, fol. 420r., Splendiani, *Tribunal de Cartagena*, 2:377.
190. *Testimonio de Diego Lopez*, AHN Inq. 1620/1/7, fol. 24v.
191. *Testimonio de Diego Lopez*, AHN Inq. 1620/1/7, fol. 24r.
192. *Testimonio de Diego Lopez*, AHN Inq. 1620/1/7, fol. 44v.; AHN Inq. 1020, fol. 379v.-380r., reprinted in Splendiani, *Tribunal de Cartagena*, 2:341.
193. AHN Inq. 1020, fol. 419v., Splendiani, *Tribunal de Cartagena*, 2:377.
194. Ceballos Gómez, "Grupos sociales y prácticas mágicas," 57-8.
195. AHN Inq. 1020, fols. 418r.-422r., Splendiani, *Tribunal de Cartagena*, 2: 375-9.
196. AHN Inq. 1020, fols. 420v.-421r.; Splendiani, *Tribunal de Cartagena*, 2:378. Ceballos Gómez explicates the societal distinctions between the types of magic (Ceballos Gómez, "Grupos sociales y prácticas mágicas," 61-2).
197. See the *Relación de las causas de fe* from 1634, AHN Inq. 1020, fols. 418r.-422r., reprinted in Splendiani, *Tribunal de Cartagena*, 2:375-9.
198. AHN Inq. 1020, fol. 422r.; Medina, *Inquisición de Cartagena*, 216.
199. AHN Inq. 1021, fol. 8r. *Relación del auto*, reprinted in Splendiani, *Tribunal*

de Cartagena, 3:43; AHN Inq. 1021, fol. 14r., 15r.-16r., 28v., *Relación de las causas de fe*, Splendiani, *Tribunal de Cartagena*, 3:48, 50, 64. As mentioned in the previous chapter, similar charges of New Christian alliance with the Dutch arose in "Portuguese" West Africa.

200. AHN Inq. 1021, fol. 28v.-29r., *Relación de las causas de fe*, Splendiani, *Tribunal de Cartagena*, 3:64. Fonseca Enríquez claims that Rodríguez Mesa possessed the logbook and served as the treasurer of the group.
201. AHN Inq. 1620/11, fol. 59; cited in Tejado Fernández, *Vida social en Cartagena*, 181.
202. Vila Vilar, "Extranjeros en Cartagena," 164, n. 54.
203. Ventura, *Portuguese no Peru*, 1:298; excerpt from the confession of Captain Estevan de Ares de Fonseca in Caro Baroja, *Judíos en la España*, 3:362-64.
204. AHN Inq. 1020, fols. 481v.; Splendiani, *Tribunal de Cartagena*, 433-4.
205. AHN Inq. 1601/18, fol. 41r.; Croitoru Rotbaum, *Documentos*, 232.
206. *Testimonio de Diego Lopez*, AHN Inq. 1620/7/1, fols. 19v.-20r.
207. Caro Baroja, *Judíos en la España*, 2:431-2; in Appendix 13, 3:331, Caro Baroja brings the letters' mention by the lawyer from Alcarez, Ignacio del Villar Maldonado, *Sylva responsorum iuris* (Madrid, 1614). The letters were proven to be a forgery by I. Loeb, "La correspondance des juifs d'Espagne avec ceux de Constantinople," *Revue des Études Juives* 15 (1887): 262-76. They are reprinted as well in Azevedo, *História dos cristãos-novos*, 464 (Appendix 10). The version printed in Loeb and Azevedo does not call for the physical destruction of churches or their idols.
208. Translated in Studnicki-Gizbert, *A Nation Upon the Ocean Sea*, 166.
209. Recorded in AHN Inq. 1600/16; Croitoru Rotbaum, *Documentos*, 486-525.
210. See AHN Inq. 1601/3/1-2; Croitoru Rotbaum, *Documentos*, 281-6. See also the testimony of the many witnesses interviewed during yet another *visita* of Inquisitor Don Pedro de Medina Rico in 1649 (AHN Inq. 1601/3/8; Croitoru Rotbaum, *Documentos*, 288-475). Complicity of varying sorts in slave trading also seems to have occurred. Uriarte and Ortiz were accused by Don Joseph de Bolibar, knight of the Order of Santiago and bailiff of the Cartagena tribunal, of using moneys sequestered by the Inquisition from the Portuguese Conversos to buy over 200,000 ducats of clothes and slaves from Angola and Guinea on one occasion, while on another purchasing from Angola and Guinea more than 450 slaves whom they sold in Cartagena for a profit of 60,000 pesos (AHN Inq. 1601/3/8, fols. 90r.-91v.; Croitoru Rotbaum, *Documentos*, 367-9; see also AHN Inq. 1601/3/8, fol. 128r.v., 165r.-166r., 187r.-191r.; Croitoru Rotbaum, *Documentos*, 402, 435-6, 456-9). Ortiz, it seems, had been a merchant before working for the Inquisition (Medina, *Inquisición de Cartagena*, 167). Another time, Uriarte, as the one in charge of the sequestered goods of João Rodrigues Mesa and Blas de Paz Pinto, ordered a girl slave of Juan Cotel to be sold at auction, though refusing to

provide the required written order, as requested by both Bolibar and Andred Fernandez de Castro, the tribunal's receiver. Cotel had owed the slave as part of his debts to either Rodrigues Mesa or Pinto, but Uriarte wanted the sale kept unofficial since Cotel also bore a debt to Uriarte's wife (AHN Inq. 1601/3/8, fol. 101r.-v.; Croitoru Rotbaum, *Documentos*, 379).

211. AHN Inq. 1601/3/8, fols. 82v.-83r.; Croitoru Rotbaum, *Documentos*, 359-60. For example, it seems Pinto was to have given some strings of pearls from the merchant Miguel Fernandez Pereira to Don Francisco Rexi, a consultant to the Cartagena tribunal, "who was his lawyer and with whom he communicated this" payment, still never paid as of 1649. See also AHN Inq. 1601/3/8, fol. 113v., 154r.; Croitoru Rotbaum, *Documentos*, 390, 424 and AHN Inq. 1600/16, fols. 12r.-v.; Croitoru Rotbaum, *Documentos*, 503.

212. As had happened with the Lima tribunal as well (Silverblatt, "Colonial Conspiracies," 268).

213. AHN Inq. 1620/7/1, fol. 17v.-18r.; AHN Inq. 1601/18, fol. 41v.; Croitoru Rotbaum, *Documentos*, 233.

214. AHN Inq. 1620/7/1, fol. 18v.-19r.; AHN Inq. 1601/18, fol. 42r.-v.; Croitoru Rotbaum, *Documentos*, 233.

215. AHN Inq. 1601/18, fol. 43r.-v.; Croitoru Rotbaum, *Documentos*, 234. João Rodrigues Mesa is also accused of being the "doctrinizer [*dotrinatisador*] of the Law of Moses and its rabbi" (AHN Inq. 1601/18, fol. 31; reprinted in Croitoru Rotbaum, *Documentos*, 223). Already the *Relación de las causas de fe* prepared for the 1638 *auto* "improved" the accusations against Pinto somewhat. Going to investigate the gatherings at Pinto's house, López claims not to have been allowed in and to have waited in the next-door house of Don Martin Felix or Feliz, who says to him, referring to the closed curtains of Pinto's house and the men assembled therein: "i do not know how the señores of the holy office sleep nor what they do, as they do not castigate these, and the said Feliz was pondering this, saying that in that House a synagogue was conducted and the whole afternoon the said don martin feliz was muttering about this with this Prisoner" (*Testimonio de Diego Lopez*, AHN Inq. 1620/7/1, 19r.). This Martin Felix/z appears never to have been interrogated. In the *Relación de las causas de fe*, the inquisitors' summation of the charges, this individual muttering supposedly produced by the daytime gatherings becomes a seemingly general "scandal and murmuring in which it was said that they had a synagogue" (AHN Inq. 1021, fol. 20v., Splendiani, *Tribunal de Cartagena*, 3:55).

216. AHN Inq. 1620, fols. 506r.-507r.; Splendiani, *Tribunal de Cartagena*, 2:441-3.

217. AHN Inq. 1601/3/8, fol. 207r., 208r.; Croitoru Rotbaum, *Documentos*, 473, 474.

218. AHN Inq. 1021, fols. 1-48r., reprinted in Splendiani, *Tribunal de Cartagena*,

3: 35-85. The *Relación del auto*, the first part of this report, read aloud at the *auto*, completely passes over the torture applied to Paz Pinto and the cause of his final and fatal illness, euphemizing the torture in the standard manner as "the charitable admonition" (AHN Inq. 1021, fol. 3v., Splendiani, *Tribunal de Cartagena*, 3:39).

219. AHN Inq. 1620, fol. 507v.; Splendiani, *Tribunal de Cartagena*, 2:443.
220. AHN Inq. 1021, fol. 5r.-v., *Relación del auto*, reprinted in Splendiani, *Tribunal de Cartagena*, 3:41.
221. From a letter by visiting inspector inquisitor Pedro Medina Rico, 31 May 1649; quoted by Medina, *Inquisición de Cartagena*, 225, n. 1. Ironically, at one point in 1636 Paula de Eguiluz was called in by the Cartagena inquisitors to minister to Manuel Alvarez Prieto, whose arms had been broken by torture (Croitoru Rotbaum, *De Sefarad*, 312-3). Taussig, basing himself on Henry Charles Lea, states that Eguiluz was initially sentenced to burning at the stake as one of the leaders of the large group of Black magical practitioners in the port of Tolú (about 65 miles south of Cartagena). After six years of imprisonment, her sentence was commuted to the punishment just described (Taussig, *Shamanism*, 219).
222. Caesar E. Farah (trans. and ed.), *An Arab's Journey to Colonial Spanish America: The Travels of Elias al-Mûsili in the Seventeenth Century* (Syracuse: Syracuse University Press, 2003), 19.

Esperanza Rodríguez: A Life In-between

223. The accused and members of her family appear under the year 1647 in the *Relación de los Reos que este Tribunal del Santo Oficio de la Iquisición de México ha Penitenciado y castigado, con otros, por la observancia de la ley de Moisén, en dos autos de fe que han celebrado; y bien desterrados perpetuamente de estos reinos y provincias [...] con testimonio de sus sentencias, edades y señas exteriores para presentarse con dichos testimonios en el Tribunal del Santo Oficio de la dicha ciudad de Sevilla [...]*, (1647; reproduced in Genaro García, *Documentos ineditos o muy raros para la historia de Mexico*, 3rd ed. (Mexico City: Editorial Porrúa, 1982), 70-74), as well as in the *Relacion sumeria del auto particular de fee, que el trbunal del santo officio de la Inquisicion de los Reyes, y Provincias de la Nueva España, celebro en la muy noble, y muy leal Ciudad de Mexico a los diez y seis dias del mes de Abril, del año de mil y seiscientos y quarenta y seis* (1646; García, *Documentos*, 137-177). In the latter, we are informed that Juan Bautista had been a sculptor and assembly worker (escultor y ensamblador; García, *Documentos*, 155). Esperanza's age is given there as seventy-four.
224. Testimony of Esperanza Rodríguez, 7 August 1642; AGN Mexico, Inq. 408, exp. 2, leg. 1, fol. 458r.

225. Testimony of 7 August 1642; AGN Mexico, Inq. 408, exp. 2, leg. 1, fol. 458r.
226. Testimony of 7 August 1642; AGN Mexico, Inq. 408, exp. 2, leg. 1, fols. 458r., 469r. and elsewhere. "[L]ibre y antes esclava de doña catalina Enríquez, reclusa en este Santo Oficio por judaizante; e hija de Isabel, negra de Guinea, que murió en Sevilla, y de Francisco Rodríguez, hebreo, cristiano nuevo; de oficio y ocupación costurera" (García, *Documentos*, 155).
227. Testimony of 7 August 1642; AGN Mexico, Inq. 408, exp. 2, leg. 1, fol. 458r.
228. Ignacio Camacho Martínez, *La Hermandad de los mulatos de Sevilla: Antecedentes históricos de la Hermandad del Calvario* (Seville: Área de Cultura del Ayuntamiento de Sevilla, 1998), 53.
229. Albert A. Sicroff, "Clandestine Judaism in the Hieronymite Monastery of Nuestra Señora de Guadalupe," *Studies in Honor of M. J. Benardete* (New York: Las Américas Publishing Co., 1965), 89-125; Ingram, "Secret Lives, Public Lies," 68-69; Marie-Theresa Hernández, *The Virgin of Guadalupe and the Conversos: Uncovering Hidden Influences from Spain to Mexico* (New Brunswick, NJ: Rutgers University Press, 2014), ch. 2.
230. Testimony of Esperanza Rodríguez, 7 August 1642; AGN Mexico, Inq. 408, exp. 2, leg. 1, fol. 459v.
231. Expediente de información y licencia de pasajero a Indias de Catalina Enríquez, 23 December 1607, AGI, Contatacion, 5297, N. 37; http://pares.mcu.es/ParesBusquedas20/catalogo/description/141979. The license lists Catalina's parents as Rodrigo Hernández and Beatriz Guerta Enríquez.
232. Testimony of Esperanza Rodríguez, 7 August 1642; AGN Mexico, Inq. 408, exp. 2, leg. 1, fol. 458v. It could be that Rodríguez is getting the dating muddled. She says she and her mistress arrived in Cartagena in 1602, where they stayed only about "fifteen or twenty days," before sailing for Havana. Arriving there, she married Del Bosque "within eight days" (ibid., fols. 459v.-460r.).
233. Testimony of Esperanza Rodríguez, 7 August 1642; AGN Mexico, Inq. 408, exp. 2, leg. 1, fol. 460v.-r. Ysavel de Silva testifies to having been aware that Blanca Enríquez maintained contact with Rodríguez during the latter's time in Guadalajara (testimony of 25 June 1643, ibid., 415, exp. 6, fol. 519r.).
234. Testimony of Esperanza Rodríguez, 7 August 1642; AGN Mexico, Inq. 408, exp. 2, leg. 1, fols. 458v., 460v.
235. Testimony of Esperanza Rodríguez, 7 August 1642; AGN Mexico, Inq. 408, exp. 2, leg. 1, fol. 460v.
236. Joan Bristol, unpublished paper, "Moving through Community: Examining the Travels of Esperanza Rodriguez in Seventeenth-Century Mexico," presented at the Society for the Study of American Women Writers, Denver, November 2018, 3. I thank the author for sharing her work with me.
237. AGN Mexico, Inq. 393, exp. 12, leg. 3, fol. 68r.

238. Testimony of 18 July 1642; AGN Mexico, Inq. 408, exp. 2, leg. 1, fol. 410r.; testimony of 18 November 1642; ibid., fol. 411r.-v. Ysavel de Silva also deposes that Rodríguez had grown up with Blanca Enriquez (testimony of 25 June 1643, ibid., 415, exp. 6, fol. 519r). In a deposition of her own, Rodríguez confirms having grown up in Seville with both Blanca de Rivera and Blanca Enriquez (testimony of 21 April 1643; ibid., fols. 357v.-468r.) and that she knew Blanca de Rivera "very well" in Seville, along with her oldest daughter Maria, who was then very little (response to the charges against her, ibid., 419, exp. 6, fol. 72r.). Indeed, Rodríguez, in her response to the charges against her, seems to say that Blanca and Margarita de Rivera are relatives of her former mistress, Catalina Enriquez in Veracruz, but that Catalina and Margarita, at least, had a falling out (ibid. 419, exp. 6, fol. 106v.-107r.).
239. Expediente de concesión de licencia para pasar a Nueva España a favor de Antonio Rodríguez Arias, 1608, AGI, Indiferente, 2073, N.7; http://pares.mcu.es/ParesBusquedas20/catalogo/description/441035. An earlier travel license had been issued to Rodríguez Arias in 1606, who likely went on his own to do business (AGI, Contratacion, 5262A, N.62. Simon Rodríguez, Esperanza's uncle had already lived in Mexico before 1605, as he is described by the Seville Inquisition as a resident of Mexico ("Relación de causas de fe, 1605," AHN, Inq., leg. 2075, exp. 24). Ana Lopez, Yna Lopez's sister, also had lived in Mexico prior to 1604 (ibid. exp. 33).
240. Testimony of Esperanza Rodríguez, 21 April 1643; AGN Mexico, Inq. 408, exp. 2, leg. 1, fol. 469r.
241. Testimony of 21 April 1643; AGN Mexico, Inq. 408, exp. 2, leg. 1, fol. 467r.
242. Testimony of Esperanza Rodríguez, 21 April 1643; AGN Mexico, Inq. 408, exp. 2, leg. 1, fol. 470v. Geronima's mother had been a Mexican mestiza who married Henrique de Miranda, whom Esperanza knew from Seville as well as from Cartagena.
243. Testimony of 25 June 1643; AGN Mexico, Inq. 415, exp. 6, fol. 519v. As had Blanca (see below).
244. Testimony of 25 June 1643, AGN Mexico, Inq. 415, exp. 6, fol. 519r.
245. *Inquisitorial Inquiries: Brief Lives of Secret Jews and Other Heretics*, ed. and trans. Richard L. Kagan and Abigail Dyer (Baltimore: Johns Hopkins University Press, 2004), 162, n. 27, 163.
246. "Relacion de las causas despachadas en el auto de la fe que se celebro en la inquisicion de Sevilla, dia de Sant Andres, treinta de nobiembre del año de 1604," AHN, Inq., leg. 2075, exp. 33. She had been arrested in 1603 (AHN, Inq., leg. 2075, exp. 21). She is mentioned in Bocanegra, *Auto general de la fee celebrada*, unpag.
247. AHN, Inquisición, leg. 1953; reprinted in J. M. García Fuentes: *La inquisición en Granada en el siglo XVI* [Granada: 1981], 432, 471-72; "Relaciones de causa pendientes y auto de fe. 1599. Sevilla," "Relaciones de causas despachadas

fuera de auto," AHN, Inquisición, leg. 2075, exp. 17. Blanca's mother and Ynes Lopez both came from Fondon, La Guardia district, Portugal.
248. "Relaciones de causa pendientes y auto de fe. 1599. Sevilla," "Relaciones de causas despachadas fuera de auto," AHN, Inquisición, leg. 2075, exp. 17.
249. Testimony of Beatriz Enríquez, 24 July 1642; AGN Mexico, Inq. 393, exp. 12, leg. 3, fol. 209v.; 24 October 1642, ibid., fol. 225v.
250. Testimony of 23 May 1643; AGN Mexico, Inq. 393, exp. 12, leg. 3, fol. 131r. For a time, Pedro lived with his grandmother (testimony of Catalina Enríquez, 3 August 1643, ibid., fol. 153v.).
251. Testimony of Gaspar Vaez Sevilla, 13 February 1644; AGN Mexico, Inq. 393, exp. 12, leg. 3, fol. 111v.
252. Testimony of Beatriz Enríquez, 24 July 1642; AGN Mexico, Inq. 393, exp. 12, leg. 3, fol. 211r.
253. Testimony of 27 May 1643; AGN Mexico, Inq. 393, exp. 12, leg. 3, fols. 132r.-v. Pedro was the son of Catalina Enríquez and Diego Tinoco. The latter had lived openly as a Jew in some non-Spanish territory (AGN Mexico, Inq. 410, exp. 4, leg. 5, fols. 524v.) or was born in such a place (according to Margarita de Rivera; testimony of 8 July 1642; ibid., fol. 527v.). Catalina testifies that Diego was circumcised (testimony of 9 November 1643; ibid., fol. 527r.). Somehow, Catalina and Margarita de Rivera knew of his being circumcised, though Catalina is not sure whether this was told to her directly (by Catalina Enríquez?) or to her mother Blanca (testimony of Catalina de Rivera, 30 June 1642, ibid., fol. 528r.; testimony of Margarita de Rivera, 8 July 1642, ibid., fol. 527v.).
254. Testimony of Beatriz Enríquez, 14 November 1642; AGN Mexico, Inq. 393/12/3, fol. 243r.-244r.
255. Testimony of 6 June 1643; AGN Mexico, Inq. 393, exp. 12, leg. 3, fols. 139r.-v. This was the parental blessing of the child, which traditionally invokes Joseph's sons, Ephraim and Menasseh, for boys and Sarah, Rebecca, Rachel and Leah for girls. Catalina Enríquez, Pedro's mother, describes the scene identically, with one difference (Testimony of 28 May 1643; ibid., fol. 149r.): each went one by one before Blanca to receive her blessing. Again, this occurred on the festival eve. Beatriz Enríquez says that they went in order of age and that it was the blessing "that Jacob gave to his grandchildren and sons" (testimony of 14 November 1642; ibid., fol. 238v.).
256. Testimony of 14 November 1642; AGN Mexico, Inq. 393/12/3, fol. 238v.
257. On the messianic expectations of this extended clan see Wachtel, "Marrano Religiosity in Hispanic America in the Seventeenth Century," 161-64.
258. Testimony of 30 July 1642, AGN Mexico, Inq. 393, exp. 12, leg. 3, fol. 156r.; ibid., 408, exp. 2, leg. 1, fols. 432v.-433r.
259. Testimony of 28 May 1642; AGN Mexico, Inq. 408, exp. 2, leg. 1, fol. 406v.
260. Blanca de Rivera knew Lopez, who was deceased by the time of her

deposition. Testimony of 18 July 1642; AGN Mexico, Inq. 408, exp. 2, leg. 1, fol. 410r.-v.; testimony of 18 November 1642; ibid., fol. 411r.-v.
261. Testimony of 18 July 1642; AGN Mexico, Inq. 408, exp. 2, leg. 1, fols. 425v.-426r.
262. Testimony of 25 June 1643, AGN Mexico, Inq. 415, exp. 6, fol. 519r.
263. AGN Mexico, Inq. 419, exp. 6, fol. 118r.
264. AGN Mexico, Inq. 419, exp. 6, fol. 108r.
265. Testimony of 30 January 1643; AGN Mexico, Inq. 408, exp. 1, leg. 1, fol. 464v.-465r. The underline was made by the inquisitorial scribe. In her response to the charges against her, Rodríguez says all this happened when she was "eight or ten" (ibid., 419, exp. 6, fol. 72r.).
266. Testimony of 30 January 1643; AGN Mexico, Inq. 408, exp. 2, leg. 1, fol. 465v.
267. Testimony of 24 September 1644, AGN Mexico, Inq. 419, exp. 6, fol. 113v.-114r. Note that if Rodríguez's mother Isabel indeed knew something of crypto-Judaism, it is not she who is credited — or blamed — for transmitting it to her daughter.
268. "Enseñó à muchas personas de su pare*tela, y estrañas la ley de Moysen, y à Esperança Rodríguez mulata su esclava ofreciandola la libertad, y ayunado con todos ellos, y otras personas, lo qual calló en su causa, y se le probó, conque murió en los mesmos delictos, è impenitente. Salió su Estatua al Auto, con vn Sābenito, y Coroza de cōdenada con vn letrero de su nombre [...]" (Bocanegra, *Auto general de la fee celebrada*, unpag.).
269. Bocanegra, *Auto general de la fee celebrada*, unpag. Catalina's husband, Pedro Arias Maldonado was also sentenced in absentia at this *auto*.
270. Charges against Esperanza Rodríguez, AGN Mexico, Inq. 419, exp. 6, fol. 62r.
271. Testimony of Catalina Enríquez, 28 May 1643; AGN Mexico, Inq. 393/12/3, fol. 149v.; eslewhere given as testimony of 18 May 1643; ibid., 408, exp. 2, leg. 1, fol. 421v.
272. AGN Mexico, Inq. 393/12/3, fols. 80v., 149v., 294v. Intriguing differences accompany the question of who washed the body of Blanca Enríquez. Her daughter Beatriz says that it was Blanca de Rivera and Rodríguez who were supposed to do so (testimony of 19 September 1647; ibid., fol. 294v.). Raphaela Enríquez says that it was Blanca de Rivera, some of Blanca's daughters and Rodríguez (response to charges, 28 September 1647; ibid., 402, exp. 1, leg. 2, fol. 343r.). Also involved in preparing Blanca's corpse was Maria Baptista, the "mestiça of the said house," as well as a Black slave woman of Rafaela Enríquez named Sicilia (only mentioned in the testimony of Antonio Lopez de Orduña, ibid., 393/12/3, fol. 177v.; and in the testimony of Maria Baptista, ibid., fol. 192v.). It seems from Maria Baptista's deposition that it was she, Rodríguez and the slave Sicilia who actually washed the body

(ibid., 193r.). As in other similar cases, it is unclear whether such arrangements reflect sentiments of intimacy, convenience or necessity. Like Blanca (and Rodríguez, for that matter), Maria Baptista was an older woman, aged fifty in 1643 (testimony of Maria Bautista, March 1643; ibid., fol. 191r.). Beatriz Enríquez testifies that before she died Blanca took from her desk an agnus dei to give to Maria, something that seems to greatly upset one of Blanca's daughters, who ran out of the room. It is not clear if Beatriz is describing her own reaction or that of one of her sisters nor whether the reaction stems from a feeling that this gift is too good for Maria Bautista (and should have gone to one of the daughters) or from sadness over Blanca's impending death (testimony of 29 October 1642; ibid., fol. 234r.-v.). It should be noted that Ysavel de Silva claims that when Blanca Enríquez was at the moment of death, she, all her daughters and Ysavel Tinoco threw out the two women who were present who were not observers of the Law of Moses, one of whom was Maria Baptista (testimony of 30 June 1643; ibid., 402, exp. 1, leg. 2, fol. 90r.). Finally, Rodríguez testifies that she noticed that after Blanca's death, Maria Baptista was "very angry that they made her eat things fried in oil" rather than in lard (testimony of 21 April 1643; ibid., 408, exp. 2, leg. 1, fol. 473r.). Baptista later testifies before the Inquisition.

273. Testimony of 17 March 1643; AGN Mexico, Inq. 408, exp. 2, leg. 1, fol. 441v.; also mentioned in the testimony Ysavel de Rivera, 22 September 1642; ibid., fol. 429v. Rodríguez confirms that Juana sent to have this garment made five days before Blanca's death (testimony of 21 April 1643; ibid., fol. 472v.).
274. Testimony of Gaspar Vaez Sevilla, 13 February 1644; AGN Mexico, Inq. 393, exp. 12, leg. 3, fols. 110v.-111r.; testimony of Catalina Enríquez, 28 May 1643; ibid., fol. 150r. Though Blanca Enríquez is not named in Vaez Sevilla's testimony, it is clearly her funeral being described. Among other clues is the discussion of the burial of her body along with some of her teeth that had fallen out while she was alive, which someone reported the tribunal was going to investigate, to the point of disinterring the body, considering it a Jewish practice to make sure all body parts were properly buried (in order to be whole for the future resurrection of the dead). Her fallen teeth are mentioned by other witnesses who describe her death or the burial. Ysavel de Silva claims that Blanca "expressly ordered" that these teeth be buried with her (testimony of 30 June 1643; AGN Mexico, Inq. 415, exp. 6, fol. 521r.).
275. Beginning with her testimony of 21 April 1643; AGN Mexico, Inq. 408, exp. 2, leg. 1, fol. 466v. and passim.
276. Testimony of 21 April 1643; AGN Mexico, Inq. 408, exp. 2, leg. 1, fols. 467v.-468r. All this was true as well with Blanca Enríquez's sister, Clara de Silva (ibid., fols. 468r.-v.).

277. Testimony of 21 April 1643; AGN Mexico, Inq. 408, exp. 2, leg. 1, fol. 469r.
278. Testimony of 21 April 1643; AGN Mexico, Inq. 408, exp. 2, leg. 1, fol. 468r. Is it possible that Juana Rodríguez was related to, was even the mother of Esperanza's father, Francisco Rodríguez?
279. Testimony of 21 April 1643; AGN Mexico, Inq. 408, exp. 2, leg. 1, fols. 467r., 466v. Rodríguez claims that when Margarita de Rivera married her cousin Miguel Nuñez de Huerta they did not even bother with the Christian wedding procedures, usually performed at some point just for appearances (ibid., fol. 467r.-v.).
280. Testimony of Esperanza Rodríguez, 21 April 1643; AGN Mexico, Inq. 408, exp. 2, leg. 1, fol. 470r. The constant maximalization of the character of the connections between Rodríguez and the others may point to a need on her part to assert her centrality, her firm standing within this White judaizing circle to her White inquisitors or to herself.
281. Testimony of 21 April 1643; AGN Mexico, Inq. 408, exp. 2, leg. 1, fol. 468r.
282. Cited in Lewin, *Singular proceso de Salomón Machorro*, 201-2. León/Machorro continues by saying that on another occasion Blanca Enríquez informed him that Rodríguez's daughter, Juana, whom he had never met, was also a secret Jew.
283. According to the Inquisition's scribe; deposition of Esperanza Rodríguez, 7 August 1642; AGN Mexico, Inq. 408, exp. 2, leg. 1, fol. 459v. After months in jail, when first moved to confess her sins/crimes, Rodríguez says that "satan [*el Demonio*] had blinded her," a phraseaology perhaps more common to Afroiberians before the Inquisition than Judeoconversos (testimony of 30 January 1643; ibid., fol. 464r.).
284. AGN Mexico, Inq. 419, exp. 6, fol. 70r.
285. Publication of charges against Esperanza Rodríguez, AGN Mexico, Inq. 419, exp. 6, fols. 80v., 81v.; charges against Esperanza Rodríguez, ibid., fol. 60r.-v. In the latter document, the person/people on whose testimony these charges are based is/are not named. The trial record against Rodríguez is not complete, though some of the missing material appears in the documentation of other trials. In her response to the accusations against her, Rodríguez denies having said these things (ibid., fol. 70r.).
286. Response to the charges against her, AGN Mexico, Inq. 419, exp. 6, fol. 70r.
287. Charges against Esperanza Rodríguez, AGN Mexico, Inq. 419, exp. 6, fol. 60r.-v. In her response to the charges against her, Rodríguez confirms that she taught this prayer to her daughters, but that they recited it only when they fasted (ibid., fol. 70r.). A slightly differing version appears in the publication of charges against Rodríguez, ibid., fol. 81r.: "Con las armas de Adonai/andare armada/con la capa de Abraham/andare cobijada/con la fe de Ysmael/en mi coraçon/por donde quiera q fuere/y viniese, buenos y malos encontrare/los buenos se me allegaiar/y los malos se me arredraran/que no

temere vara de justicia/ni alcalde, ni familiar/que no me podra maleser/ni mal empecer/ni mas mal de lo que paso/Aman sobre Mardoqueo."
288. As rendered quite traditionally in a fifteenth-century Ladino siddur for women, God is asked "non me traygas [...] ni a lugar de menos precio," and "que me escapes [...] de desverwuensamentos de façes y de desvergüensán façes, de ombre malo [...] de vesino malo, de encuentro malo [...] de ui io grave y de dueño de uicio duro, quier que es de mi ley quier que non se a de mi ley" (*Siddur Tefillot: A Woman's Ladino Prayer Book [Paris B.N., Esp. 668; 15th c.],* A Critical Edition by Moshe Lazar [Lancaster, CA: Labyrinthos, 1995], 4).
289. Silverblatt, "Colonial Conspiracies," 262, 275, n. 12.
290. Lewis, *Hall of Mirrors,* 143.
291. Quoted in Castelló, *Francisco de la Cruz,* 1:46.
292. See Robert Ricard, "Otra contribución al estudio de las fiestas de 'moros y cristianos,' " *Miscelanea P. Rivet, Octogenario Dicata* (Mexico: Universidad Nacional, 1960), 2:871-79; Nicolás Cushner, "Las fiestas de 'moros y cristianos' en las Islas Filipinas," *Revista de Historia de América* 52 (Dec. 1961): 518-20.
293. Testimony of Beatriz Enríquez, 19 January 1645; AGN Mexico, Inq. 393/12/3, fol. 278r. Blanca de Rivera states that Lopez was Portuguese (testimony of 18 July 1642; ibid., 408, exp. 2, leg. 1, fol. 410v.).
294. Testimony of 13 July 1642; AGN Mexico, Inq. 408, exp. 2, leg. 1, fol. 400v.; testimony of 15 September 1642; ibid., fol. 401r.
295. Testimony of 30 July 1642; AGN Mexico, Inq. 408, exp. 2, leg. 1, fol. 433r.
296. Testimony of 15 September 1642; AGN Mexico, Inq. 408, exp. 2, leg. 1, fol. 401v.
297. Testimony of 15 September 1642; AGN Mexico, Inq. 408, exp. 2, leg. 1, fol. 401v.
298. Testimony of 15 September 1642; AGN Mexico, Inq. 408, exp. 2, leg. 1, fol. 401v. All this took place in Guadalajara. Going out to the river to distract themselves, they eventually got trapped in an unwanted social call by a couple they knew, who would not let them return home despite their excuses. They decided that it was better to break the fast than to attract suspicion and remained and ate (ibid., fols. 401v.-402r.; testimony of Esperanza Rodríguez, 21 April 1643; ibid., fol. 471v.).
299. Testimony of 15 September 1642; AGN Mexico, Inq. 408, exp. 2, leg. 1, fol. 401v.
300. Testimony of Esperanza Rodríguez, 21 April 1643; AGN Mexico, Inq. 408, exp. 2, leg. 1, fol. 470v.
301. As reported by Ysabel de Silva, also imprisoned for judaizing; testimony of 9 July 1643; AGN Mexico, Inq. 402, exp. 1, leg. 2, fols. 107v.-108r., 109r.
302. Testimony of 24 July 1642; AGN Mexico, Inq. 408, exp. 2, leg. 1, fol. 446r.

303. Testimony of 15 September 1642; AGN Mexico, Inq. 408, exp. 2, leg. 1, fol. 402r.
304. Testimony of Catalina Enríquez, 28 May 1643; AGN Mexico, Inq. 393, exp. 12, leg. 3, fol. 151r.; testimony of Beatriz Enríquez, 7 January 1645; ibid., 271r. The latter states that up to 20 pesos went to "Justa Mendez, who was secluded in the hospital of the Indians, who was dying," transmitted by a Black slave named Ysavel. What was this Crypto-Jew doing in the hospital for Amerindians, which had been founded for that purpose in the mid-sixteenth century, endowed and sponsored by the Crown itself? Or was this hospital no longer solely serving its originally intended population? Rafaela Enríquez says that her husband, Gaspar Suarez, withdrew to this hospital because of various lawsuits and demands to pay debts brought against him (testimony of 2 January 1643; ibid., 402, exp. 1, leg. 2, fol. 249v.).
305. Testimony of 15 September 1642; AGN Mexico, Inq. 408, exp. 2, leg. 1, fol. 402r.
306. Testimoney of Maria de Rivera; AGN Mexico, Inq. 393, exp. 12, leg. 3, fol.30r.
307. Testimony of 24 July 1642; AGN Mexico, Inq. 405, exp. 8, fol. 430r. Ferry thinks that the above-mentioned masses were actually a code word for the judaizing fasts and notes the close parallel between the Catholic practice of paying priests to say masses for the souls of those who had died ("Don't Drink the Chocolate").
308. AGN Mexico, Inq. 393/12/3, fols. 13v.-14r., 325r. Pedro Tinoco, for instance requests "three or four pesos" (testimony of Beatriz Enríquez; ibid., fol. 257r.).
309. AGN Mexico, Inq. 393, exp. 12, leg. 3, fols. 68r., 127v. Núñez de Peralta's statement might be assessed in light of the assertation of Raphaela that "it is very normal that men do not declare themselves [observers of the Law of Moses] to women / es muy de ordinario no declararse los hombres con los mugeres" (ibid., 129r.).
310. Testimony of 24 July 1642; AGN Mexico, Inq. 393, exp. 12, leg. 3, fol.213r.
311. Testimony of 13 January 1643; AGN Mexico, Inq. 408, exp. 2, leg. 1, fol. 426r. Rodríguez offers a different story, saying that she and Raphaela, as well as her sister Catalina, confessed their Jewishness to one another around 1630. One source of the distance alleged by Raphaela could be Rodríguez's knowledge that both Raphaela and Catalina were carrying on extramarital affairs, or so Rodríguez told the inquisitors (testimony of 21 April 1643; ibid., fol. 469v.).
312. Testimony of 18 July 1642; AGN Mexico, Inq. 408, exp. 2, leg. 1, fol. 410v.
313. Publication of the charges against Esperanza Rodríguez, AGN Mexico, Inq. 419, exp. 6, fol. 82r.
314. Testimony of 24 July 1642; AGN Mexico, Inq. 393, exp. 12, leg. 3, fol. 213r.
315. Charges against Esperanza Rodríguez, AGN Mexico, Inq. 419, exp. 6, fols. 67v.-68r.

316. Testimony of 13 January 1643; AGN Mexico, Inq. 408, exp. 2, leg. 1, fol. 435r. According to Ysavel de Silva, the response was that Rodríguez and her daughter "were from our people / eran de los nuestros" (testimony of 10 July 1643, ibid., 415, exp. 6, fol. 524r.).
317. AGN Mexico, Inq. 419, exp. 6, fol. 121r.
318. "[E]sta confesante creyo, y entendio que la dha da Blanca enriquez se los avia dado, a la dha doña Beatriz su hija, para repartir entre pobres, observantes de la dha ley de Moisen" (AGN Mexico, Inq. 393, exp. 12, leg. 3, fols. 28v., 30r.; see also the testimony of Antonio Lopez de Orduña, 1 September 1642, ibid., fol. 175v.).
319. "Y tambien Repartio de este dinero hasta en cantidad de setenta ps. a una mulata llamada esperanza Rodríguez q aun q esta confessante sabia por Relacion q era obserbante de la ley de moissen, y la havia tratado en diferentes cossas nunca se havia declarado con ella hasta q murio la dha d. Blanca enriquez su madre q fue la dha esperansa Rodríguez a cassa de esta confessante, Y pidiendole del dho dinero la cantidad q arriba Refiere Para aiunarles por el alma de la difunta esta confessante la Pregunto q Para q queria tanto dinero junto a q la dha esperanza Rodríguez Respondio que Para ella, Y Para sus hijas Por q, Ya las havia enseñado al ley de moissen Conte q^l esta Confessante le dio les dhos setenta ps. declarandose con ella, Y ella Con la dha esperanza Rodríguez por obserbantes de la dha ley" (testimony of Beatriz Enríquez, 24 July 1642; AGN Mexico, Inq. 393, exp. 12, leg. 3, fol. 213r.). In her response to the witnesses, Rodríguez mentions that "she requested the money" from Beatriz (15 September 1644; ibid., 419, exp. 6, fol. 113r.).
320. Testimony of Ysabel Antunes, 14 December 1644; AGN Mexico, Inq. 402, exp. 1, leg. 2, fol. 152r. Rodríguez also received the two shirts which she had wet in order to wash the blood off of Blanca Enríquez's head, which Rodríguez seems to have asked to have (responses to the charges against her, ibid., 419, exp. 6, fol. 69v.) or, elsewhere in the same responses, two shirts and two sheets (ibid., fol. 110r.).
321. Charges against Esperanza Rodríguez, AGN Mexico, Inq. 419, exp. 6, fol. 63v.
322. Testimony of Juana del Bosque, 15 September 1642; AGN Mexico, Inq. 408, exp. 2, leg. 1, fol. 404r.; testimony of Raphaela Enríquez, 18 July 1642; ibid., fol. 426r.-v.; testimony of Juana Enríquez, 17 March 1643; ibid., fol. 441r.; 22 June 1643, ibid., fol. 441v. Rodríguez claims that she doesn't recall receiving alms on one occasion from Juana, but from Juana's sister Beatriz (response to the witnesses, 15 September 1644, AGN Mexico, Inq. 419, exp. 6, fol. 111v.).
323. Publication of the charges against Esperanza Rodríguez, AGN Mexico, Inq. 419, exp. 6, fol. 88v.

324. Testimony of Blanca de Rivera, 18 July 1642; AGN Mexico, Inq. 408, exp. 2, leg. 1, fol. 410r.
325. AGN Mexico Inq. 392, exp. 2, fol. 2r.
326. Descriptions such as *maltratado, quebrado, mui roto, muy viejo* abound.
327. AGN Mexico Inq. 392, exp. 2, fol. 3v.-4v.
328. AGN Mexico, Inq. 392, exp. 3, fol. 6r.
329. AGN Mexico, Inq. 393, exp. 12, leg. 3, fol. 145r.; repeated in Inq. 408, exp. 2, leg. 1, fol. 402v. It should be noted that Juana claims that Rodríguez also bought with this money an engraving or plate (*lamina*) of "our lady of the conception" and a purple christening robe.
330. Testimony of Juana Enríquez, 17 March 1643; AGN Mexico, Inq. 408, exp. 2, leg. 1, fol. 441r.
331. Charges against Esperanza Rodríguez, AGN Mexico, Inq. 419, exp. 6, fol. 65r.-v.
332. Testimony of 21 April 1643; AGN Mexico, Inq. 408, exp. 2, leg. 1, fols. 469v.-470r.
333. See, for instance, Jaffary, *False Mystics*, 118.
334. AGN Mexico, Inq. 419, exp. 6, fol. 120v.
335. Testimony of Esperanza Rodríguez, 7 August 1642; AGN Mexico, Inq. 408, exp. 2, leg. 1, fol. 459v. A note to the inquisitors in her handwriting, rather strong and legible, appears among the trial records (ibid., 419, exp. 6, fol. 130r.).
336. Testimony of 7 August 1642; AGN Mexico, Inq. 408, exp. 2, leg. 1, fol. 458v.-459r. "y aunque la dicha su hija tiene oltro niño y niña son de diferentes padres el hijo es de Don Nicolas de Alarcon hijo del governador que fue de soconuz [...]." Juana's husband was much older; Esperanza says he is 70. At some point he had gone to Caracas to work with cocoa, but never returned; they think he is dead (testimony of 21 April 1643; ibid., fol. 471v.).
337. Testimony of 7 August 1642; AGN Mexico, Inq. 408, exp. 2, leg. 1, fol. 460r. I could not confirm the identification of these two figures.
338. Testimony of Esperanza Rodríguez, 7 August 1642; AGN Mexico, Inq. 408, exp. 2, leg. 1, fol. 460r.
339. Publication of the charges against Esperanza Rodríguez, AGN Mexico, Inq. 419, exp. 6, fol. 96v.
340. A remarkably similar tale is recounted to the same effect by an unnamed modern informant of Middle-Eastern background (Susan Starr Sered, "Food and Holiness: Cooking as a Sacred Act Among Middle-Eastern Jewish Women," *Anthropological Quarterly* 61,3 [1988]: 129). I have not investigated the origins of the story, which may have been well-known among Sephardim.
341. Testimony of Esperanza Rodríguez, 7 August 1642; AGN Mexico, Inq. 408, exp. 2, leg. 1, fol. 458v. Her lack of any siblings, aunts or uncles from her mother's side might also explain her search for a community among her owners' family.

342. Joan Bristol, Unpublished paper, "Focusing Different Lenses on Esperanza Rodriguez, a mulata Jew in Seventeenth Century Mexico," presented at the Future(s) of Microhistory Symposium, University of Rochester, November 2017, 6, citing from her Inquisition trial, AGN Mexico, Inq. 408, exp. 2, leg. 1, fol. , 460.
343. Testimony of 30 January 1643; AGN Mexico, Inq. 408, exp. 2, leg. 1, fol. 465r.; repeated in the summary and sentence of the inquisitors, ibid., 419, exp. 6, fol. 117v. Ironically, or suitably, depending on one's perspective, the young Esperanza responds as one commanded, whether as a young slave girl to her masters or as a servant only of God: "she responded that she would do that which they commanded and would believe in that God of aDonay."
344. Ishac Athias, *Thesoro de preceptos adonde se encierran las joyas de los seys cientos y treze preceptos, que encomendó el señor a su pueblo israel. Con sv declaracion, razon, y dinim, conforme a la verdadera tradicion, recibida de Mosè y enseñada por nuestros sabios de gloriosa memoria* (Amsterdam: Semuel ben Israel Soeyro, 5409 [1649]; orig. Venice: Gioanne Caleoni, 1627), 67a.
345. Alberro, "Negros y mulatos en los documentos inquisitoriales," 144.
346. Cited in Alberro, "Negros y mulatos en los documentos inquisitoriales," 144.
347. For some examples from sixteenth-century Aragón, see Padilla, *Relación judeoconversa*, 15; from Spain, Graizbord, "Conformity and Dissidence among Judeoconversos," 311; from sixteenth-century Portugal, Lipiner, *Sapateiro de Trancoso*, 267.
348. Early 1640s; AGN Mexico, Inq. 403, exp. 1, leg. 2, fol. 364r. Indeed, the scribe or one of the inquisitors underlined the last statement as if to call attention to its heretical character.
349. Charges against Maria de Rivera, 1642; AGN Mexico, Inq. 403, exp. 3, fol. 379r.
350. Salomon, "Spanish Marranism Re-examined," 117.
351. Beatriz Enriquez related that Margarita de Rivera told her that Sobremonte "knew many prayers of the Law of Moses and that hearing, she was left with her mouth open, because he was very learned in the matters of the Law" (testimony of Beatriz Enriquez, 7 January 1645; AGN Mexico, Inq. 393/12/3, fol. 270v.).
352. Cited in Alberro, "Negros y mulatos en los documentos inquisitoriales," 146.
353. See *Auto General de la Fee [...]Celebrado En la Plaça mayor de la muy noble, y muy leal ciudad de Mexico, à los 19. de Noviembre de 1659. años* (Mexico: La Imprenta del Secreto del Santo Officio, n.d.), s.v. Maria de la Cruz.
354. Cited in Jaffary, *False Mystics*, 33.
355. From the summary regarding Pedro de Mercado, in Bocanegra, *Auto general de la fee celebrada*, unpag.
356. Basing himself largely on Alberro, José Piedra has likewise found that most of "the self-accusations [of prominent black citizens of New Spain] are of

being Jewish, and it remains difficult to separate fact from fiction, particularly because many blacks enjoyed a symbiotic cultural relationship with Jews" (José Piedra, "Literary Whiteness and the Afro-Hispanic Difference," in Dominick LaCapra [ed.], *The Bounds of Race: Perspectives on Hegemony and Resistance* [Ithaca Cornell University Press, 1991], 286, n. 14). Ironically, Piedra erases the negative side of this "symbiosis," ignoring the cases Alberro brings which show Afroiberians adopting the anti-Jewish prejudices of their new religion and society (a few cited in previous chapters).

357. Mello, *Gente da nação*, 25.
358. Kathryn L. Morgan, *Children of Strangers: The Stories of a Black Family* (Philadelphia: Temple University Press, 1980), 102-103.
359. Cited in Gracia Boix, *Autos de fe y causas de la inquisición de Córdoba*, 160.
360. Quoted in Gracia Boix, *Autos de fe y causas de la inquisición de Córdoba*, 83.
361. Sweet, *Recreating Africa*, 89.
362. Quoted in Villa-Flores, "Blasphemy and Slavery in New Spain," 436.
363. Quoted in Jaffary, *False Mystics*, 33. Needless to say, the inquisitors suspected Núñez of crypto-Judaism.
364. She is called *atesada*, meaning "double black" or "jet black."
365. Quoted in Gracia Boix, *Autos de fe y causas de la Inquisición de Córdoba*, 359.
366. Cited in Pullan, *Jews of Europe and the Inquisition of Venice*, 74-75, from Archivio di Stato, Venice, Santo Uffizio, b. 44, proc. Samuel Maestro, 30 April to 6 Aug. 1579. Testimony given to the Lisbon Inquisition by a visitor to Amsterdam records a 1611 encounter with Diogo Dias Querido, a prominent trader whose career had moved between Brazil, Amsterdam and the West African coast. The visitor met Querido at the synagogue: "there were three blacks at the door of the synagogue, making a great fuss because the Jews had perverted (sic) one of their black friends and turned him into a Jew" (Green, "Masters of Difference," 190). On Querido, see Schorsch, *Jews and Blacks*, 93; Green, "Masters of Difference," 189-91). What remains unclear from this testimony is whether the fuss is positive or negative, though it is probable that the understanding that the Black's conversion was a perversion belonged to the denouncer.
367. Sandoval, *Tratado sobre esclavitud*, 397; cited in Margaret M. Olsen, *Slavery and Salvation in Colonial Cartagena de Indias* (Gainesville: University Press of Florida, 2004), 111. See also Olsen's sensitive parsing of a passage in Sandoval's *De instauranda Aethiopum*, in which an African priest who converted to Christianity explains to a Muslim that Whites are free and Blacks enslaved because God created Whites first and sent those created last to serve their elders/betters (Olsen, *Slavery and Salvation*, 129-30).
368. Masarah van Eyck kindly informed me of this quotation; *The Jesuit Relations and Allied Documents: Travels and Explorations of the Jesuit Missionaries in New France, 1610-1791*, the original French, Latin, and Italian texts, with English

translations and notes, ed. Reuben Gold Thwaites, 73 vols. in 36 (New York: Pageant Book Co., 1959), 5:63.
369. Cited in Boxer, *The Church Militant*, 36. These sentiments were not limited to the Iberian Catholic sphere. Perhaps the best indication that the valences involved in such distinctions contained metaphysical import is the revealing title of a mid-seventeenth-century English translation of a conversionary tract aimed at Jews by the formerly Jewish "Samuel of Morocco": Thomas Calvert, *The Blessed Jew of Marocco: or, A Blackmoor Made White Being a Demonstration of the True Messias out of the Law and Prophets by Rabbi Samuel* (York: Thomas Broad, 1649). In this case, Jews are themselves seen as non-White; see Schorsch, *Jews and Blacks*, chs. 7 and 8.
370. For a view from other places and era, see Gauri Viswanathan, *Outside the Fold: Conversion, Modernity, and Belief* (Princeton: Princeton University Press, 1998); Van der Veer, *Conversion to Modernities*.
371. *Relacion sumeria del auto particular de fee*, in García, *Documentos*, 163. The 30 year-old Portuguese-born Pérez was said to be circumcised.
372. Testimony of 24 September 1644, AGN Mexico, Inq. 419, exp. 6, fol. 114r.
373. Charges against Esperanza Rodríguez, 2 September 1644, AGN Mexico, Inq. 419, exp. 6, fol. 68v.
374. This behavior supposedly went on for six months (summary of the case and sentencing, AGN Mexico, Inq. 419, exp. 6, fol. 121v.
375. According to E. William Monter and John Tedeschi, the "compilers of inquisitorial handbooks were unanimous in their opinion that this sentence [of life imprisonment] should be commuted when, after three years, the convicted heretic had shown signs of real contrition" (E. William Monter and John Tedeschi, "Toward a Statistical Profile of the Italian Inquisitions, Sixteenth to Eighteenth Centuries," in Henningsen and Tedeschi, *The Inquisition in Early Modern Europe: Studies on Sources and Methods*, 157, n. 73). Various cases show that such penal theory did not always triumph in practice.
376. *Relacion sumeria del auto particular de fee*, in García, *Documentos*, 155-156. Rodríguez might well be the "mulata loca" whom Francisco de la Cruz describes calling for him and asking "when the news of leaving [the jails] and the pardon arrives," a question she asked the other slaves as well (Testimony of 19 October 1643; AGN Mexico, Inq. 396/3/6, fol.535r.).
377. Summary and sentence, AGN Mexico, Inq. 419, exp. 6, fol. 126v.
378. *Relacion sumeria del auto particular de fee*, in García, *Documentos*, 160-1.
379. In the *Relación sumeria*, Isabel is said to be 24, not 25, and Juana's aunt, not sister (hermana de padre y madre de la dicha Juana del Bosque; ibid., 160).
380. *Relacion sumeria del auto particular de fee*, in García, *Documentos*, 160.
381. María is said to be 19, not 20, in the *Relación sumeria* (ibid., 169).
382. *Relacion sumeria del auto particular de fee*, in García, *Documentos*, 169.

383. Joan Bristol and Tamara Harvey, "Creole Civic Pride and Positioning 'Exceptional' Black Women," Mary McAleer Balkun and Susan C. Imbarrato (eds.) *Women's Narratives of the Early Americas and the Formation of Empire* (New York: Palgrave Macmillan, 2016), 57.
384. AGN Mexico, Inq. 419, exp. 6, fol. 130r.-v.
385 AHN, Inq., Leg. 5348, no. 1.
386 AHN, Inq., Libro 1065, Destierro.
387. The quotes are from Sweet, *Recreating Africa*, 33.

Conclusion

388. Testimony of Ysavel de Silva, 25 June 1643, AGN Mexico, Inq. 415, exp. 6, fol. 519r. My translation is intentionally loose.
389. Hernández, *Delirio*, 48.
390. Hernández, *Delirio*, 204.
391. For instance, Yirmiyahu Yovel, *The Marrano of Reason* (Princeton: Princeton University Press, 1989), 34-6.
392. Maya Restrepo, *Brujería*, 577.
393. Maya Restrepo, *Brujería*, 593.
394. Silverblatt, "Colonial Conspiracies," 262, 263, 275, n. 13.
395. I find the conclusions of Fuchs, *Mimesis and Empire*, 164-6, insightful and convincing.
396. Fuchs, Mimesis and Empire, 165.
397. Baltasar Fra-Molinero, "Juan Latino and His Racial Difference," in Earle and Lowe, *Black Africans in Renaissance Europe*, 334-5; on Muley, see Fuchs, *Mimesis and Empire*, 101-7. Morisco protest proved ineffectual. By the mid-1570s, fourteen percent of the morisco population of the city of Granada, mostly women, had been enslaved.
398. Herrera, Natives, Europeans, and Africans, 115.
399. Donald H. Akenson, If the Irish Ran the World: Montserrat, 1630-1730 (Montreal: McGill-Queen's University Press, 1997), 117-53; Richard S. Dunn, Sugar and Slaves: The Rise of the Planter Class in the English West Indies, 1624-1713 (Chapel Hill: University of North Carolina Press, 1972), 130.
400. Michel de Certeau, The Practice of Everyday Life, trans. by Steven F. Rendall (Berkeley: University of California Press, 1984), xiii-xiv; see also Pierre Bourdieu, Pascalian Meditations (Stanford: Stanford University Press, 2000), 185.
401. James C. Scott, *Weapons of the Weak; Everyday Forms of Peasant Resistance* (New Haven: Yale University Press, 1985), 42.
402. Hall, Slavery and African Ethnicities in the Americas, 167.

403. Mieke Bal, *Lethal Love: Feminist Literary Readings of Biblical Love Stories* (Bloomington: Indiana University Press, 1987), 110.
404. Horowitz, *Reckless Rites*, 174-81. Gitlitz, *Secrecy and Deceit*, 162-4, also discusses the phenomenon, coming to conclusions very similar to Horowitz.
405. Anthony Pagden, *Fall of Natural Man*, 36. Pagden cites various Inquisition cases.
406. Carlos M. N. Eire, *War Against the Idols: The Reformation of Worship from Erasmus to Calvin* (Cambridge: Cambridge University Press, 1986), 105-65; Natalie Zemon Davis, "The Rites of Violence," *Past and Present* 59 (1973): 51-91.
407. William Monter, *Frontiers of Heresy*, 228.
408. Jaffary, *False Mystics*, 10.
409. For New Spain, see Villa-Flores, "To Lose One's Soul," 435-68; for the Portuguese world, see Sweet, *Recreating Africa*, 210-14.
410. Lewis, *Hall of Mirrors*, 108.
411. Horowitz, *Reckless Rites*, 197-8, 271-2.
412. Horowitz, *Reckless Rites*, 181.
413. Though Horowitz tells us (*Reckless Rites*, 181) that this Converso behavior did not descend from rabbinic tradition, the narrative of his entire book seems to establish Jewish violence from ancient times to modern as a coherent cultural feature.
414. Gitlitz, *Secrecy and Deceit*, 162.
415. Anidjar, "Lines of Blood," 4-5; see also William A. Christian, Jr., *Local Religion in Sixteenth-Century Spain* (Princeton: Princeton University Press, 1981), 192-3; Gallagher and Greenblatt, *Practicing New Historicism*, ch. 3 ("The Wound in the Wall").
416. Gallagher and Greenblatt, *Practicing New Historicism*, 99.
417. Gallagher and Greenblatt, *Practicing New Historicism*, 104.
418. Patrick Geary, "Humiliation of Saints," in *Saints and their Cults: Studies in Religious Sociology, Folklore, and History*, ed. Stephen Wilson (Cambridge University Press, 1983), 123-40.
419. Norman Simms, *Masks in the Mirror: Marranism in Jewish Experience* (New York: Peter Lang, 2006). Though studded with insights and novel perspectives, Simms' study cannot transcend its own kind of reactive mania, a scattershot lack of methodology, over-the-top generalizations, ahistorical psychologistic speculations, idiosyncratic black-or-white maximalizations and a seeming unconcern for the most basic forms of analyzing historical actors and events (he does not cite a single solid source in Spanish or Portuguese and relies on a disturbingly high number of materials from the internet).
420. The formulation, "honorable" men, was of course ubiquitous among European elites and their creole counterparts. In 1598, the officers of the royal

audiencia in Mexico wrote to the Spanish king, warning of the consequences should the crown fail to uphold the feudal contract with its Mexican subjects. The text is suffused with the moralizing language of race and class: "Honorable men who by chance see themselves, their encomiendas exhausted, [reduced] to great poverty while others who arrived yesterday grow wealthy in the land their forefathers helped to win, taking due account of the value of their services, these men, who are unused to suffering ills, may join up with mulattoes, blacks, and other perfidious peoples and attempt some uprising" (quoted in Pagden, "Identity Formation in Spanish America," 54).

421. Burns, *Colonial Habits*, 3-4.
422. The term "maximalist" comes from Lincoln, *Holy Terrors*, 5; the quote is from Asad, *Genealogies of Religion*, 63.
423. Spinoza, *Ethics* [1677], pt. 3, prop. 9, note.
424. Stephen Greenblatt, *Renaissance Self-Fashioning: From More to Shakespeare* (Chicago: University of Chicago Press, 1980), 225.
425. The dark early modern obverse of the kind of miraculous medieval transformations treated in Caroline Walker Bynum, *Metamorphosis and Identity* (New York: Zone Books, 2001).
426. For a meditation on simultaneous status as victims and dominators, see Athalya Brenner, " 'On the Rivers of Babylon' (Psalm 137), or Between Victim and Perpetrator," in *Sanctified Aggression: Legacies of Biblical and Post Biblical Vocabularies of Violence*, ed. Jonneke Bekkenkamp and Yvonne Sherwood (London: T & T Clark International, 2003), 76-91.
427. See, for instance, Bourdieu, *Pascalian Meditations*, 156-63.
428. Yovel, Marrano of Reason, x.
429. Silverblatt, *Modern Inquisitions*, 16.
430. For examples, Stephanie E. Smallwood, "African Guardians, European Slave Ships, and the Changing Dynamics of Power in the Early Modern Atlantic," *The William and Mary Quarterly*, 3rd Series, 64,4 (October 2007): 679-716; John Thornton, "African Political Ethics and the Slave Trade: Central African Dimensions.," http://muweb.millersville.edu/~winthrop/Thornton.html.
431. Bourdieu, Pascalian Meditations, 181.
432. Some revisionist works wind up suffering from a kind of reverse imbalance. Thus Sweet's fine study does not, ultimately, convince me that "the adoption of African spiritual elements by Catholic priests was no different from the African embrace of [Portuguese] Catholic elements" or that "the impact of Christianity on Africans was no greater than the impact of African beliefs on Christians" (*Recreating Africa*, 225, 230). Or Ramón Grosfoguel: "Slaves' prayers to Catholic saints are strategies of hybridization and *mestizaje* that have nothing to do with 'syncretism.' The hybridization practiced on the

subaltern side of colonial difference represents 'subversive complicity,' 'border thinking,' and 'transculturation;' subsistence and resistance in the face of colonial power. The Catholic saints were 'transculturated' and 'transmodernized' so as to subvert and redefine them within a global, non-European cosmology. Each saint was converted into an African God" (Ramón Grosfoguel, "Hybridity and *Mestizaje*: Syncretism or Subversive Complicity? Subalternity from the Perspective of the Coloniality of Power," in *The Masters and the Slaves: Plantation Relations and* Mestizaje *in American Imaginaries*, ed. Alexandra Isfahani-Hammond [New York: Palgrave Macmillan, 2005], 125). Even Certeau's awe-inspiring analysis of mysticism proffers at one point a romanticized homogenization of 'Marrano' mysticism within Catholicism (*The Mystic Fable*, 22-3).

433. Mangan, *Trading Roles*, 11.
434. Walter D. Mignolo, "Colonial Situations, Geographic Discourses, and Territorial Representations: Toward a Diatopical Understanding of Colonial Semiosis," *Dispositio* 14,36-38 (1989): 93-140.
435. Asad, Genealogies of Religion, 3-24.
436. Asad, *Genealogies of Religion*, 4. Many of the points I argue above are made in Brian Sandberg, "Beyond Encounters: Religion, Ethnicity, and Violence in the Early Modern World, 1492-1700," *Journal of World History* 17,1 (2006): 1-25, which reached me only as this manuscript was going to press.
437. Freile, *Conquest of New Granada*, 16. The author of the Introduction is not named, but I assume it must be the translator, William Atkinson.
438. I have in mind Chava Weissler, *Voices of the Matriarchs: Listening to the Prayers of Early Modern Jewish Women* (Boston: Beacon Press, 1998), 173-6, and some of the literature she cites (255, n. 2).
439. I am paraphrasing somewhat and have taken the quote from Norman Simms, *Masks in the Mirror*, 74-5.

– Bibliography –

Abbreviations

BT = Babylonian Talmud
exp = expediente / file
JT = Jerusalem Talmud

Archival Sources

AGI = Archivo General de Indias (Seville)
AQ = Archivo de Quito
Con = *Contratación* / Transactions
Mex = Mexico
AGN Mexico = Archivo General de la Nación, Mexico
AGN Peru = Archivo General de la Nación, Peru
S.O. = Santo Oficio
Con = Contencioso
AHN = Archivo Historico Nacional (Madrid)
Inq. = Inquisition
ANTT = Arquivo Nacional Torre do Tombo
GAA = Gemeente Archief Amsterdam

Secondary Sources

Aguirre Beltrán, Gonzalo, *La población negra de México: Estudio etnohistórico* (Mexico City: Fondo de Cultura Económica, 1989).
___, *Medicina y magia: El proceso de aculturación en la estructura colonial* [Mexico City: Instituto Nacional Indigenista, 1963).
Alberro, Solange Behocaray, de, *Inquisición y sociedad en México, 1571-1700* (Mexico City: Fondo de Cultura Económica, 1988).
_____ "Negros y mulatos en los documentos inquisitoriales: rechazo e

integración," in Elsa Cecilia Frost et al (eds.), El Trabajo y los Trabajadores en la Historia de México: Ponencias y comentarios presentados en la Reunión de Historiadores Mexicanos y Norteamericanos, Pátzcuaro, 12 al 15 de octubre de 1977 (Mexico City/Tucson: El Colegio de México/University of Arizona Press, 1979).

Azevedo, J. Lúcio de, *História dos cristãos-novos portugueses*, 3rd ed. (Lisbon: Clássica Editora, 1989).

Behar, Ruth, "Sex and Sin, Witchcraft and the Devil in Late-Colonial Mexico," *American Ethnologist* 14 (Feb. 1987): 34-54.

Beinart, Haim, (ed.), *Moreshet Sepharad: the Sephardi Legacy*, 2 vols. (Jerusalem: Magnes Press/Hebrew University, 1992).

Bennett, Herman, *Africans in Colonial Mexico: Absolutism, Christianity, and Afro-Creole Consciousness, 1570-1640* (Bloomington: Indiana University Press, 2003).

Bernardini, Paolo, and Norman Fiering (eds.), *The Jews and the Expansion of Europe to the West, 1450-1800*, European Expansion & Global Interaction, Vol. 2 (New York: Berghahn Books, 2001).

Bodian, Miriam, "'Men of the Nation': The Shaping of *Converso* Identity in Early Modern Europe." *Past and Present* 143 (May 1994): 48-76.

Bowser, Frederick P., *The African Slave in Colonial Peru, 1524-1650* (Stanford: Stanford University Press, 1974).

Boxer, C. R., *The Church Militant and Iberian Expansion 1440-1770*, The Johns Hopkins Symposia in Comparative History, no. 10 (Baltimore: The Johns Hopkins University Press, 1978).

_____ The Portuguese Seaborne Empire, 1415-1825 (London: Hutchinson, 1969).

Boyajian, James C., *Portuguese Bankers at the Court of Spain, 1626-1650* (New Brunswick: Rutgers University Press, 1983).

Cañizares-Esguerra, Jorge, *Puritan Conquistadors: Iberianizing the Atlantic, 1550-1700* (Stanford: Stanford University Press, 2006).

Caro Baroja, Julio, *Los judíos en la España moderna y contemporánea*, 4th ed. (Madrid: Ediciones Istmo, 2000).

Ceballos Gómez, Diana Luz, *"Quyen tal haze que tal pague:" Sociedad y prácticas mágicas en el Nuevo Reino de Granada* (Bogotá: Ministerio de Cultura, 2002).

Certeau, Michel de, *The Mystic Fable*, vol. 1: *The Sixteenth and Seventeenth Centuries*, trans. Michael B. Smith (Chicago: University of Chicago Press, 1992).

_____ *The Practice of Everyday Life*, trans. by Steven F. Rendall (Berkeley: University of California Press, 1984).

Contreras, Jaime, Bernardo J. García García, and Ignacio Pulido (eds.), *Familia, religión y negocio: El sefardismo en las relaciones entre el mundo ibérico y los Países Bajos en la edad moderna* (Madrid: Fundación Carlos de Amberes/Ministerio de Asuntos Exteriores, 2002).

_____ and Gustav Henningsen, "Forty-Four Thousand Cases of the Spanish Inquisition (1540-1700): Analysis of a Historical Data Bank" in Gustav Henningsen and John Tedeschi (eds.) in association with Charles Amiel, *The Inquisition in Early Modern Europe: Studies on Sources and Methods* (Dekalb, Il: Northern Illinois University Press, 1986).

Cope, R. Douglas, *The Limits of Racial Domination: Plebeian Society in Colonial Mexico City, 1660-1720* (Madison: University of Wisconsin Press, 1994).

Croitoru Rotbaum, I ic, *Documentos coloniales originados en el santo oficio del tribunal de la inquisición de Cartagena de Indias (Contribución a la historia de Colombia [vol. 2])* (Bogota: Tipografia Hispana, 1971).

_____ *De sefarad al neosefardismo (Contribución a la historia de Colombia)* (Bogota: Editorial Kelly, 1967).

Curtin, Philip D., *The Atlantic Slave Trade: A Census* (Madison: University of Wisconsin Press, 1969).

Domínguez Ortiz, Antonio, *Autos de la inquisición de Sevilla (Siglo XVII)* (Seville: Servicio de Publicaciones del Ayuntamiento de Sevilla, 1981).

_____ "La Esclavitud en Castilla durante la edad moderna," *Estudios de Historia Social de España*, Carmelo Viñas y Mey (ed.) (Madrid: Consejo Superior de Investigaciones Cientificas, 1952), 2:367-428.

Dutra, Francis A. "A Hard-Fought Struggle for Recognition: Manuel Goncalves Doria, First Afro-Brazilian to Become a Knight of Santiago," *The Americas* 56:1 (July 1999): 91-113.

_____ "Blacks and the Search for Rewards and Status in Seventeenth-

Century Brazil," *Proceedings of the Pacific Coast Council on Latin American Studies*, vol. 6 (San Diego: San Diego State University, 1977-1979), 25-35.

Earle, T. F., "Black Africans versus Jews: Religious and Racial Tension in a Portuguese Saint's Play," Earle, T.F., and K. J. P. Lowe (eds.), *Black Africans in Renaissance Europe* (Cambridge University Press, 2005), 345-60.

_____ and K. J. P. Lowe (eds.), *Black Africans in Renaissance Europe* (Cambridge University Press, 2005).

Eltis, David, "Identity and Migration: The Atlantic in Comparative Perspective," in *The Atlantic World: Essays on Slavery, Migration, and Imagination*, ed. Wim Klooster and Alfred Padula (Upper Saddle River, NJ: Pearson/Prentice Hall, 2005), 108-25.

_____ "Atlantic History in Global Perspective," *Itinerario* 23,2 (1999): 141-61.

Emmanuel, Isaac S., "Seventeenth-Century Brazilian Jewry: A Critical Review," *American Jewish Archives* 14,1 (April 1962).

Farah, Caesar E. (trans. and ed.), *An Arab's Journey to Colonial Spanish America: The Travels of Elias al-Mûsili in the Seventeenth Century* (Syracuse: Syracuse University Press, 2003).

Faur, José, *In the Shadow of History: Jews and Conversos at the Dawn of Modernity* (Albany: State University of New York Press, 1992).

Ferreira Reis, Célia Maria, "A visitação de Marcos Teixeira aos Açores em 1575," Inquisição, Vol. 1: Comunicações apresentadas ao 1.º congresso luso-brasileiro sobre inquisição realizado em Lisboa, de 17 a 20 de Fevereiro de 1987 (Lisboa: Sociedade Portuguesa de Estudos do Século XVIII/Universitária Editora, 1989).

Ferry, Robert J., "Don't Drink the Chocolate: Domestic Slavery and the Exigencies of Fasting for Crypto-Jews in Seventeenth-Century Mexico," *Nuevo Mundo Mundos Nuevos* 5 (2005); http://nuevomundo.revues.org/document934.html, unpaginated.

Fuchs, Barbara, *Mimesis and Empire: The New World, Islam, and European Identities* (Cambridge: Cambridge University Press, 2001).

Gadelha, Regina Maria d'Aquino Fonseca, "Judeus e Cristãos-Novos no Rio da Prata: a Ação do Governador Hernandarias de Saavedra," in

Novinsky and Tucci Carneiro, eds., *Inquisição*.

Garcia Fuentes, Jose Maria (ed.), *La inquisición en Granada en el siglo XVI: Fuentes para su studio* (Granada: Departamento de Historia Moderna de la Universidad de Granada, 1981).

Garofalo, Leo J., "The Ethno-Economy of Food, Drink, and Stimulants: The Making of Race in Colonial Lima and Cuzco (PhD Dissertation, University of Wisconsin-Madison, 2001).

Gitlitz, David M., *Secrecy and Deceit: the Religion of the Crypto-Jews* (Philadelphia: Jewish Publication Society, 1996).

_____ "La angustia vital de ser negro: Tema de un drama de Fernando de Zárate," *Segismundo* 11 (1975): 65-85.

Gorenstein Ferreira da Silva, Lina, *Heréticos e impuros: A inquisição e os cristãos-novos no Rio de Janeiro — Século XVIII* (Rio de Janeiro: Secretaria Municipal de Cultura/Departamento Geral de Documentação e Informação Cultural, 1995).

_____ and Maria Luiza Tucci Carneiro (eds.), *Ensaios sobre a intolerância: Inquisição, marranismo e anti-semitismo (Homenagem a Anita Novinsky)* (São Paulo:Humanitas/FFLCH/USP, 2002), 65-96.

Graizbord, David Leon, "Conformity and Dissidence among Judeoconversos, 1580-1700" (PhD Dissertation, University of Michigan, 2000).

Green, Tobias, "The Role of the Portuguese Trading Posts in Guinea and Angola in the 'Apostasy' of Crypto-Jews in the 17th Century," in *Creole Societies in the Portuguese Colonial Empire*, eds. Philip J. Havik and Malyn Newitt (Bristol: Bristol University Press/Seagull/Faiolean, June 2007), 25-40.

_____ "Masters of Difference: Creolization and the Jewish Presence in Cabo Verde, 1497-1672" (PhD Dissertation: University of Birmingham, UK, 2006).

_____ "Further Considerations on the Sephardim of the Petite Côte," *History in Africa* 32 (2005): 165-83.

Grinberg, Keila (ed.), *Os judeus no Brasil: Inquisição, imigração e identidade* (Rio de Janeiro: Civilização Brasileira, 2005).

Grosfoguel, Ramón, "Hybridity and *Mestizaje*: Sincretism or Subversive Complicity? Subalternity from the Perspective of the Coloniality of

Power," in *The Masters and the Slaves: Plantation Relations and Mestizaje in American Imaginaries*, ed. Alexandra Isfahani-Hammond (New York: Palgrave Macmillan, 2005), 115-29.

Haliczer, Stephen, *Inquisition and Society in the Kingdom of Valencia, 1478-1834* (Berkeley, Calif.: University of California Press, 1990).

Hall, Gwendolyn Midlo, *Slavery and African Ethnicities in the Americas: Restoring the Links* (Chapel Hill: University of North Carolina Press, 2005).

Hall, Stuart, "Pluralism, Race and Class in Caribbean Society," in Race and Class in Post-Colonial Society: A Study of Ethnic Group Relations in the English-Speaking Caribbean, Bolivia, Chile and Mexico (Paris: UNESCO, 1977).

Henningsen, Gustav, "The Eloquence of Figures: Statistics of the Spanish and Portuguese Inquisitions and Prospects for Social History," in *The Spanish Inquisition and the Inquisitorial Mind*, ed. Angel Alcalá (Boulder: Social Science Monographs/Columbia University Press, 1987).

_____ "The Archives and the Historiography of the Spanish Inquisition," in Henningsen, Gustav, and John Tedeschi (eds.) in association with C. Amiel, *The Inquisition in Early Modern Europe: Studies on Sources and Methods* (Dekalb, Ill.: Northern Illinois University Press, 1986).

Hernández, Marie Theresa, *Delirio — the Fantastic, the Demonic, and the Réel: The Buried History of Nuevo León* (Austin: University of Texas Press, 2002).

Hernández Asensio, Raúl, *La frontera occidental de la audiencia de Quito: Viajeros y relatos de viajes (1595-1630)*, Travaux de l'Institut Français d'Etudes Andines, 203 (Lima: Instituto de Estudios Peruanos/Instituto Francés de Estudios Andinos, 2004)

Hernández Cuevas, Marco Polo, *Africa en el carnival mexicano* (Mexico City: Plaza y Valdés, 2005).

Herrera, Robinson A., *Natives, Europeans, and Africans in Sixteenth-Century Santiago de Guatemala* (Austin: University of Texas Press, 2003).

Ingram, Kevin, "Secret Lives, Public Lies: The Conversos and Socio-religious Non-conformism in the Spanish Golden Age" (PhD Diss.: University of California San Diego, 2006).

Isfahan-Hammond, Alexandra (ed.), *The Masters and the Slaves : Plantation*

Relations and Mestizaje in American Imaginaries (Palgrave Macmillan, 2004).

Israel, Jonathan I., *Diasporas Within a Diaspora: Jews, Crypto-Jews and the World Maritime Empires (1540-1740)*, Brill's Series in Jewish Studies, 30 (Leiden: Brill, 2002).

_____ *European Jewry in the Age of Mercantilism, 1550-1750* (Oxford: Clarendon Press, 1989).

_____ "Menasseh Ben Israel and the Dutch Sephardic Colonization Movement of the Mid-Seventeenth Century (1645–1657)," in Kaplan, *Menasseh Ben Israel and His World*.

_____ *Race, Class and Politics in Colonial Mexico, 1610-1670* (Oxford: Oxford University Press, 1975).

Kagan, Richard L., and Abigail Dyer (eds. and trans.), *Inquisitorial Inquiries: Brief Lives of Secret Jews and Other Heretics* (Baltimore: Johns Hopkins University Press, 2004).

Kagan, Richard L., and Philip D. Morgan (eds.), *Atlantic Diasporas: Jews, Conversos, and Crypto-Jews in the Age of Mercantilism, 1500-1800* (Baltimore: Johns Hopkins University Press, 2009).

Kaplan, Yosef, *Judios nuevos en Amsterdam: Estudios sobre la historia social e intelectual del judaísmo sefarí en el siglo XVII* (Barcelona: Gedisa Editorial, 1996).

___, Henry Méchoulan and Richard H. Popkin (eds.), *Menasseh Ben Israel and His World* (Leiden: E. J. Brill, 1989).

_____ "The Travels of Portuguese Jews from Amsterdam to the 'Lands of Idolatry' (1644-1724)," in Yosef Kaplan (ed.), *Jews and Conversos: Studies in society and the inquisition* (Jerusalem: World Union of Jewish Studies/The Magnes Press/The Hebrew University, 1985), 197-224.

_____ "The Portuguese Jews in Amsterdam: From Forced Conversion to a Return to Judaism," *Studia Rosenthaliana* 15, 1 (March 1981): 37-51.

Lewis, Laura A., *Hall of Mirrors: Power, Witchcraft, and Caste in Colonial Mexico* (Durham, NC: Duke University Press, 2003).

Lipiner, Elias, *Gonçalo Anes Bandarra e os cristãos-novos* (Trancoso/Lisbon: Câmara Municipal de Trancoso/Associação Portuguesa de Estudos Judaicos, 1996).

_____ *Izaque de Castro: o mancebo que veio preso do Brasil* (Recife:

Fundação Joaquim Nabuco/Editora Massangana, 1992).

———— Os judaizantes nas capitanias de cima: Estudos sobre os cristãos-novos do Brasil nos séculos XVI e XVII (São Paulo: Editôra Brasiliense, 1969).

López Belinchón, Bernardo, *Honra, libertad y hacienda: Hombres de negocios y judíos sefardíes* ([Alcalá de Henares, Madrid]: Universidad de Alcalá, 2001).

Lopez Garcia, José Tomás, *Dos defensores de los esclavos negros en el siglo XVII* (Maracaibo/Caracas: Biblioteca Corpozulia/Universidad Catolica Andres Bello, 1981).

Lutz, Christopher H., *Santiago de Guatemala, 1541-1773: City, Caste, and the Colonial Experience* (Norman, Okla.: University of Oklahoma Press, 1994).

Mangan, Jane E., *Trading Roles: Gender, Ethnicity, and the Urban Economy in Colonial Potosí* (Durham: Duke University Press, 2005).

Mark, Peter, and José Da Silva Horta, *The Forgotten Diaspora: Jewish Communities in West Africa and the Making of the Atlantic World* (New York: Cambridge University Press, 2011).

———— "Two Early Seventeenth-Century Sephardic Communities on Senegal's Petite Cote," *History in Africa* 31 (2004): 231-56.

Martínez López, María Elena, "The Spanish Concept of *Limpieza de Sangre* and the Emergence of the 'Race/Caste' System in the Viceroyalty of New Spain," (PhD Dissertation, University of Chicago, 2002).

Martínez Villada, Luis G., *Diego López de Lisboa* (Córdoba: Imprenta de la Universidad, 1939).

Maya Restrepo, Luz Adriana, *Brujería y reconstrucción de identidades entre los africanos y sus descendientes en la Nueva Granada, siglo XVII* (Bogota: Ministerio de Cultura, 2005).

Medina, José Toribio, *Historia del Tribunal de la Inquisición de Lima, 1569-1820*, Prólogo de Marcel Bataillon, 2nd. ed., 2 v. (Santiago de Chile: Fondo Histórico y Bibliográfico J. T. Medina, 1956 [orig. 1887]).

———— *Historia del Tribunal del Santo Oficio de la inquisición en Chile* (Santiago de Chile, Fondo Histórico y Bibliográfico J. T. Medina, 1952 [orig. 1890]).

———— *El tribunal del santo oficio de la inquisición en las provincias del Plata*

(Buenos Aires: Editorial Huarpes, 1945).

———— Historia del Tribunal del Santo Oficio de la Inquisición de Cartagena de las Indias (Santiago de Chile: Imprenta Elzeviriana, 1899).

Melammed, Renée Levine, A Question of Identity: Iberian Conversos in Historical Perspective (New York: Oxford University Press, 2004).

———— Heretics of Daughters of Israel? The Crypto-Jewish Women of Castile (New York: Oxford University Press, 1999).

———— "María López: A Convicted Judaizer from Castile," in Mary E. Giles, ed., Women in the Inquisition: Spain and the New World (Baltimore: Johns Hopkins University Press, 1999), 53-72.

———— "Judaizing Women in Castille: A Look at Their Lives Before and After 1492," in Le Beau, Bryan F. and Menachem Mor (eds.), Religion in the Age of Exploration: the Case of Spain and New Spain (Creighton University Press, 1996), 15-37.

———— "Some Death and Mourning Customs of Castilian Conversas," in Exile and Diaspora: Studies in the History of the Jewish People Presented to Professor Haim Beinart (Jerusalem: Ben-Zvi Institute of Yad Izhak Ben-Zvi/the Hebrew University of Jerusalem/Consejo de Investigaciones Científicas, Madrid, 1991), 157-67.

———— "The Conversos of Cogolludo," Proceedings of the Ninth World Congress of Jewish Studies, Division B, Vol. I (Jerusalem: World Union of Jewish Studies, 1986), 135-42.

Mellafe, Rolando, La introducción de la esclavitud negra en Chile: Trafico y rutas (Santiago de Chile: Universidad de Chile, 1959).

Mello, José Antônio Gonsalves de Gente da nação: Cristãos-novos e judeus em pernambuco, 1542-1654 (Recife: Fundação Joaqium Nabuco/ Editora Massangana, 1989).

Memmi, Albert, The Colonizer and the Colonized (Boston: Beacon Press, 1967 [1957]).

Mignolo, Walter D., The Darker Side of the Renaissance: Literacy, Territoriality, and Colonization (Ann Arbor: University of Michigan Press, 1995).

Molinero, Baltasar Fra, "Juan Latino and His Racial Difference," in Earle and Lowe, Black Africans in Renaissance Europe, 326-44.

_____ *La imagen de los negros en el teatro del Siglo de Oro* (Madrid: Siglo Veintiuno Editores, 1995).

Newson, Linda A., and Susie Minchin, *From Capture to Sale: The Portuguese Slave Trade to Spanish South America in the Early Seventeenth Century* (Leiden: Brill, 2007).

Novinsky, Anita, "The Myth of the Marrano Names," *Revue des Études Juives* 165,3-4 (2006): 445-56.

_____ *Inquisição: Prisioneiros de Brasil - séculos XVI-XIX* (Rio de Janeiro: Editora Expressão e Cultura, 2002).

_____ "Marranos and the Inquisition: On the Gold Route in Minas Gerais, Brazil," in Bernardini and Fiering, *Jews and the Expansion of Europe to the West*, 215-41.

_____ "A Critical Approach to the Historiography of *Marranos* in the Light of New Documents," *Studies on the History of Portuguese Jews from their Expulsion in 1497 through their Dispersion*, ed. Israel J. Katz and M. Mitchell Serels (New York: Sepher-Hermon Press, 2000).

_____ "Jewish Roots of Brazil," in Judith Laikin Elkin and Gilbert W. Merkx (eds.), *The Jewish Presence in Latin America* (Boston: Allen & Unwin, 1987).

_____ *Cristãos-novos na Bahia, 1642-1654* (São Paulo: Pioneira/EDUSP, 1972).

Olsen, Margaret M., *Slavery and Salvation in Colonial Cartagena de Indias* (Gainesville: University Press of Florida, 2004).

Pagden, Anthony, "Identity Formation in Spanish America," in Nicholas Canny and Anthony Pagden (eds.), *Colonial Identity in the Atlantic World, 1500-1800* (Princeton; Princeton University Press, 1987), 51-93.

Palmer, Colin A., *Slaves of the White God: Blacks in Mexico, 1570-1650* (Cambridge: Harvard University Press, 1976).

_____ "Religion and Magic in Mexican Slave Society, 1570-1650," in Engerman, Stanley L. and Eugene D. Genovese (eds.), *Race and Slavery in the Western Hemisphere: Quantitative Studies* (Princeton: Princeton University Press, 1975), 311-28.

Popkin, Richard H., and Gordon M. Weiner (eds.), *Jewish Christians and Christian Jews: From the Renaissance to the Enlightenment* (Dordrecht:

Kluwer Academic Publishers, 1994).
Rout, Leslie, *The African Experience in Spanish America, 1502-present* (New York: Columbia University Press, 1976)
Salomon, Herman Prins, "Spanish Marranism Re-examined," *Sefarad* 67,1 (Jan.-June 2007): 111-54.
Schorsch, Jonathan, *Jews and Blacks in the Early Modern World* (New York: Cambridge University Press, 2004).
Schwartz, Stuart B., *All Can Be Saved: Religious Tolerance and Salvation in the Iberian Atlantic World* (New Haven: Yale University Press, 2008).
_____ "Spaniards, *Pardos*, and the Missing Mestizos: Identities and Racial Categories in the Early Hispanic Caribbean," *Nieuwe West-Indische Gids* 71,1&2 (1997): 5-19.
_____ "Panic in the Indies: The Portuguese Threat to the Spanish Empire, 1640-1650," in Werner Thomas and Bart De Groof (eds.), Rebelión y resistencia en el mundo hispánico del siglo XVII: Actas del Coloquio Internacional Lovaina, 20-23 de Noviembre de 1991 (Leuven: Leuven University Press, 1992), 205-26.
_____ "The Formation of a Colonial Identity in Brazil," in Canny and Pagden, *Colonial Identity in the Atlantic World, 1500-1800*, 15-50.
_____ Sugar Plantations in the Formation of Brazilian Society: Bahia, 1550-1835 (Cambridge: Cambridge University Press, 1985).
Scott, James C., *Weapons of the Weak; Everyday Forms of Peasant Resistance* (New Haven: Yale University Press, 1985).
Silva, Filipa Ribeiro da, "A inquisição na Guiné, nas Ilhas de Cabo Verde e São Tomé e Príncipe," *Revista Lusófona de Ciência das Religiões* 3,5-6 (2004): 157-73.
Silverblatt, Irene, "Colonial Conspiracies," *Ethnohistory* 53,2 (Spring 2006): 259-80.
_____ Modern Inquisitions: Peru and the Colonial origins of the Civilized World (Durham: Duke University Press, 2004).
_____ "New Christians and New World Fears in Seventeenth-Century Peru," *Comparative Studies in Society and History: An International Quarterly* 42,3 (July, 2000): 524-546.
Silverman, Joseph H., "On Knowing Other People's Lives, Inquisitorially and Artistically," in Mary Elizabeth Perry and Anne J. Cruz (eds.),

Cultural Encounters: the Impact of the Inquisition in Spain and the New World (Berkeley: University of California Press, 1991), 157-75.

Solano Alonso, Jairo, *Salud, cultura y sociedad: Cartagena de Indias, siglos XVI y XVII* (Bogota: Fondo de Publicaciones de la Universidad del Atlántico/Colección de Ciencias Sociales Rodrigo Noguera Barreneche, 1998).

Splendiani, Anna-María, *Cincuenta Años de Inquisición en el Tribunal de Cartagena de las Indias, 1610-60*, 4 vols. (Bogotá, 1997).

Studnicki-Gizbert, Daviken, "*La Nación* among the Nations: Portuguese and Other Maritime Trading Diasporas in the Atlantic, Sixteenth to Eighteenth Centuries," Richard L. Kagan and Philip D. Morgan (eds.), *Atlantic Diasporas: Jews, Conversos, and Crypto-Jews in the Age of Mercantilism, 1500-1800* (Baltimore: Johns Hopkins University Press, 2009), 75-98.

_____ *A Nation upon the Ocean Sea: Portugal's Atlantic Diaspora and the Crisis of the Spanish Empire, 1492-1640* (New York: Oxford University Press, 2007).

Sweet, James H., *Recreating Africa: Culture, Kinship, and Religion in the African-Portuguese World, 1441-1770* (Chapel Hill: University of North Carolina Press, 2003).

Swetschinski, Daniel M., *Reluctant Cosmopolitans: The Portuguese Jews of Seventeenth-Century Amsterdam* (London: Littman Library of Jewish Civilization, 2000).

Thornton, John, *Africa and Africans in the making of the Atlantic world, 1400-1800*. Second ed. (Cambridge, UK: Cambridge University Press, 1998).

Uchmany, Eva Alexandra, "The Participation of New Christians and Crypto-Jews in the Conquest, Colonization and Trade of Spanish America, 1521-1660," in Bernardini and Fiering, *Jews and the Expansion of Europe to the West*, 186-202.

_____ *La vida entre el judaísmo y el cristianismo en la Nueva España, 1580-1606* (Mexico City: Archivo General de la Nación/Fondo de Cultura Económica, 1992).

Ventura, Maria da Graça A. Mateus, *Portugueses no Peru ao tempo da união ibérica: Mobilidade, cumplicidades e vivências*, 2 vols. in 3 pts. (Lisbon:

Imprensa Nacional-Casa da Moeda, 2005).

_____ "Los Judeoconversos portugueses en el Perú del siglo XVII: Redes de complicidad," *Familia, religión y negocio: El sefardismo en las relaciones entre el mundo ibérico y los Países Bajos en la edad moderna*, ed. Jaime Contreras, Bernardo J. García García and Ignacio Pulido (Fundación Carlos de Amberes/Fernando Villaverde Ediciones, 2002).

_____ *Negreiros portugueses na rota das Índias de Castela, 1541-1556* (Lisbon: Edições Colibri/Instituto de Cultura Ibero-Atlântica, 1999).

Vilar, Enriqueta Vila, "Extranjeros en Cartagena (1593-1630," *Jahrbuch für Geschichte von Staat, Wirtschaft und Gesellschaft Lateinamerikas* (Koln Wein, 1979): 147-84.

_____ *Hispanoamerica y el comercio de esclavos: los asientos portugueses* (Seville: EEHA, 1977).

Villa-Flores, Javier, " 'To Lose One's Soul': Blasphemy and Slavery in New Spain, 1596-1669," *Hispanic American Historical Review* 82,3 (2002): 435-68.

Wachtel, Nathan, *La foi du souvenir: Labyrinthes marranes* (France: Éditions du Seuil, 2001).

_____ "Marrano Religiosity in Hispanic America in the Seventeenth Century," Paolo Bernardini and Norman Fiering (eds.), *The Jews and the Expansion of Europe to the West, 1450 to 1800* (New York: Berghahn Books, 2001), 149-71.

Yerushalmi, Yosef Hayim, *Assimilation and Racial Anti-Semitism: The Iberian and German Models*, Leo Baeck Memorial Lecture, 26 (New York: Leo Baeck Institute, 1982).

_____ *From Spanish Court to Italian Ghetto: Isaac Cardoso, A Study in Seventeenth-Century Marranism and Jewish Apologetics*, 2nd ed. (Seattle: University of Washington Press, 1981 [orig. 1971]).

Yovel, Yirmiyahu, *The Marrano of Reason* (Princeton: Princeton University Press, 1989).

– Index –

Abravanel, Isaac 98
Acosta, Antonio de 28
Acosta, Manuel de 28
Afroamerican 121
Afroiberian history 9
Afroiberians 6, 9, 10, 13, 15, 16, 70, 99, 101-103, 105, 113-119, 121-128, 133, 158, 164
Alberro, Solange 99, 171
alms 67, 89, 90, 92, 93, 95, 96, 161
alumbrado (*also* alumbrar, alumbrasse, alumbrada) 94, 102, 105
Amerindians 4, 10, 19, 56, 115, 118, 143, 160
Amsterdam 3, 21, 61, 68, 71, 78, 98, 132, 163, 164, 171, 177, 182
Angola 4, 5, 22, 28, 48, 49, 51, 52, 145, 150, 175
Anidjar, Gil 120, 134
Antunes, Isabel 87
Antunes, Ysavel 77
anti-Portuguese hysteria 24
Ariu (heresiarch) 35
Asad, Talal 126
asiento (slave contract) 19
auto de fé 27, 34, 41, 60, 65, 67, 76, 80, 103, 137, 154, 155
Auto general de la fee celebrada 154, 156, 163
Azevedo, J. Lúcio de 172

Bal, Mieke 117, 167
Behar, Ruth 172
Beinart, Haim 131, 172, 179
Bennett, Herman 132, 172
blasphemy 9, 104, 105, 134, 164
blood purity 11, 15, 37
Bodian, Miriam 172
Bourdieu, Pierre 166
Bowser, Frederick 10, 172
Boxer, Charles R. 19
Boxer, C. R. 135, 172
bozales 31, 47
bruja / brujo / brujeia 17, 31, 41, 45, 53, 58, 60, 67, 141, 146

Buenos Aires 48, 179
burial 90, 157
Burns, Kathryn 122
Cabo Verde 175, 181
Cañizares-Esguerra, Jorge 172
Carmen Convent 81
caste (caste system) 11, 13, 14, 28, 67, 134, 177, 178
Cartagena 10, 15, 17-26, 29, 30, 37-39, 41, 44, 48, 49, 51, 53-55, 59-63, 65, 67, 69-71, 73, 95, 96, 114, 134, 136-138, 141, 143-145, 147-154, 164, 173, 179, 180, 182
Carvajal, Luis de 102
Certeau, Michel de 116, 166, 173
Claver, Pedro 10, 20, 65, 134, 136, 147
colonialism 2, 4, 125, 142
Colombia 23, 59, 136, 173
concubinage 70
confession 28, 49, 50, 105, 150
Conversos 4, 9, 24, 27-29, 61, 70, 131, 132, 139, 145, 150, 153, 174, 176, 177, 179, 182
Cope, R. Douglas 173
creole 145, 166, 167, 175
crypto-Jews 2, 14, 15, 17, 32, 36, 69, 73, 97, 102, 117, 119, 121, 131, 132, 137, 139, 145, 174, 175, 177, 182
crypto-Judaism 88, 112, 145, 156, 164
cultural intermediaries 15

denunciation / denunciations 15, 24, 25, 44, 57, 118, 129
desecration 120
diaspora 124, 132, 133, 144, 145, 177-179, 182
domination 117, 119, 122, 125, 127-129, 131, 173

Edicts of Faith / Edicts of the Faith / *edictos de fé* 26, 28, 141
England 3, 140
Esther, Queen 76, 80, 81
ethnicity (ethno-racial identity) 9, 125, 135, 144, 169, 178

ethnocentrism 122
ethnographic 13
execution 80, 101

fasting 83, 87, 137, 174
Felipe, King 37
Ferry, Robert 174
Foucault, Michel 126
Franciscan order 70

Gallagher, Catherine 120
Gómez, Diana Luz Ceballo 33
Graizbord, David 175
Green, Tobias 27, 48, 175
Greenblatt, Stephen 120, 168
Guiné 48, 145, 181

Horowitz, Elliott 118, 139

imprisonment 29, 56, 60, 65, 74, 88, 108-113, 152, 165
Islam 12, 104, 131, 174
Israel, Jonathan 3, 10, 48, 132-134, 145, 177
Israel, Menasseh ben 21, 133, 136, 177

Johnson, Willis 35, 139
judaizer / judaizing (*see also* crypto-Jews, crypto-Judaism) 14, 24, 28, 49, 60, 69, 73, 75, 87, 89, 90, 92, 94, 96, 99, 102, 105, 106, 122, 124, 128, 135, 148, 158-160, 179

Latour, Bruno 11
Law of Moses 24, 26, 28, 49, 50, 58, 60, 62, 64, 75, 77, 79, 81-83, 85, 87, 89, 90, 92, 93, 96, 97, 101, 105, 108-111, 151, 157, 160, 163
León, Juan de 82, 122
León, Pedro López de 38, 141, 148
Lewis, Laura 177
Lipiner, Elias 177

Machorro, Salomón 82, 122, 145, 158
magic 17, 31, 38, 45, 46, 60, 85, 115, 134, 141-143, 146, 149, 180
magical gatherings 41, 53, 58
magical practices 31, 46
Marranos 119, 131, 133, 180
marronage 47, 97, 115

Melammed, Renée Levine 131, 179
mestizos 8, 10, 19, 59, 181
Minas Gerais, Brazil 180
Moriscos 10, 85, 103, 116, 118, 140
Mulato 17, 30, 53, 85, 101, 134, 138
mystics 2, 142, 143, 162-164, 167

Nação 164
The Nation 52, 69, 131, 132, 136, 147, 150, 172, 182
neophyte 10
New Christians 1, 4, 6, 9, 10, 21, 24, 29, 42, 48, 49, 70, 82, 102, 103, 114, 121, 122, 131, 133, 144, 145, 181, 182
New Granada / Nueva Granada 12, 19, 20, 21, 47, 82, 127, 145, 169, 178

old Christians 36, 37

Pagden, Anthony 118, 167, 180
Palenques 45
Pernambuco 61, 103, 118, 179
Peru 5, 17, 19, 45, 115, 132-137, 144-148, 150, 171, 172, 181, 182
prayers 64, 84, 89, 104, 121, 163, 168, 169

rebellion 46, 123
Reconquista 1, 10, 85
religion 9, 11, 13, 16, 79, 81, 97, 104, 107, 118, 119, 131, 134, 135, 146, 164, 167-169, 175, 179, 180, 182
Rio de Janeiro 175, 180
Roth, Cecil 14, 119, 133
Rufina 15, 31-35, 37-48, 50, 51, 53-58, 113, 114, 116, 141, 142, 144, 146, 149

Sandoval, P. Alonso de 10
Santiago de Chile 136, 141, 178, 179
São Tomé 181
Schwartz, Stuart 181
Sentence 45, 67, 92, 109-111, 152, 163, 165
Sephardim 162, 175
Spinoza, Benedict (Baruch) 131
spiritual economy 122
Sweet, James H. 182

Torquemada, Tomás de 1
torture 26, 28, 29, 55, 64, 74, 104, 113, 137, 152

trade 3, 27, 48, 49, 51, 70, 132, 133, 135,
   136, 145, 168, 173, 180, 182

Ventura, Maria 61, 133, 147, 182
visions 124, 143

West India Company 61

Yerushalmi, Yosef Hayim 141
Yovel, Yirmiyahu 124, 166

zambos 8, 59

— About the Author —

Jonathan Schorsch holds the Chair in Jewish Religious and Intellectual History at the University of Potsdam (Germany), having taught previously at Sarah Lawrence College, Columbia University and Emory University. Among his books are *Swimming the Christian Atlantic: Judeoconversos, Afroiberians and Amerindians in the Seventeenth-Century Iberian World* (2008) and *Jews and Blacks in the Early Modern World* (2004). With Sina Rauschenbach he co-edited *The Sephardic Atlantic: Colonial Histories and Postcolonial Perspectives* (2018).

www.ingramcontent.com/pod-product-compliance
Lightning Source LLC
Chambersburg PA
CBHW032253150426
43195CB00008BA/439